CONFLICT IN NORTHERN IRELAND

Northern Ireland

John Darby

CONFLICT IN NORTHERN IRELAND:

The Development of a Polarised
Community

GILL AND MACMILLAN, DUBLIN
BARNES & NOBLE BOOKS, NEW YORK
a division of Harper & Row, Publishers, Inc.

First published in 1976
Reprinted in 1977

Gill and Macmillan Limited
15/17 Eden Quay
Dublin 1
and internationally through association with the
Macmillan Publishers Group

Published in the USA in 1976 by
Harper & Row Publishers, Inc.
Barnes & Noble Import Division

Gill and Macmillan SBN: 7171 0780 9
Barnes & Noble ISBN: 0-06-491580-8
Library of Congress Catalog Number: LC 76-15689

Printed and bound in Great Britain by
REDWOOD BURN LIMITED
Trowbridge & Esher

For my father and mother

Contents

Preface

IT has almost become traditional to preface new books on Northern Ireland with an apology by the author for adding to an already considerable literature on the subject. In this case the opposite applies; the variety, both in extent and in quality, of the new literature on the Northern Ireland problem supplies part of the reason for the production of this book.

Until 1969 anyone writing about Northern Ireland's community conflict had a similar problem to that facing the selectors of the province's football team : the available talent was scanty and their freedom of choice correspondingly restricted. One feature of both situations has been a tendency to place too much reliance on inferior resources, simply because they existed. Since 1969 the situation has altered considerably. The civil disorder of the early 1970s has stimulated interest in Ulster's problems and there is now a much greater quantity of evidence to test some of the speculations of earlier years, and to remedy some imbalances. There is also much greater need for caution in assessing the new material.

It is still true that many of the problems which are widely believed to have relevance to the development of a divided society have not been properly researched. The effect of segregated schooling is one such problem; the influence of the media another. In other areas, notably conflict theory, demography and the administration of justice, research of the highest quality has been carried out. Some of this material has not been printed and many of the published papers have only appeared in specialist journals. As a result, debate on important policy matters in Northern Ireland has been based more often on speculation than information. It is a major function of this book to draw together the various studies which have been produced and to evaluate their importance.

Most recent research has been related to the causes and consequences of Northern Ireland's community divisions. It is my intention to go a stage further, and to consider the relationship between the conflict and the social institutions in the province. As well as examining institutions both as agencies for social control and as arenas for conflict, my object is to look at their influence on the nature of the conflict—how the institutions which reflect community polarisation in the province have themselves further polarised the community.

Considerable licence has been taken with the opening and closing dates. Where appropriate, and especially in the first chapter and the chapters on demography and education, I have started as far back as the seventeenth century Plantation of Ulster; at the other extreme, there are references to publications which appeared in 1975, which was as late as publication schedules allowed. The emphasis in the book, however, is on the period between the 1920 Government act, which established the state of Northern Ireland, and the fall of the Northern Ireland Executive in 1974.

I make no apology for the frequent use of the terms 'Catholic' and 'Protestant'. They are not only the most common means of referring in Northern Ireland to its main community groupings, but much more accurate than any of the alternatives. It is not intended to imply by their use that there is a theological basis to the province's divisions.

John P. Darby,
New University of Ulster.

Chronology: 1912-1975

1912   Almost 500,000 Ulster people sign the 'Ulster League and Covenant' to resist the threat of Home Rule.

1914   Military build-up north and south: Larne and Howth gun-runnings. Britain declares war on Germany.

1916   Easter rising in Dublin.

1919–21   Anglo-Irish war—the war of Independence: First meeting of Dail Eireann in 1919.

1920   Government of Ireland act: partition established.

1921   Anglo-Irish treaty. First Northern Ireland parliament opens.

1921–22   Violence in Northern Ireland: 232 people killed in 1922 alone.

1922   Irish Free State established, followed by Irish Civil war (1922–23).

1922–23   Northern Ireland establishes its institutions: Civil service: Local government: Royal Ulster Constabulary: Civil Authorities (Special Powers) act (1922): Education act (1923)—the Londonderry act.

1929   Proportional Representation abolished.

1930–39   Northern Ireland's unemployment rate never fell below 25%.

1932   Fianna Fail government under de Valera in Free State, which becomes Irish Republic: 'Vigorous Northern policy'.

1932–38   Economic war between Britain and Free State.

1932–35   Intermittent violence in Northern Ireland.

1937   New constitution for Irish Free State: 'Special position' of Catholic church incorporated in it, as was claim that 'the national territory consists of the whole island of Ireland'.

1939–45 Second World War : economic boom in Northern Ireland.
IRA campaign in Britain.

1945–53 Social advance in Northern Ireland : Housing Trust established (1945): Industrial development policy launched (acts in 1945, 1953 and 1966): Education act (1947) establishes compulsory and free secondary education: National assistance and health services introduced (1948).

1949 Irish Republic leaves Commonwealth.
The Ireland act guarantees Northern Ireland's position within the United Kingdom.

1950–53 Economic co-operation between Northern Ireland and Republic: Joint Erne scheme (1950): Joint takeover of Great Northern Railways (1953): Joint takeover of Foyle fisheries (1952).

1956–62 IRA campaign in Northern Ireland.

1963 Terence O'Neill replaces Lord Brookeborough as Prime Minister.

1964 Northern government recognises the Irish Congress of Trade Unions.
Campaign for Social Justice in Northern Ireland begins.
Disturbances in Belfast during elections. 'Tricolour incident'.

1965 Premiers of Northern and Southern governments (O'Neill and Lemass) meet at Stormont.
Lockwood committee recommends that New University be established in Coleraine.
Wilson plan for economic expansion heavily concentrates growth areas in the east.

1966 Ulster Volunteer Force declares war on 'the IRA and its splinter groups'.
Malvern St murders: UVF members convicted and jailed.

1967 Northern Ireland Civil Rights Association (NICRA) formed.
Republican Clubs declared illegal.

1968   *12 June.* Phelim O'Neill expelled from Orange Order for attending Catholic ceremony.

20 June. Austin Currie takes possession of house in Caledon, Co. Tyrone, which he claimed had been unfairly allocated.

24 August. First Civil Rights march from Coalisland to Dungannon.

5 October. Civil Rights march to Derry, despite government ban : RUC charge marchers and rioting continued during the night.

9 October. Five Civil Rights organisations in Derry form the Derry Citizens Action Committee.

30 November. Ian Paisley, Ronald Bunting and their followers occupy Armagh to prevent Civil Rights march, which was diverted.

22 November. Terence O'Neill announces reform programme, including a points system of housing allocation, an ombudsman, franchise reform, a review of the Special Powers act and the dissolution of Derry Council.

9 December. NICRA declares truce : no marches or demonstrations.

11 December. William Craig, Minister of Home Affairs, dismissed from cabinet.

20 December. People's Democracy (PD) announce a Belfast-Derry march.

1969   *4 January.* PD march attacked by loyalists at Burntollet.

11 January. PD march in Newry followed by rioting.

30 January. Twelve Unionist MPs call for change of leadership.

6 February. New Ulster Movement formed to support policies of Terence O'Neill.

24 February. Elections to Northern Ireland parliament : the 'O'Neill election'.

28 April. Terence O'Neill resigns : replaced on 1 May by James Chichester-Clark.

2 July. White paper on *Reshaping of local government:* 73 councils to be replaced by 17.

12 August. Apprentice Boys' march in Derry attacked:

xiii

Bogside stormed by RUC: rioting which later led to establishment of 'Free Derry'.

13–14 August. Rioting spreads to Dungannon, Dungiven, Lurgan, Newry and Armagh. In Belfast four men and a boy killed.

15 August. Units of British army intervene between Falls and Shankill roads in Belfast, establishing what later became the 'Peace line'.

29 August. Joint communique from British and Northern Ireland Prime Ministers.

12 September. Cameron report on August riots: allegations of police misconduct confirmed.

10 October. Hunt report on police reform: RUC to be disarmed: 'B' Specials to be abolished: security to become a military responsibility.

27 November. Commissioner for Complaints office established: John Benn first Commissioner.

2 December. Maurice Hayes becomes first chairman of Community Relations Commission.

1970   *1 January.* Ulster Defence Regiment comes into operation.

11 January. Two hundred and fifty-seven delegates walk out of Sinn Fein congress in Dublin—they were to form the nucleus of the Provisional IRA.

5 February. Public Order (Amendment) act: stricter control of marches and demonstrations.

17 April. Ian Paisley and William Beattie first Protestant Unionist party MPs elected to Stormont.

21 April. Alliance party formed: policies moderate and 'firm on the constitutional issue'.

19 June. Elections to Westminster parliament.

1 July. Minimum Sentences act, relating to rioting offences, passed.

4 July. British army imposes curfew on Lower Falls area of Belfast following rioting.

July-August. Intermittent rioting in Belfast and Derry.

21 August. Social Democratic and Labour party (SDLP) formed.

1971   *23 March.* Brian Faulkner becomes Prime Minister,

replacing Chichester-Clark who had resigned three days earlier.

April. A number of bodies, including the Republican Clubs and forty priests, advocate boycott of census as protest against the administration of justice.

27 May. Three men charged under new Incitement to Hatred act: later acquitted.

16 July. SDLP announce boycott of Stormont, following two deaths in Derry, and set up alternative assembly.

9 August. Internment introduced: 300 people arrested: widespread violence and intimidation: 11 deaths and 240 houses burned down: Rent and Rates strike.

19 August. Thirty prominent Roman Catholics withdraw from public office, to be joined three days later by 130 non-Unionist councillors.

30 October. Democratic Unionist Party (DUP) formed.

16 November. Compton report on interrogation of internees: found evidence of ill-treatment, but not of brutality.

1972   *3 January.* Northern Ireland Housing Executive takes over its responsibilities.

30 January. 'Bloody Sunday' in Derry: Thirteen men killed by army: Followed by four days' rioting in Derry, Belfast and Dublin.

9 February. Maurice Hayes resigns as chairman of Community Relations Commission.

9 February. Ulster Vanguard launched by William Craig as umbrella movement for traditional unionists.

22 February. Bombing of Parachute regiment's headquarters at Aldershot by Official IRA in retaliation for 'Bloody Sunday': Six civilians and one padre killed.

28 February. Foreign Affairs sub-committee of US House of Representatives begins three days hearings on Northern Ireland.

2 March. Parker committee's report on interrogation

procedures : Found, Lord Gardiner dissenting, that methods were justified in exceptional circumstances.

13 March. Amnesty International report on treatment of internees : Found that the 'ill-treatment used amounted to brutality'.

24 March. British proposals to Northern Ireland government include border plebiscite, the phasing-out of internment and the transfer of 'law and order' to Westminster: Direct rule introduced with William Whitelaw as Secretary of State: Vanguard call two-day strike.

19 April. Widgery report on 'Bloody Sunday': army's behaviour generally vindicated.

23 April. Sunday Times report on 'Bloody Sunday' critical of army.

21 May. UDA set up barricades for second consecutive weekend : Army remove them.

26 June. IRA ceasefire.

5 July. UDA announce 14 days of 'peace and grace' during the 'Twelfth' celebrations.

9 July. IRA ceasefire ends : violence in Belfast.

21 July. 'Bloody Friday' : 22 IRA bomb explosions in Belfast : 9 dead and 130 injured.

31 July. Operation 'Motorman': Army move into positions in Andersonstown and Bogside : Claudy car bomb : 8 killed.

11 September. UDA, Vanguard and the Loyalist Association of Workers amalgamate under William Craig : Strike by power workers in protest against army shooting two Protestants on 7 September.

24 September. Darlington conference on future of Northern Ireland attended by Northern Ireland Labour party, Alliance and the Unionist party.

28 October. Provisional IRA lay down three demands —the Irish people should decide Ulster's future; a date for withdrawal of British troops; and an amnesty for political prisoners.

6 November. Three Commissioners appointed to hear appeals from those in detention.

8 December. Plebiscite in Irish Republic votes to delete the clauses of the Irish constitution on the special position of the Catholic church.

20 December. Diplock report suggests temporary changes in administration of justice, including trial without juries.

22 December. Provisional IRA confirm their Christmas truce.

1973   *15 February.* Burgess report advocates the abolition of the 11+ examination.

8 March. London car bombs: One killed and 180 injured.

Border poll: 41% abstained, 57·4% favoured the British union and 0·63% a united Ireland.

20 March. White paper proposed an 80-member Assembly, PR and a Council of Ireland.

30 March. Vanguard Unionist Progressive party (VUPP) formed with UDA support.

2 April. Northern Ireland (Emergency Provisions) act passed, based on Diplock report.

30 May. Local government elections, the first on universal adult suffrage.

28 June. Elections to Northern Ireland Assembly.

18 July. Northern Ireland Constitution act, abolishing Stormont parliament, becomes law.

31 July. First meeting of Northern Ireland Assembly: Loyalists stage sit-in.

5 October. Talks between those parties which accepted Constitution act—SDLP, Unionist party and Alliance party.

31 October. Kilbrandon report: suggested Northern Ireland should have 17 rather than 12 MPs at Westminster.

18 November. UVF 43-day ceasefire begins (later extended indefinitely).

22 November. Whitelaw announces composition of new Executive—6 Unionists, 4 SDLP and 1 Alliance.

3 December. The ten anti-Executive Unionists in the Assembly form new political group, and are joined by five of the seven Unionist MPs at Westminster.

Francis Pym replaces William Whitelaw as Secretary of State.

9 December. Sunningdale agreement between pro-Executive parties : accepted by Assembly five days later.

1974 *1 January.* Northern Ireland Executive takes office.

5 January. Ulster Unionist party rejects the power-sharing policy of Brian Faulkner.

23 January. Official Unionists, VUPP and DUP withdraw from Assembly as protest against Executive.

28 February. Elections to Westminster parliament : Labour win election : Eleven of Northern Ireland's twelve seats go to loyalists, campaigning under United Ulster Unionist Council (UUUC) banner.

5 March. Merlyn Rees becomes Secretary of State.

30 April. Basil McIvor, Minister of Education, announces intention to introduce 'shared schools'. Ivan Cooper, Minister of Community Relations, announces plans to abolish the Community Relations Commission.

14 May. General strike called by Ulster Workers' Council (UWC) as protest against Executive.

17 May. Four car bombs in Monaghan and Dublin : 28 killed and 100 injured.

28 May. Unionists forced by UWC strike to resign from Executive, which collapses : Direct rule restored.

24 June. Brian Faulkner and his followers form new party, later named the Unionist party of Northern Ireland.

4 July. British government White paper proposes elections to a Constitutional Assembly.

10 October. Elections to Westminster parliament : Labour win : Ten Northern Ireland seats go to UUUC.

2–8 November. Prevention of Terrorism bill allows deportation of people from Britain.

8 December. Irish Republican Socialist party formed.

22 December. Provisional IRA suspend operations for limited period.

1975   *30 January.* Gardiner report recommended continu-
        ation of detention.
        10 February. Provisional IRA ceasefire: Incident
        centres established.
        26 March. Government announce plan to nationalise
        Harland and Wolff.
        1 May. Elections to Northern Ireland constitutional
        assembly.

Events since 1969 must be seen against a backcloth of violence
which is not easily represented in a chronology. A cold look at
official statistics, however, will give some appreciation of its
scope :

	1970	1971	1972	1973	1974
Shootings	213	1,756	10,628	5,018	3,206
Explosions	153	1,022	1,382	978	685
Armed robberies		£303,787	£790,687	£612,015	£572,152
Deaths: Army and police	2	59	146	79	50
Deaths: Civilians	23	115	322	171	166
Injuries: Army and police	811	707	1,044	839	718
Injuries: Civilians		1,800	3,813	1,812	1,680
Houses searched	3,107	17,262	36,617	74,556	71,914

CHAPTER I

Dates and slogans:
The historical background

Both Northern Ireland and the Irish Free State owe their origin not to the force of argument, on which the national movement from O'Connell to Redmond had relied, but to the argument of force, and their history bears the marks of that tragic but inescapable fact.
T.W. Moody, 1967

A fifty-years' experience has not given Northern Ireland either unity or stability; but it has defined the political, economic and social problems of the area in specifically local terms. Even if Northern Ireland, as a separate political unit, were to be abolished, it would, in a real sense, survive, and carry into the foreseeable future the characteristics that have developed from the settlement imposed in 1920.
J.C. Beckett, 1972

W.C. SELLAR and R.J. YEATMAN in their comic history of Britain, *1066 and all that*, decided to include only two dates in the book, because all others were 'not memorable'. They would have had much greater difficulty writing an equivalent volume on Irish history. 1170, 1641, 1690, 1798, 1912, 1916, 1921, 1968—all these dates are fixed like beacons in the folklore and mythology of Irishmen. They trip off the tongue during ordinary conversation like the latest football scores in other environments, and are recorded for posterity on gable walls all over Northern Ireland.

To some extent this chapter is a history of the above, and other, dates. It is not intended as a pocket history of Northern Ireland, and anyone who wishes a more comprehensive account of the history of Ulster or Ireland will have no difficulty in finding suitable books.[1] The intention here is to construct a

1

short historical framework into which the developments and events which are considered in the rest of the book can be fitted. Since the book is concerned mainly with the interactions between the inhabitants of the state of Northern Ireland and their relations with their immediate neighbours, this chapter attempts to isolate some of the historical events and developments which illumine or at least are germane to this theme. In a sense, it is a history of community relations in the province.

Such a subject cannot be considered in isolation from the neighbouring areas. For centuries Ulster was one of the three partners in a trinity of relationships with Britain and with the rest of Ireland. Today, as in the past, its relationship with its immediate neighbours has been the most explicit method of determining political allegiances within the province.

Nevertheless Ulster* has a history of separateness which is not explainable in purely regional terms. Before the plantation of the early seventeenth century it was, apart from a few precarious coastal fortresses, the most Gaelic part of the country, and had successfully resisted English colonial ambitions. Nor were the relationships between its chiefs and those in the rest of Ireland particularly close, except when they faced each other across interminable battlefields. Links with Scotland, however, were close; western Scotland and eastern Ulster exchanged immigrants long before the middle ages.

It would be a mistake to regard pre-Plantation Ulster as a cohesive unit. Like the rest of Ireland it was dominated by a number of territorially jealous chiefs, and internal wars and vendettas were not uncommon. But the dominance of the O'Donnells in Donegal, the MacDonnells in Antrim and particularly the O'Neills in the centre of the province did produce some stability; it also produced military cohesion against Elizabeth I's armies and, for a time, success. It took nine years and a blockade of the province to bring the Ulster chiefs to their knees.

* The term 'Ulster' is popularly used in Ireland to describe two different areas. The first is the nine counties of the traditional province—Antrim, Down, Armagh, Derry, Tyrone, Fermanagh, Donegal, Monaghan and Cavan. The other area is the administrative and political unit which since 1921 has formed the state of Northern Ireland: it comprises the first six counties in the list above. In this book the term 'Northern Ireland' will be preferred when describing the latter area.

It was this very intransigence that accounted for the comprehensiveness of the Plantation of Ulster in 1609. There had been earlier attempts at colonising parts of Ireland during the sixteenth century, but they had usually consisted of little more than the confiscation of land and the grafting on of a new aristocracy. This also happened in Ulster. The leaders of the Ulster families were forced to flee to Europe and their lands were confiscated. By 1703, less than a century later, only 14% of the land in Ireland remained in the hands of the Catholic Irish, and in Ulster the figure was 5%. But these figures are not a real measure of the changes introduced with the Plantation of Ulster. What made it unique in Irish plantations was the comprehensive attempt made to attract, not only British gentry, but colonists of all classes, and the fact that the colonists were Protestant and represented a culture entirely alien to Ulster. This policy of comprehensive colonisation was a result of the advice of the Solicitor General to James I, and was an attempt to replace one entire community with another. The Catholic Irish remained, of course, but in conditions which emphasised their suppression. They were relegated to a state below servility, because the Planters were not allowed to employ the native Irish as servants in the new towns which they built. The towns themselves were unashamedly fortresses against the armed resentment of the Irish. Outside the town they were banished from the land they had owned and worked, and were confined to the boggy and mountainous regions. The reality differed from the intention however. There were simply not enough settlers to achieve comprehensive control, and Irish servants were quietly admitted to the towns.

The sum of the Plantation then was the introduction of a foreign community, which spoke differently, worshipped apart, and represented an alien culture and way of life. It had close commercial, cultural and political ties with Britain. The more efficient methods of the new farmers, and the great availability of capital, which allowed the start of cottage industries, served to create further economic differences between Ulster and the rest of Ireland, and between Catholic and Protestant within Ulster. The deep resentment of the native Irish towards the planters, and the distrustful siege mentality of the planters towards the Irish, is the root of the Ulster problem.

The next two centuries supplied a lot of the dates and other trappings essential to the conflict. The Rising of 1641 against the Planters provided a Protestant massacre, and the Cromwellian conquest in the 1650s a Catholic one. Most important of all was the battle of the Boyne in 1690, sanctified on a hundred gable walls and Orange banners as the victory of the 'Prods' over the 'Mikes'. Historians keep trying to debunk these myths, but historical scholarship has never had any effect on a folklore socialised into generations of Ulster people.

The aftermath of William of Orange's victory at the Boyne was much more important than the campaign itself. It was a mark of the sustained hostility between Planter and Gael that the Penal laws, often included in the catalogue of England's evils in Ireland, were enacted by Irishmen through the Irish parliament in Dublin. The laws were of vital importance in broadening the differences between the Irish establishment and its opponents. Having established an exclusively Protestant legislature in 1692, a comprehensive series of coercive acts against Catholics were implemented during the 1690s and after. They were excluded from the armed forces, the judiciary and the legal profession as well as from parliament; they were forbidden to carry arms or to own a horse worth more than £5; all their bishops and regular clergy were banished in 1697, although secular clergy could remain under licence; Catholics were forbidden to hold long leases on land, to buy land from a Protestant, and were forced to divide their property equally among their children in their wills, unless the eldest conformed to the Anglican faith; they were prohibited from conducting schools, or from sending their children to be educated abroad. Some of these laws, and notably those affecting property, were rigidly enforced, while others were unenforceable. Their main effects were to entrench the divide between Catholics and Protestants, to strengthen Irish Catholicism by adding a political component to it, and to drive underground some aspects of the Catholic Gaelic culture, notably education and public worship.

During the second half of the eighteenth century relations between the religious communities in Ireland were in a situation of considerable flux. Acting as a counterbalance to tendencies dividing Catholics and Protestants, the coerced and the

4

coercors, was the rivalry between Presbyterians and members of the Church of Ireland. The fact that there were also penal laws against the Presbyterians which excluded them from a share of political power—although certainly not as severe or comprehensive as those against Catholics—created a Catholic-Presbyterian relationship which was in some ways closer than that between the Protestant sects. This was particularly true in Ulster, and some of its fruits have persuaded some historians that this was an age of tolerance. Most of the Penal laws were repealed by the 1790s; a convention of the Irish Volunteers—an exclusively Protestant body aimed at creating greater Irish independence from Britain—met at Dungannon in 1782 and passed a resolution 'that as men and as Irishmen, as Christians and as Protestants, we rejoice in the relaxation of the Penal laws against our Roman Catholic fellow-subjects'.[2] Belfast Volunteers, Protestant to a man, formed a guard of honour for Father Hugh O'Donnell as the first Catholic Church in Belfast, St Mary's in Chapel Lane, was opened, and Protestants contributed £84 towards the cost of its building.[3] The early success of the Society of United Irishmen in attracting both Presbyterians and Catholics into a revolutionary republican movement during the 1790s appeared to indicate a new Irish cohesion which disregarded religious denominationalism and was determined to establish an independent republic of Ireland. The abortive 1798 rebellion, best known for the Catholic rising in Wexford, also included risings in Antrim and Down; in the resulting judicial investigations 30 Presbyterian clergymen were accused of participation, three of them were hanged, seven imprisoned, four exiled or transported and at least five fled the country.[4]

Such a benign interpretation of the late eighteenth century ignores equally powerful evidence pointing towards the existence of strong community divisions. Secret organisations like the Defenders, the Peep o' Day Boys and the Steelboys, strongly sectarian and determined to ensure that tenancies must be prevented from passing into the hands of the other religion, waged persistent and occasionally bloody skirmishes with each other in the country areas. Indeed it was one of these skirmishes in Armagh which produced the Orange Order, an organisation which stressed the common interests of all Protestants and effectively challenged the Presbyterian-Catholic alliance in the

United Irishmen. Inside Belfast the tolerance towards Catholics was not unrelated to their numbers in the city. In 1707 George McCartney the Sovereign of Belfast reported to his superiors that 'thank God we are not under any great fears here, for . . . we have not among us above seven papists'.[5] The industrial expansion of the city towards the beginning of the nineteenth century attracted very large numbers of Catholics to the city. Between 1800 and 1830 the proportion of Catholics in the city rose from 10% to 30%[6] and the first signs of serious urban conflict occurred as a result of competition for jobs and for houses. The same period saw considerable changes within the Presbyterian church. The liberals within the church came under increasing challenge from hardline opinion which was represented by Henry Cooke and closely linked with the Orange Order. The dispute was along both theological and political lines, and resulted in a complete victory for Cooke and his supporters. The liberals under Henry Montgomery broke away and formed the Non-subscribing Presbyterian Church. The community divisions in Ulster began to assume a form similar to that well-known today.

The first serious communal riots in Belfast took place in Belfast on July 12, 1834, and a woman was killed. An English witness to the riot, John Barrow, contrasted Belfast with the industrial cities in Britain where such disturbances were frequent. 'In Belfast, where everyone is too much engaged in his own business, and where neither religion nor politics have interfered to disturb the harmony of society, it could not fail to create a great and uneasy sensation.'[7] It was a sensation which Belfast citizens were to experience frequently ever since. Andrew Boyd mentioned eight other years 'of the most serious rioting' during the rest of the nineteenth century, and indeed few years passed without some disturbances.[8] The main effect of these riots was to ensure that the expanding population of the city was separated into sectarian areas, and to fortify the communal differences between Catholics and Protestants.

The nineteenth century also witnessed the growth of conscious separatism between Ulster and the rest of Ireland. The effects of the industrial revolution in Ireland were confined almost entirely to the northern part of the country, strapping even closer its industrial and commercial dependency on Britain.

6

The greater prosperity of the north, its economic structure, even its physical appearance, increased its alienation from the rest of Ireland. The potato famine of the 1840s, undoubtedly the most far-reaching event in nineteenth-century Ireland, had much more severe consequences in the south than in the north and had profound effects on political, economic and social developments there which were less dramatic in Ulster. Economic differences found a political voice when the campaign for the repeal of the act of Union with Britain caused a petition to be organised as early as 1834 against repeal or, if a Dublin parliament was restored, in favour of a separate legislature in Ulster. In 1841 Daniel O'Connell, the champion of repeal, visited Belfast. His coach had to avoid an ambush, the meeting hall was stoned, and his entourage was protected by a strong police force on its way southwards.

It was the Home Rule campaign in the 1880s which was to give Protestant Ulster its organised basis and its tradition. As late as the general election of 1885, 17 out of 33 Ulster seats were carried by the Home Rule party. The next two decades transformed this picture and stiffened Ulster's resistance to Home Rule. The resistance was strengthened by the growing identification between Ulster unionism and the Conservative party in Britain. Two remarks of Lord Randolph Churchill, a leading Conservative politician, identified the basis of the new alliance. 'We have got the old man hooked' he wrote jubilantly to Salisbury when the Liberal leader Gladstone announced his advocacy of Home Rule. 'The Orange card is the one to play.' And he told an enthusiastic crowd in Belfast 'Ulster will fight and Ulster will be right.'[9] The basis of the new Conservative policy was an identification with Protestant fears, and particularly with the province of Ulster. If the motive was frank political opportunism from the Conservatives, the Ulster Unionists were glad of such powerful support. Nevertheless, although this support was important, it was events inside Ulster which gave the anti-Home Rule campaign its real power. Amidst the outbursts against Home Rule by churchmen, Unionists, MPs and Conservative politicians, it was the Orange Order which emerged to provide the leadership and organisation to maintain the union. The Order's fortunes during the eighteenth century had been chequered; outlawed and abused on many

7

occasions, it had nevertheless, survived. The anti-Home Rule campaign served to transform the Order from a disreputable to a respectable body. For its part the Order supplied the ready-made framework of an effective organisation for growing Protestant dissatisfaction, especially in Ulster. By 1905 it had played a major role in uniting disparate unionist voices within the Ulster Unionist Council—the coalition from which the Unionist party was to emerge.

The Home Rule campaign against which this unionist re-organisation was aimed was not confined to parliamentary strategies. The Irish parliamentary party, which attempted to achieve Home Rule by legislative action, was at times complemented and at times rivalled by revolutionaries of both the physical force and the cultural variety. The Irish revolutionary tradition, represented by the Fenians from the 1850s, and later by the Irish Republican Brotherhood, the IRA and others, loomed over the parliamentary campaign. It was strategically useful to Charles Stewart Parnell, the Irish Nationalist leader, as evidence of what would happen if Home Rule were rejected—but it became a serious and in the end a more powerful rival to the parliamentary party as public impatience grew. The formation of the Gaelic Athletic Association to encourage Irish sports, and the Gaelic League to encourage interest in Irish language and literature, reflected a growing nationalism which was more closely tuned to the revolutionary than the parliamentary tradition. These developments were adopted with enthusiasm by nationalists in the north of Ireland, just as the organisation of the anti-Home Rule campaign included branches all over the country. But as the crisis came to a head between 1906 and 1914, the quarrel was regarded in increasingly general geographical terms as one between the northern and southern parts of the country. Lip-service was paid to the existence of minorities within the enemy camps, but their causes did not receive really serious attention until the 1920s when their minority conditions had been confirmed within separate states.

The decade between 1912 and 1922 was a momentous one for Ireland. Civil conflict between north and south, where private armies were openly drilling, was averted by the outbreak of the First World War; the Easter 1916 rising in Dublin and the subsequent guerrilla campaign shifted the spotlight southward; the signing in 1921 of a treaty between the British government and Sinn Fein, the political wing of the Irish Republican Army, established a state from which Northern Ireland opted out. These events and the first years of both new states were accompanied by civil disorder. Belfast experienced a guerrilla campaign and sectarian conflicts. The new state was created in the midst of the troubles and divisions which were to characterise its history.

As J.C. Beckett has pointed out, it is not correct to regard the establishment of Northern Ireland as a response to the current European demand for self-expression. 'The six north-eastern counties of Ireland were grouped together and given a parliament and government of their own, not because anyone in the area wanted (let alone demanded) such an arrangement, but because the British government thought that this was the only possible way of reconciling the rival aspirations of the two Irish parties.'[10] Indeed it was intended as part of a wider settlement which never materialised. The Government of Ireland act (1920) proposed two states in Ireland, one for the six counties and the other for the remainder of Ireland. Each was to have its own parliament to deal with domestic matters; each was to have representatives at Westminster; and a Council of Ireland was to deal with matters of common interest. In fact the terms only came into operation in Northern Ireland, and the Council of Ireland never met. Having fought against Home Rule for almost a century Unionists were, in the words of Rev. J.B. Armour, 'compelled to take a form of Home Rule that the devil himself could never have imagined'.[11]

The size of the new state was a case in point. The county boundaries had never been intended as anything more than local administrative limits, and fairly arbitrary ones at that. Now some of them became international frontiers. As to why six counties had been selected rather than four or nine or any other number, the reasons were unashamedly straightforward. The traditional nine counties of Ulster held 900,000 Protestants, most of whom supported the British connection, and 700,000 Catholics, most of whom wanted to end it. However, in the six counties which were later to become Northern Ireland, the religious breakdown was 820,000 Protestants and 430,000 Catholics. In 1920 James Craig, the first Prime Minister of

9

Northern Ireland, expressed the case frankly in the House of Commons 'If we had a nine-county parliament, with sixty-four members, the Unionist majority would be about three or four: but in a six-county parliament, with fifty-two members, the Unionist majority would be about ten.'[12] It was this more than any other consideration which persuaded the Unionists to accept the six-county area.

The two most pervasive problems of the new state of Northern Ireland were the continuing polarisation of the nationalist and unionist communities which occasionally flared into violence, and relations with its two closest neighbours, Great Britain and the southern part of Ireland. Both of these problems were closely related to economic circumstances. The troubles of the 1930s were triggered off by the depression and indeed accusations of economic discrimination were among the most bitter reasons for discontent by the Northern minority. And the relationships with southern Ireland and Britain became increasingly dependent on economic ties and divisions.

Northern Ireland: Internal Matters

The new state was born amid bloodshed and communal disorder. In 1922 232 people were killed in the violence in Northern Ireland, and almost 1,000 wounded. The nationalist minority refused to recognise the new state; the ten anti-partitionist MPs refused to attend parliament; Catholic teachers shunned the educational system, submitting pupils for examinations in Dublin and even refusing salaries. At the very time when the institutions of the new state were being established, a considerable minority of its citizens were refusing to participate on committees or to perform any action which might lend support to its authority.

As time passed, and the state remained, most nationalists decided on a reluctant acceptance of the need to come to some accommodation, at least in the short term. In some cases they found that the institutions which had been established and those which were still being set up were so arranged as to effectively exclude them from positions of power. Partly as a result of Catholic unwillingness to participate in a state whose existence they opposed, and partly as a result of bias by the establishment against a section of the community which it considered

10

as traitorous, many of the institutions were heavily biased in favour of Unionists. The local government franchise, for example, which remained unreformed until 1969, reflected property rather than population, excluding non-ratepayers and awarding many people with more than one property extra votes. Housing allocation and the gerrymandering of constituency boundaries were actively used in some cases, notably Derry* city, to maintain Unionist majorities. In the membership of the police force and the Ulster Special Constabulary, formed to help combat the IRA threat in 1921, a combination of nationalist unwillingness and Unionist distrust created forces which were largely Protestant. As late as 1961 only 12% of the Royal Ulster Constabulary was Catholic, and the 'B' Specials were exclusively Protestant. Education too was an area where Catholics felt bitterly that the system established by the Education Act (NI) of 1930 was one which had been tailored by Protestant pressure, producing a state education system which was in fact Protestant, and forcing Catholic schools to find 50% of the cost of education. In the administration of justice Catholics have long alleged that the Special Powers Act, which placed considerable powers in the hands of the Minister of Home Affairs and which, although emergency legislation, operated permanently within Northern Ireland, was designed exclusively against the nationalist minority. Further allegations have been made, and vindicated by the Cameron Report in 1969, about discrimination against Catholics in public employment. The most serious general allegation in this field was that the government operated a policy of deliberate discrimination against part of the province—counties Derry and Fermanagh in particular—creating conditions which encouraged emigration to counter the higher Catholic birth rate in these areas. Disputes about the extent of institutional discrimination, and about the reasons for it, have always been particularly bitter, but one point is clear. Far from resolving intercommunal suspicion and fear, the establishment of the state actually served to render them more precise.

Professor Beckett's judgement that 'between the early 1920s and the late 1960s Ireland enjoyed a longer period of freedom

---

* The name of Derry is used for Londonderry throughout.

11

from major internal disturbance than it had known since the first half of the eighteenth century',[18] holds less validity if confined to the Northern state. The years which followed immediately upon the establishment of the state were among the most violent in the history of Ulster, although they were clearly related to political opposition to the new state. The familiar relationship between economic recession and inter-communal strife was bloodily revived in the depression of the 1930s. The dependency of Northern Ireland on exports made her particularly vulnerable to world trends. The linen industry was severely restricted; in 1933 no ships were launched from Belfast shipyards for the first time in over 100 years. Between 1930 and 1939 the unemployment rates in the province never fell below 25%. The bitter competition for too few jobs inevitably took a sectarian turn, which was exacerbated by worsening relations between the United Kingdom and the Irish Free State. The Ulster Protestant League was formed in 1931 and encouraged Protestants to employ other Protestants exclusively, a sentiment endorsed by Basil Brooke, the Minister of Agriculture and future Prime Minister. Whether this was a concerted policy or, as Hugh Shearman claims, merely caused by 'the nervous and vituperative atmosphere of the early 1930s'[14] made little difference to those who were jobless.

Certainly the early 1930s were nervous and vituperative years. Widespread riots in 1931, some of which involved the IRA, resulted in between 60 and 70 people being injured. 1932 saw riots in Belfast, Larne, Portadown and Ballymena. In 1935 the troubles reached their peak. Twelve people were killed and six hundred wounded. Incidents like the 1932 Shankill riots in support of the Falls hunger marchers who had been baton charged by the police disturbed the pattern but did not alter it. The frequency of sectarian violence gradually faded as the employment situation improved, but few believed that it had retreated far below the surface.

The comparative peacefulness, by Northern Ireland standards, of the next twenty years set the scene for the important changes which appeared to be taking place in the 1950s and 1960s. This period of communal peace, or rather of absence of overt conflict, coincided with a growing and deliberate emphasis on economic expansion for the province. In the first

12

place, the war years brought unprecedented prosperity to Northern Ireland. Her shipbuilding, engineering and aircraft production boomed; agricultural production shot up; and the economic expectations of the people rose accordingly. The post-war years consequently saw determined attempts on the part of the Northern Ireland government to attract foreign capital and industry, and its success was considerable. As a result of various incentive schemes 150 new factories, supplying 55,000 new jobs, were established. The new industries, many of which were branches of international combines, brought with them alien ideas about employment, employing their workers without regard to religious affiliation. These new industries offered hope to Catholics, especially from the middle and lower managerial classes who had formerly found promotion prospects restricted.

An improvement in the prospects and conditions of the minority was also evident in other spheres. The post-war legislation which greatly broadened the social benefits of the welfare state particularly benefited the poorer classes in society, and in Northern Ireland this included a disproportionate number of Catholics. The 1947 Education act opened doors of educational opportunity by introducing free secondary education, and the remarkable rise in the number of Catholics attending University was one measure of its effectiveness. Although the extent of these changes is often debated, there is no doubt that the 1950s saw a growing tendency for Catholics to see their future in terms of a Northern Ireland context rather than in an all-Ireland state. The most dramatic pointer to this change was the failure of the IRA offensive of 1956–62. Its defeat owed more to apathy than to the efficiency of law enforcement machinery, and this was recognised by the IRA in its statement formally ending the campaign. The decision taken by the IRA shortly afterwards to abandon military methods and concentrate on socialist objectives by political means seemed to promise that the 1960s would be free of republican violence. This coincided with a Social Studies conference at Garron Tower in 1958, where G.B. Newe called for greater participation by Catholics in Northern Ireland affairs and Terence O'Neill, the future Prime Minister, appeared to indicate that they would be welcomed. In 1959 there were other signs of a possible erosion of traditional attitudes. The republican party, Sinn Fein, lost its two seats at Westminster, their percentage of the votes plummeting from 26% to 14%. Just as dramatic was the attempt by some leading Unionists to suggest that Catholics might be permitted to join the party. The attempt was thwarted by the obduracy of the Orange Order, but that it had been made at all was seen as a sign of changing times.

So the 1960s started as the decade of hope. The retirement in 1963 of the Prime Minister, Lord Brookeborough, who was to many Catholics the personification of right-wing Unionist opinion, and his replacement by Terence O'Neill, appeared to be another victory for moderation. The policies of the new premier encouraged this view. In 1964 he declared, 'my principal aims are to make Northern Ireland prosperous and to build bridges between the two traditions.'[15] The same year saw an important step in facilitating both aims. The southern connections of the Irish Congress of Trade Unions, to which most Northern workers were affiliated, had ensured its non-recognition by the Brookeborough administration. In 1964 a compromise was reached whereby the Congress was recognised by Stormont in return for greater independence being granted to its Northern Ireland Committee. But the most dramatic gestures towards reconciliation were the exchange visits between Captain O'Neill and the southern premier, Mr Lemass, in 1965. As a direct result of this visit the Nationalist party in Northern Ireland agreed to become the official opposition party in Stormont.

Such developments persuaded many contemporaries and not a few later observers to regard the 1960s as an age of tolerance reminiscent of the 1780s and 1790s. Like the earlier epoch, however, there were many warning signals remembered in retrospect but underrated in the exuberant optimism of the 1960s, that basic attitudes had not altered significantly. Moderate values in Ulster have their mythology, just as extremist values; and, like all mythologies, they ignore those pointers which challenged the popular view of the tolerant sixties. The traditional Ulster values, which would have been threatened by reconciliation, may have been in temporary hiding, but they soon emerged with banners flying. Indeed the flying of a banner and an attempt to remove it—in this case a tricolour in the Divis Street headquarters of Liam McMillan, the Republican candidate for West Belfast—provoked a riot in 1964, when liberal mythology had republicanism at its lowest ebb. A man who played a leading role in demanding the removal of the flag was to provide leadership to those Unionists and Protestants who opposed the current doctrines of political reconciliation and religious ecumenism. The attitudes expressed by Ian Paisley, head of the Free Presbyterian Church and the Protestant Unionist Party, had roots which stretched far into history. But the classic duel between liberal and right-wing Presbyterianism fought between Cooke and Montgomery in the 1820s was repeated when the Presbyterian General Assembly was picketed and attacked by Paisley in 1966. In the same year the Malvern Arms murders and the apprehension of the murderers revealed the existence of the UVF (Ulster Volunteer Force) which saw itself as the loyalist equivalent of the IRA. The pressures for change in Northern Ireland society had produced defenders of the status quo.

The changes which they were resisting seemed less substantial to some Catholics. Indeed the failure of the O'Neill administration to translate its intentions into practice caused considerable frustration and resentment. A series of measures —notably the closure of the rail link to Derry, the decision to establish a new university at Coleraine instead of in Derry where a University college was already operating, and the establishment of a new growth centre at Craigavon—were seen by both Catholics and Protestants in the west of the province, and especially in Derry city, as blatant discrimination against the disadvantaged west. In March 1967 the Republican Clubs, which represented an attempt by Republicans to find a legitimate method of political expression, were declared illegal by the government, a move which seemed narrow and repressive by many people who did not share republican views. As late as 1969, the failure of a Catholic to secure the Unionist nomination as a parliamentary candidate led to his resignation from the party. Louis Boyle, in his resignation statement, declared: 'One of my main hopes and guiding aims as a member of the party, has been to work towards a newly structured Unionist Party in which Protestants and Catholics could play a part as equal partners in pursuing a common political end. Now I know this is not possible. . . . The Unionist Party arose out of, and is still essentially based on a sectarian foundation, and only a reconstitution of the party away from its sectarian foundation could make Catholic membership a real possibility.'[16]

Other Catholics too had decided that reform would not come without pressure, believing that, whether Captain O'Neill wanted reform or not, the conservatism of his party would sabotage any changes. Housing allocation provided the issue for this pressure, and the success of the Civil Rights campaign in America suggested non-violent protest as the means. The Campaign for Social Justice in Northern Ireland, formed in Dungannon in 1964, developed through Housing Action committees in many parts of the province. In 1967 the broader-based Northern Ireland Civil Rights Association (NICRA) was formed. Its campaign, followed with increasing interest by international news media, was to make the Northern Ireland problem an international issue, and ushered in the most dynamic years in the history of Northern Ireland.

Any attempt to assess the internal performance of the Northern Ireland state between the early 1920s and the late 1960s must consider its record in economic matters. After an abysmal inter-war record in housing and employment, considerable advances were made after the Second World War—changes which altered the economic and social structure of the province. When it comes to measuring attitudes, the most significant development had been on the Unionist side. The downright opposition to or reluctant acceptance of the new state in 1920 had been converted to a pride and loyalty towards its institutions. The steadfast prime loyalty to Great Britain was both fortified and challenged by this more local pride. But no significant improvement had been made in the age-old community problem within Northern Ireland. The very processes and institutions which had created fierce loyalties among Protestants had deterred Catholics from accepting the state as their own. The apparent willingness of Catholics to accept the status quo in the post-war years was always conditional. For a genuine transition towards full participation in the new states Catholics demanded a number of institutional and social changes. The failure of the government to produce these changes made pressure inevitable. The pressure was applied seriously from 1967.

16

Northern Ireland: External Relations

Her relationships with the southern part of the country and with Britain provide Northern Ireland with the issue which determined prime political loyalties. In simple terms this issue has been whether the Northern Ireland area should be included within the United Kingdom or within an all-Ireland state. The state of diplomatic relations between southern Ireland and Britain to some extent was reflected in the relationship between the two communities inside Northern Ireland, as were the interactions between the two parts of Ireland.

The relationship between the Northern Ireland and British legislatures was not defined in any great detail by the Government of Ireland act (1920). Nevertheless some indisputable guidelines were laid down. One of these was the superiority of the Westminster parliament to which Northern Ireland sent twelve representatives. The subservience of the Northern Ireland assembly precluded it from some areas of government, notably foreign affairs and defence, which remained the responsibility of Westminster. This meant that all dealings between the northern and southern parts of Ireland were outside the jurisdiction of Northern Ireland's legislature.

During the first decade after the treaty, both Irish governments were more preoccupied with internal affairs to court conflict between each other; Britain was determined to remain, as far as was possible, outside Irish affairs. The Cosgrave administration, which remained in power in Dublin from 1922 until 1932, was almost exclusively occupied with domestic matters, but its attitude towards Northern Ireland was co-operative. In 1925 an agreement was signed by Great Britain and both Irish administrations which formally acknowledged the existing partition of the island.

Governments are transitory things, and the history of Ireland from the 1920s was to demonstrate that fluctuations in North-South relations depended more on governmental changes south of the border than on those in Northern Ireland. The coming to power of de Valera and the Fianna Fail party in 1932 had an immediate effect on these relations. Their aggressive policy of separatist nationalism immediately affected the Irish Free State relations with Britain. De Valera's decision in 1932 to end the annuities which had been repaid to the British government since

17

it had financed land purchase schemes for Irish tenants, produced retaliatory British tariffs on Irish cattle and finally led to the raising of general tariff walls between the two countries. The new Irish constitution of 1937 introduced a distinctly Catholic and Irish flavour, recognising the 'special position of the Holy Catholic Apostolic and Roman Church as the guardian of the faith professed by the great majority of the citizens.' Northern Ireland was directly affected by these new policies. In 1933 de Valera marked the new Northern policy by standing as an abstentionist for a seat in South Down. More important, Article 2 of the 1937 constitution stated unequivocally 'The national territory consists of the whole island of Ireland, its islands and its territorial seas.' The trade war between Eire and Great Britain ended with the trade agreement of 1938. But the challenge against partition was not so readily dropped.

Paralleling the deterioration of relations between Northern Ireland and the Irish Free State during the 1930s was a less spectacular but critical tightening of the bonds between Northern Ireland and the rest of the United Kingdom. This development particularly applied to the economic links between the two areas. Originally it was thought that taxes levied in Northern Ireland would adequately cover its expenditure, and even leave a surplus for an imperial contribution which was determined at £6·7 million for 1922–23.[17] With the rise of United Kingdom social expenditure and a decline in Northern Ireland's industrial expansion, it soon became clear that such hopes were illusory. Although a token Imperial contribution was maintained—descending to £10,000 p.a. during some of the depression years—a situation was rapidly reached where the rest of the United Kingdom was subsidising Northern Ireland's social benefits. The British Chancellor of the Exchequer recognised and supported this situation in 1938. The Simon declaration of that year not only acknowledged Northern Ireland's entitlement to similar social standards as Great Britain, but that the Westminster exchequer must supply the necessary funds for this if a deficit occurred in Northern Ireland. This principle of parity was naturally welcomed in Northern Ireland. Its short-term effect was to further widen the standards of social services north and south of the border; it was some time before it became clear that such financial concessions might imply conditions and obligations from Westminster which had been avoided in the early years of the new state. The increase in Britain's financial involvement in Northern Ireland following the Second World War—the establishment of the welfare state —led to the first British insistence that Stormont was obliged to adopt British standards in legislation. The Education Act (NI) in 1947 and the increase in family allowances in 1956 were two examples of British intervention to prevent the possibility of social services funds being distributed in a discriminatory fashion.

The immediate post-war years also saw statements in both Southern Ireland and Great Britain about the position of Northern Ireland. Ironically enough the declaration of an Irish Republic and its withdrawal from the British Commonwealth was carried, not by Fianna Fail which had lost office in 1948, but by a coalition government under John Costello. Sheehy may exaggerate when he claimed that these actions 'set the seal on Irish disunity'[18] but they certainly aroused fervour among Northern Ireland unionists. The 1949 general election there is known as the Union Jack election, and was fought largely on the issue of the union, thought by some to be in danger from a Labour government in Britain. In 1949 the Ireland act was designed to dispel such fears :

> It is hereby declared that Northern Ireland remains part of His Majesty's dominions and of the United Kingdom, and it is hereby affirmed that in no event will Northern Ireland or any part thereof cease to be part of His Majesty's dominions and of the United Kingdom without the consent of the parliament of Northern Ireland.

This strong British guarantee, and the severing of the Commonwealth relationship between Southern Ireland and Great Britain, might have been expected to inflame passions between the two parts of Ireland and within Northern Ireland itself. There were indeed communal stresses in the North following the election, and the Republic launched an international anti-partition campaign. But by the early fifties matters returned to normal, and a period of comparative stability returned for almost two decades. Britain had Conservative governments between 1951 and 1964. Never keen to enter the murky waters of Irish politics and diplomacy unless dragged in, they confined their interest to the economic field. Today Britain takes almost 70% of the Republic's exports, and supplies more than half her imports; and this relationship is reflected in emigration patterns from the Republic. Before 1936 well over half of Ireland's emigrants went to the United States; after that date, Great Britain became the main destination. The economic dependency on Britain is conspicuous enough for Boserup to claim that, in economic terms, the union between the Republic of Ireland and the United Kingdom was being restored. Nor was this all. The Republic of Ireland, quite apart from her relations with Britain, developed a much more outward-looking foreign policy from the 1950s, becoming actively involved in the United Nations movement, and eventually joining the European Economic Community in 1973.

It was in this new context of internationalism that the first few cautious steps of North-South co-operation began. Significantly, they were largely confined to economic interests which affected both areas. Thus in 1952 agreement was reached that both governments should take over the Foyle fisheries. This was followed by joint involvement in draining the Erne basin and in a hydro-electric development there.[19] Between 1953 and 1958 the Great Northern Railway, which included the Belfast-Dublin line, was operated jointly by the two governments and has since been operated jointly.

The meeting which took place in 1965 between the Northern and Southern premiers, Terence O'Neill and Sean Lemass, was a logical extension of these developments, but its symbolism was not lost in both parts of the island. They seemed to many to represent the new Ireland which had at last shaken off the past, men interested in prosperity rather than politics, in opportunities for co-operation instead of excuses for conflict. The effect inside Northern Ireland was considerable. The Nationalist party agreed to become the official opposition at Stormont, and the Catholic hierarchy appointed a chaplain to parliament. 'Twin towns' were established across the border, their citizens exchanging visits and experiences. Relations between north and south, and between both of them and Britain, had never been closer, and the prospects of a period of community harmony seemed good. They were to be destroyed by a mixture of majority tardiness and minority impatience. The events following from the Civil Rights campaign of 1967 were to radically alter both internal relations inside Northern Ireland, and Northern Ireland's relations with her immediate neighbours.

Civil Rights and After

One of the most remarkable aspects of the Civil Rights campaigns of 1968 was their success in forcing through some reforms.[20] After two marches, to Dungannon in August and to Derry in October, the O'Neill administration agreed to replace Derry City Council with a Development Commission, to establish an Ombudsman and to abolish the unfair company vote. Certainly complaints remained, notably about the Special Powers act and remaining inequalities in the franchise (one man, one vote), but promises were given that the schemes for allocating publicly-owned houses would be clarified and the Special Powers act reviewed. These successes ultimately split the Civil Rights movement. Those, like the members of the People's Democracy (PD) who were moving towards a more radical position, believed that it would be foolish to abandon a successful campaign before it had achieved all its objects.[21] Others felt that both the reforms and the dismissal from office in December of William Craig, the Minister of Home Affairs, demonstrated the government's good intentions, and that a suspension on marches should be agreed to enable the passing of further reforms. The decision by the People's Democracy unilaterally to march from Belfast to Derry in January 1969, and the violent opposition to the marchers at Burntollet Bridge, destroyed any hopes of non-violent protest. Many Protestants and liberal Catholics who had participated in the early campaigns now drifted out. The campaign became more radical. Nineteen sixty-nine was one of the seminal years in Irish history. Although the Civil Rights campaign continued, largely spurred by PD, the centre of the stage was dominated in the first few months by internal dissension within the Unionist Party. The January elections of that year gave hints of this combustion, and the replacement of Captain O'Neill as premier by Major Chichester-Clark was an attempt to find a compromise between inter-party views which were becoming increasingly incompatible.

It was the events of the summer which set the province on a

21

new and violent course. Community tensions had been increased by the events of 1968, and the months leading up to the traditional celebrations were marked by riots in Strabane, Derry and Belfast. On 12 August the Protestant Apprentice Boys of Derry held their march and were attacked. The violence of the police reaction in the Catholic Bogside produced two important responses. The Prime Minister of the Irish Republic, Jack Lynch, made his famous 'we will not stand by' speech, the strong language of which it is now clear was intended to compensate for his inability to do anything else; and the violence spread to Belfast. In August the Catholic Lower Falls area was invaded by a hostile mob, seven people were killed, more than 3,000 lost their homes, and the situation was changed utterly.

The events of August introduced two new elements which were soon to dominate the Northern Ireland stage. On 14 August the British government sent the army into Derry, and on the next day to Belfast. Up until August 1969 the violence of the campaign was certainly no greater than it had been on many earlier occasions. The extra ingredient in the Civil Rights campaign was the massive coverage by the international news media, which put unprecedented pressure on the British government to intervene more directly in Northern Ireland. This intervention took the form of sending the army to protect the Catholic areas against further attacks, and installing two senior civil servants in Northern Ireland to supply directly accurate information. The soldiers were received rapturously in Catholic areas. People were later to remember Bernadette Devlin's words in August 1969, 'You're giving them tea now. What will you be giving them in six months?' Her time scale was inaccurate, but the sentiment proved true.

The Provisional IRA was officially formed in January 1970, when its founder members rejected the socialism of the Official IRA. But the Provisionals' birthplace was Belfast in August 1969. The growing pacificism of the IRA during the early 1960s was blamed for the vulnerability of the Falls in 1969. 'IRA I Ran Away', chalked derisively on the walls of the city, determined some members that this must never happen again. The new organisation built up its support to a background of community strife in early 1970. There were riots in Ballymurphy in April. During June of that year five people died in civil disturb-

22

ances and 248 were injured. The imposition of a curfew on the Falls by the army in July greatly increased Catholic disenchantment with the army, and the tea stopped flowing. On 31 October 1970 the Provisionals killed their first soldier, and the campaign escalated during the winter and the following spring.

Curiously enough the same period witnessed a number of reforms which would have been gratefully accepted two years earlier, but which passed almost unnoticed. Following the Hunt Report the 'B' Specials had been disbanded in October 1969 and the Royal Ulster Constabulary disarmed the following month. During the second half of 1970 a central Housing Authority, a Ministry of Community Relations, a Community Relations Commission, and a Commissioner for Complaints were all established. An Incitement to Hatred bill was introduced, and universal suffrage—the famous *One Man, One Vote*—was extended to local elections. All these were swamped in a sea of violence.

Brian Faulkner's rise to the premiership in March 1971 presaged the introduction of internment. Protestant frustration had been steadily increasing as the Provisional IRA's bombing and shooting campaign increased. In March shipyard workers had marched through the centre of Belfast to demand the introduction of internment. Despite army and other advice that such a policy would merely consolidate Catholic support for the Provisionals' campaign, internment started on 9 August. It was followed by riots, gun battles, heavy casualties and the intimidation of about 2,500 families from their homes during that month. The opposition Social Democratic and Labour Party withdrew from Stormont and set up a short-lived Alternative Assembly. And the Provisionals' campaign continued with even greater violence. There is little doubt that internment and the interrogation methods used by the army and police hardened minority opinion and assisted the Provisionals.

It is difficult to chronicle the events of the next three years. Indeed every initiative and every development between 1970 and 1974 was acted out against a constant backcloth of violence and death, interrupted only by new terrorist or anti-terrorist techniques or particularly shocking incidents. The murder of the three Scottish soldiers in March 1971; Bloody Sunday and the Aldershot bomb; Bloody Friday; the Vanguard strike follow-

23

ing the imposition of Direct Rule from Westminster in March 1972; the Provisional IRA truce in July 1972; the growth of the assassination campaign; all these are milestones in a saga of death, intimidation and destruction. The people in Northern Ireland had adjusted to abnormality. Outside Northern Ireland, feelings of shock were soon replaced by boredom.

The decision by the British government to prorogue the Northern Ireland parliament and government, and to rule directly from Westminster through a Secretary of State, was primarily an attempt to lay foundations for a new beginning. It had little discernible difference on the rate of escalation of violence. As well as the bombings and shootings, 1972 was the year in which loyalist militarism became organised and increasingly active in the Ulster Defence Association; it also saw an increase in murders which were solely sectarian in character, with victims often selected at random on account of their religion. Local politicians argued that the growing ability of violent and paramilitary groups to call the political tune during the period of Direct Rule was due to the absence of a local legislature. But an attempt to form a power-sharing Executive from three parties whose mandate was based on election results to a new Northern Ireland Assembly in 1973 was unsuccessful. A strike by loyalist workers in May 1974 forced its resignation and Direct Rule returned. In the meantime, after a decade of political chaos, with old parties disappearing and new ones emerging, the wheel had swung full circle. By the end of 1974 the unionist parties had united in the United Ulster Unionist Council, the old Nationalist voters were supporting the Social Democratic and Labour Party, and the parties of the centre could claim the support of only 10–15% of the population. The permanence of the Ulster problem had reasserted itself.

CHAPTER II

Who lives where:
The demographic background

The extremity to which party and religious feeling has grown in Belfast is shown strikingly by the fact that the people of the artisan and labouring classes . . . dwell to a large extent in separate quarters, each of which is given up almost entirely to persons of one particular faith, and the boundaries of which are sharply defined.
Official report; 1886 riots

The church is plainly the focal point, and then the school. Around these two buildings cluster the population they serve, and so a ghetto is born.
Harold Jackson, 1971

JUST as one cannot hope to understand the Northern Ireland conflict without an acquaintance with its history, it is impossible to appreciate its pervasiveness without some knowledge of the background, extent and effect of residential segregation between Catholics and Protestants. This is both the cause and consequence of the province's history of turbulence.

It is inaccurate to regard Ireland's population as twenty-six southern Catholic counties divided by a border from six northern Protestant ones. While it is true that Protestants represent only 5% of the Republic of Ireland's population, there are considerably larger concentrations of Protestants in Donegal, Monaghan and Cavan, the counties which fringe the border. Similarly with Northern Ireland. In 1961 65·1% of Northern Ireland's population was Protestant, but this disguises the fact that there are regions within the province with considerable Catholic majorities. Most of these are in the areas nearest the border, but they also include west Belfast and parts of north Antrim. In some parts of Northern Ireland

Catholic and Protestant homes and farms exist alongside each other; in others, especially some urban centres, districts, streets and quarters are exclusively inhabited by one religious group.

The implications of residential segregation are more than a matter for abstract speculation. In a polarised community, where few voters are prepared to alter their allegiances, the politics of population assume particular importance. What are the relative Protestant and Catholic birth and emigration rates? Do electoral boundaries favour one group? Is there a possibility of the minority's higher birth rate eventually converting them into a majority? It was questions like these which determined the size and composition of the Northern Ireland state, and which guided major political attitudes after its formation.

But the importance of Northern Ireland's demographic structure is not confined to general political considerations. On a more local level it is often religious segregation, especially in towns, which converts distrust and dislike into violence. Most towns which have escaped the worst community conflict are those where the houses of both communities are integrated; the worst communal violence has been concentrated in urban centres where one polarised religious bloc adjoins its rival— towns like Belfast, Derry, Lurgan and Portadown. Obviously other factors also contribute to the prevalence of community tension in these towns, but it is clear that a concentration of one religious group in a particular district provides a focus for its opponents. The relationship between sectarian violence and residential segregation is an integral one.

In this chapter the origins and growth of this segregation, especially in urban areas, will be examined, and its current extent and effects discussed. Finally those dynamic factors which affect and alter population balance—factors like emigration, birth rates and intimidation—will be described and considered.

The Development of Residential Segregation

The historical roots, as usual, go back to the early seventeenth century, when the Plantation of Ulster introduced a large number of alien settlers to the province. It is an appropriate starting point for any consideration of residential segregation, because the

26

arrival of the Planters established demographic patterns which are essentially those dividing Northern Ireland's communities today. In particular they brought with them a foreign concept of towns.

The entrepreneurs who bought the planted land at low prices were required to build and maintain towns as fortresses from which the native Irish were excluded. In Derry, for example, citizens were forbidden to employ the natives as servants 'in order that the city might not in future be peopled with Irish'.[1] Such injunctions were soon found to be unenforceable. Not only was it difficult to attract a sufficient number of English and Scots tenants, but it was almost impossible for them to find fellow-countrymen willing to carry out the more menial tasks. So Catholics were accepted as farm labourers and occasionally as tenants on the land which they had recently owned. Even in the towns there was need for servants, labourers and other residents who would service the Planters. Gradually the restrictions which excluded Catholics from towns were relaxed or ignored, especially in the eighteenth century. By the 1790s there were enough Catholics in Belfast to justify the building of the city's first Catholic church, St Mary's in Chapel Lane.

The new Catholic citizens were excluded from the parts of the towns inhabited by Protestants and settled in closely-knit exclusive clusters. In Belfast, where they had been prohibited from the original walled city, Catholics congregated in the western reaches; the name of the 'Irish Quarter' in Carrickfergus clearly proclaimed its origin; Lurgan and Portadown were other towns where the two main religious groupings developed apart from each other. But the most powerful barrier between the Planter and Gael, both real and symbolical, were the stern walls of Derry. 'To the west of the walls, behind the city and beneath the Mall Wall and the fluted Doric column erected to the memory of Governor Walker and the great siege, symbolising Protestant power, was another Derry.'[2] The other Derry, where the Catholic immigrants, most of whom came from Donegal, settled, was appropriately called the Bogside.

It was the expansion of Belfast during the nineteenth century that produced the most volatile urban problems. The Industrial Revolution left few traces in Ireland outside the Lagan valley;

27

Belfast began to grow, pushing her boundaries out in every direction to meet the demands of the new textiles and shipbuilding industries. The drift to the city was encouraged as much by acute land shortage throughout Ireland as by the attraction of industrial wages, and the combined effect was the emergence of a raw sprawling industrial complex. Barrow, an English tourist, noted in 1834 that 'some four or five thousand raw uneducated Catholic labourers from the south had, within a few years, poured into the city to supply the demand for labour.'[3] In the decade preceding 1841 Belfast's population increased by 40%, and one third of these were Catholics. 'Almost immediately the tolerance which had characterised Protestant attitudes before the turn of the century turned to mistrust. The second half of the nineteenth century saw a series of conflicts and the growth of intolerance which was to reach its greatest bitterness in this century.'[4] It was in the parts of Belfast where the workers congregated that the violence was closest to the surface. Although a Catholic bourgeoisie arrived in the city to service the growing population—priests, lawyers, teachers, manufacturers and merchants—they did not represent a similar threat to their Protestant counterpart as the new workers; in both Belfast and Derry the nineteenth century saw the withdrawal of the middle classes, both Protestant and Catholic, to the suburbs. Among the workers, however, a different pattern emerged. The main Catholic colony expanded outwards along the Falls road with the Protestant working-class Shankill road shadowing it to the north. Similarly across the river in east Belfast, the small Catholic enclave of the Short Strand contracted into a fortress within predominantly Protestant east Belfast. The pattern was similar in Derry and in many of the other towns like Lurgan and Portadown. Catholic and Protestant workers lived in the same general urban areas, but were divided into religious ghettos, compact, mutually exclusive and leaning on each other.

The recurrent riots of the nineteenth and early twentieth centuries hardened the religious boundaries in Belfast. The fact that many of these riots were followed by eviction of the minority families, usually from the same working-class districts on each occasion, shows that even short periods of peace produced some residential mixing—a blurring of the ghetto boundaries.

But it was the families who lived in alien territory who were usually the first victims of violence. Consequently since the 1830s there was a steady progression towards single-religion communities in the working-class parts of Belfast. The process was described in a number of official investigations, like the report on the 1857 riots : 'Since the commencement of the late riots, however, the districts have become exclusive, and by regular systematised movement on both sides, the few Catholic inhabitants of the Sandy Row district have been obliged to leave it, and the few Protestants of the Pound district have been obliged to leave that district.'[5]

So there were strong forces which maintained sectarian districts in Belfast, and community sanctions against any family which disturbed the pattern. The same phenomenon has been observed during the violence of 1969 and the early 1970s. The building of a number of public housing estates in Belfast's suburbs during the years following the Second World War introduced a new living environment for many families; some of them were integrated. One effect of the latest troubles has been to divide and polarise these new estates. It has been estimated that between 5% and 10% of Belfast's population were so intimidated by violence between 1969 and 1973 as to leave their homes and seek the security of living among their co-religionists.[6] The erection by the army of a 'Peace Line' in 1969 not only physically cut off Belfast's Falls and Shankill communities from each other; it symbolised a situation where Catholics and Protestants in many parts of the city no longer felt that they could live together with any degree of security.

Living Apart
Where People Live
Visiting journalists and observers of the Northern Ireland scene, bemused already by its nuances, were further bewildered by a bland announcement in 1971 that Dr Paisley's latest Free Presbyterian church was to be built in the Irish Republic. Similarly surprise is expressed on each 12 July when Orange lodges from Donegal, Cavan and even Dublin attend the great Orange processions in Northern Ireland. Even considerable acquaintance with the reality of the situation has not banished the widely accepted belief in religious stereotypes. So the South is seen as

29

a priest-ridden, economically backward Catholic bastion and the North as a puritanical hard-bitten Orange dictatorship. All this divided, it is believed, by what Brian Friel described as a drunken line that 'reels across the country and stumbles into Lough Foyle at a place appropriately called Muff'. The belief that the border accurately divides two cohesive populations is as inaccurate as the religious stereotypes. Brendan Walsh, one of Ireland's leading population experts, put it like this: 'The religious division of the country into Roman Catholics and other denominations is, from a demographic viewpoint, far more real than the political division into Northern Ireland and the Republic.'[7]

While this may appear to be an academic point, it is a matter of deep concern in the counties which touch the border. There are considerable Protestant minorities in the three counties of traditional Ulster which were excluded from the state of

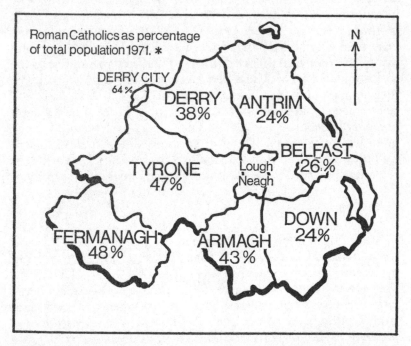

Roman Catholics as percentage of total population 1971. *

DERRY CITY 64%
DERRY 38%
ANTRIM 24%
BELFAST 26%
TYRONE 47%
Lough Neagh
FERMANAGH 48%
ARMAGH 43%
DOWN 24%
N

* These percentages should only be taken as approximate guides, since large numbers of people in all parts of Northern Ireland refused to state their religious affiliations in the 1971 census.

Northern Ireland. At the start of this century 22% of the population of Donegal and Monaghan was Protestant—in Cavan the figure was 19%.[8] While these figures have since declined to 14% and 12%, they comprise minorities which tend to cluster in particular parts of these counties, some of which represent formidable enclaves.

In Northern Ireland the situation is similar. In very general terms the areas nearest the border have larger Catholic proportions than those furthest away. It is also interesting to note that, since partition, the Catholic percentage has only increased in one of the Northern counties touching the border. In counties Derry, Fermanagh and Down it has declined, while it has stayed constant in County Tyrone.

The Protestant heartlands are firmly established in the areas west of the River Bann. In counties Antrim and Down and in Belfast the population is more than 70% Protestant. In demo-

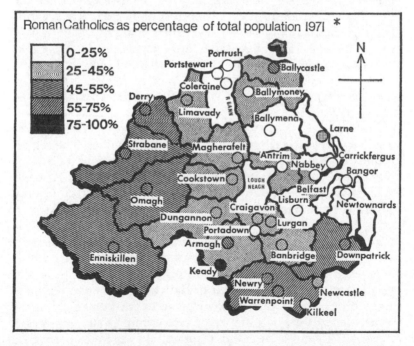

Roman Catholics as percentage of total population 1971 *

0-25%
25-45%
45-55%
55-75%
75-100%

*These percentages should only be taken as approximate guides, since large numbers of people in all parts of Northern Ireland refused to state their religious affiliations in the 1971 census.

31

graphic terms, the east-west division of Northern Ireland is a real one, and nothing reflects this more than their political allegiances.

The last election which took place in Northern Ireland before the introduction of Direct Rule was the 'O'Neill' election of 1969. An analysis of voting patterns clearly reveals their connection with religious adherences. Twenty-nine of the thirty-nine Unionist MPs came from Belfast, County Antrim, or County Down and six of the remainder from Counties Derry and Armagh, the areas with the largest Protestant populations.[9] The city of Belfast, on a smaller scale, showed a similar consistency of voting behaviour. Every election since 1920 shared the same general pattern.

So it is tempting to think of Northern Ireland's population in terms of generalisations. A Protestant core east of the River Bann: Catholics strongest in rural areas: a high correlation between Catholicism and proximity to the border. Under the microscope the pattern is much more complicated. Areas which appear at first sight to be entirely green or orange have in fact a much more mottled appearance. It is not true on a whole that Protestants and Catholics in Northern Ireland only live among people of their own religion. The picture is rather one of a series of religious enclaves. It is certainly true, especially in the towns, that these religious enclaves are sometimes large and denominationally exclusive. More often, however, the enclaves vary in size from small groups to individual families. The region around Ballycastle in County Antrim, for example, is a Catholic area in the Protestant heartland; so are the towns of Armagh and Keady in County Armagh. The northern part of County Tyrone is predominantly Catholic, but the town of Cookstown within it has a Protestant majority. Even the most overwhelmingly Protestant town has areas where Catholics and Protestants live in haphazard demographic patterns; and Catholic farms are worked alongside Protestant in many parts of the province, as Rosemary Harris described it in Ballybeg.[10] The two religious communities are in fact interwoven into the human fabric of the province. It is not a matter of two ethnic groups glowering at each other across the Bann. Contact takes place in every part of the province; indeed it is often impossible to avoid such contacts, especially in country regions. The relevant point is

32

that the enclaves, whether they are large groups or mere individuals see themselves as ethnic units distinct from the other ethnic units beside or around them. And it is this factor which is perhaps the most important in maintaining their distinctiveness.

The Towns

It is in the larger towns that tensions were most keenly felt. Belfast and the areas surrounding it has more than its fair share of resources in relation to the rest of the province. According to the 1971 census, 36% of the province's population and a much higher percentage of its industrial employees live in Belfast and its environmental areas.[11] Indeed the eastern concentration is even greater than this; almost two thirds of Northern Ireland's population live within thirty miles of Belfast.

How much housing segregation is there within the Greater Belfast area? To start with, about 26% of this population is Catholic, and most of this minority—81% of it in fact[12]—live in the Falls and Ardoyne areas. In 1968 two thirds of Belfast's families lived in streets in which 91% or more of the households were of the same religion. On the other hand, 27·5% of Belfast Catholics live in streets in which less than 40% of the households are Catholic.[13] Similarly with occupations, although there is undoubtedly occupational segregation as well as discrimination, many Catholics and Protestants work with people of the other religion. So considerable contact takes place between the communities, although, as J.C. Beckett wrote, 'they mingle with a consciousness of the differences between them'.[14]

Belfast is not the only city in the world with residential segregation, and it is far from being the most polarised. Racial segregation in Birmingham is roughly similar in extent to religious segregation in Belfast. In the United States many minorities, notably black people, are segregated to a much greater extent than Catholics in Belfast. The difference is that none of these cities have the tradition of communal violence which Belfast has. Few people would argue that the proximity of the two sides created communal riots. What it in fact did was to ensure that normal neighbourhood differences often assumed sectarian form and were correspondingly more likely to lead to

33

violence, inter-communal rivalry often providing the initial arguments. So the two communities did not fight each other because they were close together; but the closeness made violence more likely. It may be true that increased familiarity with opposing points of view helps to erode sectarian myths; Belfast demonstrates that a combination of proximity and lack of contact ensures their propagation.

There have been recent indications of important changes in the city's population pattern. Many cities are experiencing conditions in which citizens are abandoning the centre for the suburbs. Belfast is no exception. The city's population declined by 39,405 between 1966 and 1971.[15] In the same period the environmental areas on its outskirts increased by 27,378. This was partly due to the government's Resettlement Grants scheme, which offers financial inducements to leave Belfast and move to designated growth points. Even before the introduction of this scheme there had been a considerable voluntary exodus from the city; poor housing conditions and a housing shortage accentuated by the city's redevelopment were the main reasons, and the trickle became a flood when violence further deteriorated living conditions. The trouble was that the new Resettlement Grants scheme encouraged families to leave Belfast, but no steps were taken to ensure that the city's sectarian problems were left behind. It is hardly surprising that they were not. Many of those who moved, especially since 1969, have been intimidated families, seeking security and peace after experiences which were often traumatic. Their arrival in towns, villages and estates outside the city was seen by local inhabitants as threatening the stability of the neighbourhood—a spreading of the Belfast disease. No serious attempts were made to acclimatise the new arrivals to new conditions, or to reassure their new neighbours about the extent or effects of the infusion of newcomers. The result has been the disruption of some settled communities and bitter disillusionment for the new families. Forced by violence to seek stable conditions, their very arrival in the new area often destroyed the stability which they sought.

The very name of Northern Ireland's second city is one of the symbols which helps betray the ethnic background of an Ulsterman. To many Protestants it is Londonderry, Catholics

34

preferring the pre-plantation name Derry. Manoeuvring conversations to include the city's name is a common Northern Ireland gambit to discover the religion of one's companion—like employers asking potential employees what school they attended, the answer usually reveals a person's religion.

There is residential and occupational segregation in Derry as there is in Belfast, and there it was actively encouraged by the housing allocation policies of the local council. The Bogside is as Catholic as the Fountain is Protestant. But the city has a number of other particular qualities which make it unique. It has been claimed that its birth rate of 31·8 per 1,000 may be the highest in Europe.[16] An unemployment rate which has scarcely dropped below 20% in the last fifty years has contributed towards a remarkably high adult male emigration rate, especially among Catholics. This situation was widely believed to result from governmental decisions which discriminated against the city. One of many such decisions which are quoted in support of this view was the controversy about the siting of Northern Ireland's second university. Derry with a population of 52,000 (1971 census) is the largest population centre outside the Belfast area; it also had a long-established University College. Nevertheless it was decided in 1965 to establish the New University of Ulster in Coleraine, which had a population of 10,000–11,000. It is hardly surprising that this was interpreted in Derry as yet another instance of governmental bias against the areas west of the Bann.

The effect of this was to make Derry, despite its bitter internal divisions, a city which has many integrating factors. There is an intense local pride which is not present in Belfast.[17] Certainly Derry Catholics, with their physical closeness to the Republic and their many cross-border family ties in Donegal, are anti-partitionist. But the city can be regarded in some respect as a unit, forged by a common bond of grievance against an unsympathetic government. The reaction to the 1965 Lockwood report, which rejected Derry's proposals for the new university, was one which overcame sectarian differences. The mass meetings and the motorcade which travelled to Belfast to protest against the decisions were organised by both unionist and nationalist local leaders. So it is with many other issues. In Belfast problems are often seen in terms of hostile communities;

Derry is more concerned with the institutions which created its problems—Westminster, Stormont, the City Council. Issues are debated at a state rather than a community level. Derry is the microcosm of the Northern Ireland problem, where contrasts are seen more sharply—a community fashioned by its grievances. It is no coincidence that the civil rights campaign got off its feet there, and the first 'no go' areas were established within its boundaries.

As in Belfast and Derry, so in some smaller towns. Lurgan,[18] in County Armagh, with a population of 24,000, is one example of a segregated town. Its population growth was similar to that of some other Northern Ireland towns. Belfast's first Catholics had settled in the west of the city near the Bog Meadows and Derry's in the Bogside. In Lurgan it was the fenlands beside Lough Neagh which housed its first Catholics. Once again the two religious communities ranged themselves in separate parts of the town and a typically segregated situation began.

In Lurgan however there was an attempt to break the pattern. The first modern estates in the town were integrated. But over the years people drifted towards their own ghetto areas. One of the reasons for this was a simple factor which is still not sufficiently considered in planning. The new estates, while excellent in some ways, were sited too far away from the Catholic churches and schools. In Lurgan at any rate there is considerable evidence that a major motive for segregation was convenience rather than fear.

One concept which throws light on the reluctance of Catholics and Protestants to live together in some part of Northern Ireland is that of 'territoriality'. This has been defined by Robert Ardrey: 'Everyone has an area of territory where they feel more secure, which acts as a haven from a hostile world and a place where they can seek refuge among their own kind. This area need not have a physical boundary and varies from one individual to another. Such personal territory represents the mental conception of the physical-social space around the individual and is referred to as "territoriality".'[19]

A number of observers, in attempting to explain the way in which Northern Ireland people define their 'personal territory', emphasise the importance of the religious structures which distinguish one community from the other. As already mentioned,

36

Kirk stressed the importance of the siting of churches and schools when Lurgan people were deciding where they wished to live. Harold Jackson made a similar point about Belfast: 'The church is clearly the focal point, and then the school. Around these two buildings cluster the population they serve, and so a ghetto is born.'[20] Whether or not this is true, the most valid way to look upon Belfast's community is as a collection of urban villages. The man from the Shankill road may not think he has much in common with the man from Ardoyne, but they share a prime loyalty to their immediate locality rather than to Belfast. Sometimes, as Jackson suggested, the parish is the main unit, as it is in Clonard or Ardoyne; but it is just as likely to be a housing estate like Turf Lodge or Ballymurphy, or one of the city's traditional communities, like Sandy Row or the Falls or the Shankill. Whatever their basis it is these enclaves which are the significant communities in Belfast, and possibly in some other towns in Northern Ireland.

Because these urban fortresses are ideological as well as territorial there is strong pressure towards social conformity within them. A survey in 1971 found that 58% of both religious groups believe that co-religionists should 'stick together and do a lot to help each other'. Church attendance in Northern Ireland is remarkably high.[21] Attitudes towards people who marry outside their religious group are not favourable in either community. Consequently it is not surprising that a high percentage of marriages are between partners from the same immediate area, creating numerous complex family relationships which further strengthen its cohesion. The result of all these factors is the creation of remarkably stable segregated communities, and segregation, once established, shows a strong tendency towards inertia. The changes which do take place—for example the inflow and outflow which accompany sectarian rioting—tend to further strengthen the bonds with the enclaves, as when intimidation uproots minority families and forces them to seek the security of their co-religionists.

The greater the hostility between Catholic and Protestant communities, the more one would expect to find conformity in each one. Dr Boal from Queen's University, Belfast, has carried out surveys to examine territoriality in parts of Belfast. His results show a high degree of segregation, not only in the places where people live, but in their everyday social habits.[22]

The areas which he selected were the Clonard area in the Lower Falls Road, and part of the adjoining Shankill Road. The first was 98% Catholic and the second 99% Protestant. Clonard is part of a constituency which then returned a Republican Labour MP, while a Unionist represented the Shankill. The slogans on the walls were the brands which identified the boundary between the two areas. In addition to these obvious divisions, Boal found significant differences in the pattern of living in the two areas. They read different newspapers, for example; while 83% of the Clonard families read the *Irish News*, only 3% of those on the Shankill did. They supported different football teams, and no one in either area favoured the team supported by the majority in the other community. A small minority did their shopping in the alien territory, but well over 90% supported shops in their own community although this often involved considerable inconvenience. Even the name which they applied to the small area (population less than 5,000 persons) in which they lived was a symbol of their differences: No one in Clonard described his area as part of the Shankill Road; no one in the Shankill saw himself as part of the Falls or Clonard community. Boal sums up his evidence briefly: 'The cumulative evidence indicates the presence of two very distinct territories.'[23]

Such polarisation is not confined to Belfast. A study conducted in Derry city in 1969[24] found very similar territorial differences between the Long Tower district (99·5% Catholics) and the Fountain district (85·4% Protestant). Interaction between the two groups was confined to their places of work and Derry's shopping centre, although it was commonplace in an adjoining mixed district which was also studied.

So polarisation between Catholic and Protestant areas is extensive in some urban areas. Equally revealing however was a comparative study carried out by Boal, also in 1968. This time he selected two neighbouring Protestant estates in Belfast, one comprising council housing and the other expensive private residences—Taughmonagh and Upper Malone. Similar activity tests were conducted and contact between the two areas was found to be as low as in the Shankill-Clonard region. For

38

example, the schools attended by children from the two estates were significantly different. None of the children in Taughmonagh estate attended grammar school preparatory departments, which were favoured by 44% of the children of Upper Malone. During a period when visits in and out of the areas were monitored, not one single visit from one area to the other took place. The conclusion was clear. 'Socio-economically based territories exist that are every bit as sharply divided as are the more publicised religious territories of Belfast.'[25]

It may be true that Catholic areas would not show the same sharp contrasts as Upper Malone and Taughmonagh because they tend to be more socially mixed, but this has not yet been tested by researchers. However the territoriality studies which have been carried out indicate that Belfast urban fortresses are frequently divided by class as well as by religion. If social divisiveness is seen as Northern Ireland's main problem, it may be that public concentration on the problem of sectarian divisions has obscured class divisions which are at least as marked.

Dynamic Factors

Most of the demographic factors in Northern Ireland—segregated housing, tradition, territoriality—contribute towards the permanence of its divisions. It is not surprising that contrary influences, those which might threaten the carefully constructed differences, are particularly important. At the national level, a radical change in the balance between the communities would threaten the very existence of the state, since the state would have been abolished by a Nationalist victory at the polls. The balance is equally important at community level, where the extent and type of segregation critically affects living conditions, safety and even life. Since the state was established, three variables in particular have threatened the demographic balance of the province; they are birth and emigration rates, and intimidation.

Birth and Emigration Rates

'In culturally divided communities differences in demographic behaviour frequently become a focal point of prejudice and controversy. The higher birth rate generally found among the poorer or disadvantaged group is typically seen as a threat of eventual outbreeding by the rest of the population.'[26] Brendan Walsh's remarks apply particularly to the Northern Ireland situation. Many Unionists have seen the state which they created being threatened by a larger Nationalist birth rate. At times the main political strategy of the Nationalist party appears to have been merely to wait for their supporters to out-breed their opponents.

The figures superficially seem to bear these fears out. In both Northern Ireland and the Republic the Catholic birth rate has been about 50% higher than that of other denominations. This gap has been declining slightly recently, but the size of Catholic families is still larger than the average. Emrys Jones, writing about Belfast in 1960, demonstrated the higher fertility in the Catholic parts of the city, and went on to say 'there is a clear indication that, other things being equal, an increasing rate of growth of the Catholic population compared with the Prot-estant population will continue'.[27]

The most important words in that sentence are 'other things being equal'. In fact a number of factors seriously modify the picture of Catholics inexorably outbreeding Protestants for the cause of Irish unity. In the first place, although Catholic mar-riages in Ireland are remarkable for their high fertility rate, people tended to marry much later than usual or not at all. There is a strikingly high level of celibacy among Catholics of both sexes.[28] This phenomenon of a high marriage fertility without the consequence of a high birth rate is seen by de-mographers as an archaic method of population control, and it particularly applies in country areas. It is a regulating factor on what would normally be a steady increase in the Catholic per-centage of the population of Northern Ireland.

Emigration, more than anything else, has countered the effect of the high Catholic birth rate. Ireland's population is unique among western states as being still considerably lower than it was 150 years ago. An agrarian economy with too many depen-dents often relies on emigration as a safety valve, and Ireland's tradition of exporting her population dates back many years. Protestant emigration from Ulster was extensive during the eighteenth century—it was not unusual for Minister and congregation to move *en bloc* to America. But it was the great famine of the 1840s which really produced a large-scale exodus. In 1851, for example, one quarter of Liverpool's population had been born in Ireland. In addition to steady emigration figures, seasonal migration was and is common. In 1841 no fewer than 57,651 Irishmen went to England for the harvesting season and returned home when it ended.[29]

The partition of Ireland added a new dimension to the migration question, although a temporary one. Despite the scepticism of many politicians about the chances of such an artificial division lasting for long, Lloyd George's forecast that 'frontiers once established, harden into permanence', was soon vindicated. However, partition was followed by considerable demographic changes. The most radical of these was Protestant migration from the south to the north. Between 1911 and 1926 the Protestant population of the South declined by a third, and has continued to decrease by about 10% each decade since then.[30] The 1961 census reveals that 53,124 Northern Ireland residents had been born in the Republic— twice as many as the number of residents of the Republic born in Northern Ireland, despite the Republic's greater population. So the trend once again was towards more clearly defined religious units.

A sorting-out period was to be expected following partition, but there is no evidence of extensive migration between the two parts of Ireland after the 1920s. But the traditional pattern of emigration from both North and South, especially to Britain, continued unimpaired. One of its most important consequences was its relative effect on the two religious communities in Northern Ireland.

F.S.L. Lyons estimated that between 55% and 58% of those who emigrated between 1937 and 1961 were Catholic, despite the fact that Catholics account for only about one third of the population.[31] Brendan Walsh reckoned that as many as two thirds of male emigrants and three quarters of female were Catholic. Equally significant is the fact that emigrants were highly concentrated into the 15–39 age groups. In the inter-censal period 1951–1961, for example, no less than 31·7% of male Catholics aged between twenty-five and twenty-nine had left Northern Ireland, largely because of emigration. The equivalent figure for other denominations was 19·3%.[32] None

41

of this is very surprising, except perhaps in extent. It is not remarkable for those who are economically less well off to be most ready to leave. But the figures do not apply equally to Catholics all over the province. A comparative study of emigration rates between Counties Antrim and Fermanagh from 1951 to 1961 shows how the denominational differences were greater in the case of Fermanagh and less in County Antrim.[38] In County Antrim the Catholic population rose by about 6·8% in the decade, as against 4·7% for other denominations. In Fermanagh both communities declined in number, but at different rates; the Catholic population fell by between 14% and 15%, and that of other denominations by between 2% and 5%. Antrim's increase is largely explained by its relative prosperity, and Fermanagh's decline by economic depression there. Poverty and the resulting higher emigration rate in Fermanagh and the west, where Catholics were more numerous, were not numerically compensated by the increase in County Antrim's population, and there have been numerous allegations that the west's high Catholic population was one cause of the governments' inertia towards its decline.

But whatever the reasons, there can be little doubt about the outcome. In net terms, the higher Catholic birth rate is almost entirely offset by the higher Catholic emigration rate. The result is virtual stability in the overall population picture. In 1926, the first census in the Northern Ireland state, Catholics formed 33·5% of the population; in 1961 it was 34·9%. Indeed, in some particularly sensitive areas like County Fermanagh the Catholic percentage has actually gone down.

The seriousness of the population numbers game should not be forgotten. It consists of projecting from past trends what will be the future balance between Catholics and Protestants. In its simplest form the question is, do the present patterns indicate that Protestants will be outbred in Northern Ireland? Brendan Walsh has studied this question and reckons that, given equal emigration rates and the maintenance of the birth rate differential, Catholics would outnumber Protestants in 55 years from 1970. The lesson of the last fifty years however, is that such bald statements are futile. Emigration rates have not been equal; the birth rate differential has varied considerably. It is true that the stability of the Northern Ireland population was due to the interaction of a number of variables, and any change in their composition could have dramatic effects. If, for example, the Protestant emigration rate rose as a result of civil disorders or any other factor, the way would be left clear for the Catholic superior birth rate to assert itself. Equally, if the Catholic birth rate were to decline and its emigration rate were to be maintained, the Protestant percentage in Northern Ireland would gradually increase. Such a decline has taken place in Catholic countries before—in post-war Italy and Spain, for example—and there were signs of a reduced Catholic birth rate in Ireland between 1961 and 1965.

Intimidation

Intimidation is not new to Northern Ireland. Both communities have taken advantage of the regular sectarian disturbances since the 1830s to remove potential enemies from their midst. Intimidation and evictions accompanied every nineteenth-century riot as well as the violence of the 1920s and early 1930s. It seems doubtful, however, that anything in the past came even close to the population movements which have taken place since 1969. In August and September of that year more than 3,500 families were forced to leave their homes, 85% of them Catholic.[34] Two years later, during three weeks in August 1971, a further 2,069 recorded families left their homes.[35]

Between and after these two periods of exceptional violence, a less spectacular but steady flow of families abandoned their homes from fear or intimidation. Darby and Morris calculated this at between 8,000 and 15,000 families in the Greater Belfast area alone.[36] The extent of enforced housing movement in the towns outside Belfast has never been researched, but Darby and Morris suggested that some of these urban centres experienced comparable disruption.[37]

Apart from the suffering of the victims, who were forced by general pressure or personal threat to seek more secure living areas, the main result of the process has been to increase greatly housing segregation in the Belfast urban area. Recent research indicates that there is a definite pattern in the way in which areas have become polarised :[38]

Stage 1	Predominantly Protestant	Mixed	Predominantly Catholic
Stage 2	Predominantly Protestant		Predominantly Catholic
Stage 3	Exclusively Protestant		Exclusively Catholic

In the affected areas the first stage is often a sorting-out of the mixed region between the two religious groups. Thus in August 1971 it was not unknown for a family to exchange its house for one on the other side of the road, creating a recognisable boundary between the two communities. In some parts of the city this boundary has been sanctified by the establishment of army barriers, as in the so-called Peace Line between the Shankill and the Falls roads.

The next stage, and one which had been reached in a number of city areas by 1973, is a further clarification of the boundary by the intimidation and consequent removal of the isolated families who now lived in alien territory.

There are indications that there may be further stages in the model. Indeed the process is capable of infinite refinement for, in a desperate search for security, any non-conformist is a possible danger. Thus the city has witnessed pressure against people whose marriage partners had a different religion to themselves, people who were not sufficiently enthusiastic about the IRA or UDA, even families which offended community standards by sexual promiscuity or drug-taking. In a puritan community on both Catholic and Protestant sides of the religious divide, it was not difficult to disturb such standards.

This process has had a significant effect on the demography of Belfast. Apart from the numbers involved, there was clearly a different pattern in the movements of Catholics and Protestants. Although the population of Belfast is about 74% Protestant, more than 80% of housing movements resulting from intimidation were Catholic. Protestant victims generally found new homes in the predominantly Protestant estates of north and east Belfast; but the choices available to Catholic victims were much more restricted since the exclusively Catholic parts of the city are confined to a wedge of territory in west Belfast and a few other.enclaves, all but one west of the River Lagan. The resulting situation was that large numbers of Catholic refugees poured into already overcrowded areas. In such circumstances it was inevitable that the Catholic areas of the city would expand. This in turn applied pressure to adjoining Protestant estates, producing further evacuations.

The main consequences of these latest population movements has been to further concentrate the urban working class into increasingly polarised communities. This had an extra significance in a situation of communal violence, inter-communal rioting becomes more likely; the bombing of a particular public house or the machine-gunning of a bus heading towards a particular estate could be carried out with the knowledge that any casualties would almost certainly belong to one or other of the two main sectarian groupings.[39] As Ardrey put it, 'Territory is not the cause of war. It is the cause of war only in the sense that it takes two to make an argument. What territory promises is the high probability that if intrusion takes place, war will follow.'[40]

Evaluation

No other aspect of Northern Ireland's problems has attracted such a consistently high standard of research as demography. Apart from the excellent work carried out by such members of the Geography department at Queen's University as Estyn Evans, Emrys Jones and F.W. Boal, other researchers like Brendan Walsh, Alan Robinson and Rosemary Harris have discovered a great deal about the extent, effects and nature of residential segregation, and about the factors which influence it.

The picture which they and others have produced is a surprisingly constant one. There is no doubt that Northern Ireland's general demographic outlines—those parts of the country where Protestants and Catholics concentrated—were pencilled in by the seventeenth-century plantation. Subsequent pressures on the province's population have etched in the lines more clearly—the development of urban segregation, famine, emigration, political upheavals and the population movements which followed riots and intimidation. Given this turbulent

45

background, the most remarkable phenomenon is how these pressures have balanced each other out and produced a situation similar to that which preceded them. Since population data have been recorded in Northern Ireland, they have altered surprisingly little.

An equally strong conclusion is that, although population patterns in Northern Ireland have been influenced to some extent by governmental policies, the reason why most people live among their co-religionists is because they choose to do so. It matters little whether this is caused by hostility, fear or simply a desire to live among neighbours with whom they feel most comfortable; the effect is the same.

The resulting polarisation has particular implications for planners, who are increasingly at the mercy of events entirely beyond their control. One acute example is the problem of Belfast's Catholic areas. Badly overcrowded and poorly housed even before the recent violence began, the influx of Catholics into west Belfast produced an urgent need for more houses. The difficulty is that the only available building land lies on the western outskirts of the city, between Andersonstown and Twinbrook estates three miles further out. If houses are to be built in an area acceptable to those who need them, planners are left with no option but to build in this area.

While this trend towards polarised estates may particularly affect Catholics in west Belfast, it is common to almost all working-class areas of the city. Indeed it is difficult to foresee any development in the near future which could erode segregation housing patterns, and there is not very much planners can do about it. This is particularly frustrating for those who regard community integration as an integral function of planning, but it is clear that people will not be forced to live in inimical areas. Rather than do so, some of them have been prepared to live in appalling conditions, fleeing to derelict or incompleted houses, without gas, water, electricity or even a roof.

But while this is true, it is not universal. Not everyone can find refuge in segregated estates. Mixed-marriage families—those whose husbands and wives have different religions—often find that increased polarisation deprives them of any safe place in which to live, and this occasionally applies to their relations as well. Northern Ireland's few immigrants have some-

46

times experienced the same difficulties. But, even apart from these groups who may be rejected by both communities, there is evidence that a number of families living in segregated districts would prefer to live in an integrated community. This was particularly noticeable, for example, among families who had been forced by intimidation to leave mixed areas and seek the security of their co-religionists.[41]

Clearly it would be unrealistic for planners to ignore the demand for segregated housing estates; but this does not mean that the minority which desire integration should not be considered. It is not difficult to envisage the construction of experimental housing projects which would be advertised as mixed-religion areas, and where prospective tenants would be required to sign a covenant agreeing to live alongside families of other religions, no religion or mixed religion. Such areas exist spontaneously in many of the less troubled parts of Northern Ireland; given the necessary extra precautions and protection, there is no reason why they could not be encouraged in at least some of the districts which have experienced violence.

To attempt imposing such a policy in all new housing estates, however, would be to ignore the facts of the present situation, and perhaps to invite violence. Circumstances may change in the future; but the realities of the present cannot be avoided.

CHAPTER III

The state and state institutions

To discover what the liberty of a people is, we must live among them, and not look for it in the statutes of the realm. The language of written law may be that of liberty, but the situation of the poor may speak no language but that of slavery. There is too much of this contradiction in Ireland; and where manners are in conspiracy against law, to whom are the oppressed to have recourse?
Arthur Young, 1780

Human rights is a pleasing abstraction impregnated with our notion of our own benevolence. But minority rights evoke a sudden sharp picture of 'that lot' with their regrettable habits, extravagant claims and suspect intentions. Special rights for them? Not likely.
Conor Cruise O'Brien, 1973

UNTIL 1921 Ireland's state institutions were recognisably based on the British system of government. There were similarities between the British and Irish judiciaries, systems of local government and general structure of government. These similarities were based on the fact that the conquest of Ireland was followed by the establishment of a governmental system based on the institutions of the English and Scottish colonists. Local variations emerged as British and Irish institutions developed separately, but by 1920 the similarities were still more marked than the differences.

The constitutional settlement of 1920, however, produced obvious changes. In the first place, twenty-six of the thirty-two counties established their independence and began to evolve new institutions. The six counties of Northern Ireland neither became independent nor did they remain an integral part of the United Kingdom. A compromise settlement was reluctantly agreed, which involved both new relationships and new institutions. What were the main components of this settlement?

Three levels of authority were established in Northern Ireland. The United Kingdom parliament at Westminster still retained control over some major policy areas, notably peace and war, the armed forces, treaties with foreign countries, external trade and coinage. It also retained the ultimate power of repealing or proroguing the 1920 Government of Ireland act, a power which it exercised in 1972. Northern Ireland elected twelve members of parliament to sit at Westminster.

The second level of authority resided in the parliament and government of Northern Ireland at Stormont. These were entitled to legislate and govern on matters local to Northern Ireland; these matters included the control of policing, social welfare, education, industry and agriculture. Fifty-two members were elected to the Northern Ireland House of Commons, and the upper house, or Senate, had twenty-six members.

Northern Ireland also controlled its own judiciary.

Apart from these central institutions, the system of local government in Northern Ireland remained similar to that practised in England. Until local government reorganisation in the early 1970s, which reduced the number of local authorities to twenty-six, there were seventy-three local councils in Northern Ireland, with some functions relating to education, health, welfare, housing and a number of services, for which they were empowered to employ whatever workers were required to administer the system.

The Westminster parliament and the local authorities, therefore, were features which had been present before 1920; but the Northern Ireland parliament and government at Stormont were new institutions. The stability of electoral loyalties in the province ensured that the exercise of power remained in the hands of a succession of Unionist governments. Their opponents have alleged that this power has been exercised in a discriminatory fashion, both at Stormont and at local government level. At the former level, the allegations have been most frequently aimed at the Northern Ireland government's control of the electoral system, its legislative programme, its direction of the police and the administration of justice and its distribution of those resources under its control. At the local authorities level, the main grievances have been caused by the allocation of public housing and by alleged discrimination in employment by some local authorities. These charges will be examined in this chapter.

Public Representation

The slogan 'One man, one vote', which became identified with the Northern Ireland Civil Rights Association from its very early days, represented one of the most persistent grievances of the nationalist minority against the Unionist government. The charges were in essence simple ones—that the restrictions on the local government franchise operated against the nationalist minority, and that some constituency and local government boundaries were deliberately gerrymandered to ensure disproportionately high unionist representation.

The local government franchise which operated in Northern Ireland until 1969 was certainly an antiquated one. Two categories of people were entitled to vote in local government elections. The first category was 'resident occupiers', i.e., the owner or tenants of a house; under this category only two people in each house might vote—usually the householder and his wife; other lodgers, and indeed children over the minimum voting age, had no franchise. The other category was 'general occupiers', or occupiers of property with an annual valuation of £10 a year or over. Those fortunate enough to own property valued at more than £10 a year were permitted to appoint a voting nominee for each additional £10, up to a maximum of six nominees. This property qualification naturally mitigated against the poorer sections of the community, and in Northern Ireland amounted to a de facto advantage to the Unionist party. The situation was well illustrated by Derry city. Although its population of 53,762 (1961 census) was comprised from 36,073 Catholics and 17,689 Protestants, the voting population was 14,429 Catholics and 8,781 Protestants. In other words, 40% of the city's Catholics were entitled to vote, and 50% of Protestants.

It is difficult to estimate how much difference this made in terms of council seats won and lost, and impossible to judge whether the franchise was directed specifically against Catholics, generally against the working classes or merely arose from an unwillingness to change existing practices; but the franchise issue assumes a greater importance when considered together with the more serious charge of gerrymandering. This is, briefly, the claim that some critical electoral boundaries, both at Stormont and local government levels, were deliberately manipulated to ensure Unionist majorities.

It is in the field of local government that the most serious allegations of gerrymandering have been made, and once again it is the city of Derry which offers the archetypal case. In 1967 there were just over 23,000 qualified voters in the city. There were distributed among three wards, each of which elected a number of councillors :

Table 1   Londonderry Local Authority Returns 1967

	Catholic Voters	Other Voters	
North	2,530	3,946	8 Unionists
Waterside	1,852	3,697	4 Unionists
South	10,047	1,138	8 Non-Unionists
TOTAL	14,429	8,781	12 Unionists and 8 non-Unionists

So although more than two-thirds of the city's total population, and 60% of its adult population, were Catholic, they were only able to secure eight seats in a twenty-man council. As F.S.L. Lyons put it, 'The particular form this segregation has taken in Londonderry city has resulted in a pattern of Unionist control which has been too consistent for too long to be anything other than deliberately contrived.'[1]

Derry is a particularly well-publicised case, but not unique. Despite Nationalist majorities in a number of other towns, and in County Fermanagh, the local councils still produced considerable Unionist majorities.[2]

Table 2 Political Composition of Local Authorities with Large Catholic Populations, 1972

	Catholic population	Unionists	Non-Unionists
Co. Tyrone	(%)		
Dungannon UD	50	14	7
Dungannon RD	52	16	6
Omagh UD	61	12	9
Omagh RD	60	24	18
Castlederg RD	50	13	6
Clogher RD	51	14	5
Cookstown RD	55	12	7
Strabane RD	49	22	9
Other Counties			
Armagh UD	58	12	8
Magherafelt RD	54	20	8
Fermanagh CC	53	33	17
East Down RD	50	19	5
Lurgan MB	46	15	0

It is important to point out, however, that the majority of the local councils were not contested on a sectarian basis and that the entire local government system in the province was radically re-organised in 1973, when proportional representation was introduced for local government elections.

It is frequently asserted that similar practices operated at Stormont and Westminster elections as those which pertained at local level. Two instances are quoted which point to election manipulation in these spheres: the first was the abolition of proportional representation in 1929 to protect the Unionist party against splinter unionist groupings; and the second was the retention of the four Stormont seats for Queen's University Belfast until 1968, during which time forty Unionists and two Independent Unionists were returned out of a total of fifty-three University members; in the latter case the Unionist dominance arose from the fact that the franchise was confined to graduates of Queen's University, most of whom were Protestant. In addition, the fact that there was no general adjustment of electoral boundaries between the abolition of Proportional Representation in 1929 and its return in 1973, coupled with the Unionist Party's ability to consistently hold between 32 and 40 of the 52 Stormont seats, might suggest that gerrymandering was practised in these elections also. When it comes to specific cases, however, the only serious allegation has been made in respect to the three Fermanagh seats in the Stormont parliament. Despite a Catholic majority in the county which varied between 53% and 55% the Enniskillen and Lisnaskea constituencies have returned Unionists in every Stormont election, and South Fermanagh has always returned a Nationalist. The 1949 election was the only one in which all three constituencies were contested between 1921 and 1969, and the results were as follows :

Table 3   N.I. Parliamentary Elections in Fermanagh, 1949

	Unionist vote	Nationalist vote	Majority
Enniskillen	5,706	4,729	997 (U)
Lisnaskea	5,593	4,173	1,420 (U)
South Fermanagh	2,596	6,680	4,084 (N)
TOTAL	13,895	15,582	

Despite this particular case, Barritt and Carter rejected the claim that gerrymandering was widely practised in elections to the Stormont parliament :

> Our general conclusion is that in its composition the Northern Ireland parliament reflects the views of the people with no more distortion than there is normally to be found in democratic parliaments.[3]

Indeed Terence O'Neill was able in 1968 to neatly turn the argument against his opponents :

> There *are* some undue disparities between the sizes of constituencies for the Northern Ireland parliament. Electorates vary between three of under 10,000 and two of over 40,000; but the fifteen seats with the largest electorates are *all* held

53

by Unionists, mainly very comfortably, while four of the six with the smallest electorates are held by Opposition parties. Mr Gerry Fitt, for instance, represents the tiniest electorate in Northern Ireland at Stormont. At the last Ulster General Election his *poll* of 3,326 votes in an electorate of 7,620 compares with fourteen Unionist majorities of more than 3,000 in average electorates of almost 23,000.[4]

Such figures cannot be disputed. Apart from County Fermanagh there were no anomalies in the Stormont election results which could not be explained either by normal demographic vagaries or by Nationalist incompetence. It is also worth mentioning that anti-partitionist candidates have never succeeded in winning more than three of the twelve Westminster seats, although no one has ever seriously suggested that those electoral boundaries, which are determined by Westminster, were gerrymandered. In the 1974 general election, for example, only two of the twelve Westminster seats were won by anti-partitionists.

Central Government
Legislation and Policy
To some nationalists every act passed by the Stormont parliament discriminated against them, since all were based on the discriminatory Government of Ireland act which established the state. In a more detailed sense, however, it was the legislation related to the social services and to security which had aroused most bitter feelings. In the provision of social services the principle of parity of services with Britain, which came to mean an increasingly large annual Westminster subsidy (usually estimated at between £200 and £300 million[5] in 1974), effectively reduced the control of Stormont over its welfare spending and consequently its ability to discriminate. One episode in particular demonstrated the point: in 1956 the Westminster government increased British family allowances from 40p a week for all children except the first-born to 40p for the second child and 50p for all subsequent children. The Northern Ireland Minister of Labour and National Insurance, Ivan Neill, attempted to reverse the pattern in the province by awarding 48p for the second and third children, and 40p for all subsequent children. This scheme would have worked to the detriment of Catholics, who tended to have larger families, but was eventu-

54

ally dropped as a result of pressure from Westminster. Since then any changes in the provision of cash benefits in Britain have followed automatically in Northern Ireland.

Another running sore in the relationships between the Catholic community and the state has been the question of state aid to religious institutions. The schools question is discussed in Chapter V; suffice it to say here that, although clearly the Catholic hierarchy would like all its educational expenses to be paid by the state, negotiations with the Ministry of Education have been notably cordial. Since 1968 the subsidy to most Catholic schools has covered 80% of building costs and all bills for maintenance and equipment—a settlement which is considerably superior to that which exists in Britain. Similar in some respects to the education dispute was the controversy over the Mater Infirmorum Hospital in Belfast, which operated without any financial aid from government as a Catholic hospital.[6] When hospitals were nationalised in 1948, the Minister of Health did not adopt the British clause which permitted grant aid to those voluntary hospitals which wished to remain outside the service, but simply offered them the choice of joining the service or receiving nothing. The Catholic authorities refused to accept guarantees that the character and religious associations of transferred hospitals would be preserved. Despite recurrent negotiations no settlement was reached, and the hospital was financed entirely from voluntary contributions until 1971. In that year the issue was harmoniously resolved and the Mater controversy at last ended.

The disputes about extraordinary legislation in relation to security were much more bitter than those about social services. The Civil Authorities (Special Powers) act (NI) of 1922 was not novel;[7] similar powers had been used in Ireland long before partition was introduced, notably under the Defence of the Realm Consolidation act (1914) and the Restoration of Order in Ireland act (1920). The regulations contained in the schedule of the Special Powers act have varied from time to time, but included such specific powers as the right to search without warrant, to detain people without warrant and, most notably, to intern. In addition to these specified regulations, more vague powers were allowed under Section 1 and Section 2, subsection 4 of the act. The former allowed the Minister of Home Affairs to 'take all such steps and issue all such orders as may be necessary for preserving the peace and maintaining order', and the latter stated that 'if any person does any act of such nature as to be prejudicial to the preservation of the peace or maintenance of order in Northern Ireland and not specifically provided for in the regulations, he shall be deemed to be guilty of an offence against the regulations'.

There has been constant opposition to the Special Powers act and its administration, both in Northern Ireland and from abroad. In 1936 the National Council for Civil Liberties appointed a commission of enquiry which reported strongly against the operation of special powers in the province.[8] The Civil Rights Association has, since its formation, regarded the act's repeal as one of its most important objectives. In the main those who attacked the act have not taken a stand against extraordinary legislation as such, but against the wide powers permitted under the Special Powers act and the manner in which they were exercised. Indeed the necessity of the state having powers to protect itself in emergencies is one recognised in international law, although there are stringent regulations about the limits of such powers. That these regulations were ignored in Northern Ireland was recognised by the British government, and indeed by the government at Stormont, when they published their joint statement of reforms in 1968. This included the agreement that 'such of the Special Powers as are in conflict with international obligations will as in the past be withdrawn from current use',[9] although the Northern Ireland government was, rather surprisingly, given the power to reactivate them. At any rate opposition to the act has focused on three main points.

The first was the powers which the act placed in the hands of the Minister of Home Affairs. The requirement that he must place before parliament all regulations not specified in the act only slightly restrained the wide discretionary powers which the act allowed him. F.S.L. Lyons hardly exaggerated when he described it as a bill which 'only needed to have one clause: the Minister of Home Affairs shall have power to do what he likes, or let somebody else do what he likes for him'.[10] A book written in 1973 by James Callaghan, who had been British Home Secretary with responsibility for Northern Ireland,

56

clearly revealed another *de facto* weakness in the operation of the act. His enquiries revealed that 'the Minister of Home Affairs seemed totally dependent on the Inspector-General (i.e. of the Royal Ulster Constabulary). He was the Minister's sole source of intelligence and professional advice, and the Minister seemed to take second place to him'.[11] This predominance of police influence in determining the operation of the Special Powers act caused considerable concern at the time of the early Civil Rights marches.

The use of extraordinary powers on a permanent basis, whether or not a guerrilla campaign was in operation, was the second main cause of complaint. The 1922 act was intended as a temporary measure, but in 1933 another Civil Authorities act placed it on an indefinite footing, until its repeal in 1973. In the first instance opposition to the bill was not confined to one side of the House; George Boyle Hanna, a Unionist member, opposed it on the grounds that it permitted a civil authority to use martial law powers. Harry Calvert, the constitutional lawyer, spoke on behalf of many lawyers in 1968 when he expressed his concern at the government's constant preference for extraordinary rather than normal processes of law. He wrote, 'The Special Powers act has been invoked to proscribe organisations suspected of criminal activities but it has not been claimed that their proportions were such as to have overtaxed the resources of the administration of justice in the normal course or that prosecution to conviction on charges of criminal or seditious conspiracy was rendered impossible by intimidation of witnesses. Nor does it seem that the proportions of the evil to be combated are such as to require running the risk of oppressing the innocent.'[12] In effect neither the legislature nor the judiciary were restraints on the executive.

The use of the act for political rather than community advantage and its application almost exclusively against antipartitionists was the third and most bitter complaint of its opponents. For example, the banning of the Republican Clubs in 1967 when they appeared to have been engaged in legitimate political activities, could not be justified by the presence of an emergency situation at the time. Furthermore, the government's failure to use the act against loyalist militants—until 1966 the IRA was the only body proscribed by law—caused constant

57

allegations of bias against Unionist governments. Professor Mansergh, for example, claims that the Orange Order was promised immunity from the act when it was first passed.[18] To the minority the failure to include any loyalists in the lists of people interned in August 1971 was merely further evidence that loyalist illegalities would never be seriously tackled by Unionist administrations in Stormont, and provided a particular focus for what had previously been more general grievances. Although internment is essentially a secondary issue, introduced as a strategy to deal with more basic problems, on every occasion of its imposition in Northern Ireland it has rapidly superseded all other grievances and its abolition has become a prerequisite for political advances.

Policing
The Royal Irish Constabulary (RIC) from which the Royal Ulster Constabulary (RUC) evolved, had a semi-military function since its foundation in the 1800s, and policemen were trained in the use of arms as a matter of course. In addition to their normal duties of crime prevention and detection, the RIC and later the RUC had the extra responsibility of security duties, thus creating the dichotomy that the policeman who directs traffic one day may be involved in anti-terrorist activities the next.

It is not surprising that the difficulties inherent in this situation were not resolved when the state of Northern Ireland was established. When the first Minister of Home Affairs established a committee of enquiry into policing in 1921, it met to a backcloth of violence and civil disorder. Any thoughts of removing its security role from the RUC or disarming it must have been instantly dismissed as hopelessly unrealistic. The legislation which eventually established the RUC was strictly limited by the Government of Ireland act, which allowed the Northern Ireland government to legislate and administer on matters of 'peace, order and good government'—a power which included policing and home affairs, but not defence. The Inspector-General of the RUC and the Northern Ireland Ministry of Home Affairs controlled training, management, deployment and size, and a single command was established instead of the local control which operated in the rest of the

United Kingdom. Since Northern Ireland was the only part of the United Kingdom which had a land frontier, the delicate matter of security was not underlined. It appears to have been accepted as a practical necessity that the police would be occasionally used for security duties.

The size of the new force was set at 3,000 places, of which one-third were to be reserved for Catholics. This ceiling remained until 1962, when it was raised to 3,200, and had reached 3,400 by the time of the Hunt report. The percentage of Catholics in the force never approached the optimistic 33% advocated in 1921. In 1961 only 12% of the force was comprised of Catholics, and the troubles of the early 1970s have subsequently reduced it further to 9·4%.[14]

Despite this small percentage of Catholics, there is no evidence that discrimination was practised in the employment of policemen. The Hunt Committee, for example, 'heard no evidence of discrimination on religious grounds with regard to promotion within the RUC'.[15] The fact is that Catholics have never been attracted in large numbers into the RUC because they have associated the force with the Unionist government. The Hunt and Cameron Committees, while making little comment on the substance of the charge, recognised that it was widely believed and accepted 'that the Catholic minority believed the police to be amenable to political pressure'. The antagonism of this minority towards the police is perhaps best illustrated in the Black Paper published in 1973 by the Central Citizens' Defence Committee, a body which is located in the strongly Catholic Falls Road area.[16] It detailed a number of instances which present the RUC as a body which invariably acted against the Catholic side in a riot situation, even when the riot was provoked by Protestant extremists. Many of the instances quoted took place in the early months of the Civil Rights campaign, the period covered by the investigations of the Scarman Tribunal and the Cameron Commission, and some of them were confirmed by the reports of these bodies. Reference was made, for example, to the tendency of the RUC to face the Catholic crowd in a riot situation and ignore the Protestant violence behind them, and to the small number of Protestant rioters arrested by the police. Police misconduct or inefficiency was detailed on a number of instances; two will suffice for purposes of illustration: after the Derry march in January 1969 the Cameron Report remarked that there was 'a breakdown of discipline' and that during the subsequent invasion of the Bogside by the police, 'our investigations have led us to the unhesitating conclusion that on the night of 4/5 January a number of policemen were guilty of misconduct which involved assault and battery, malicious damage to property in streets in the predominantly Catholic Bogside area, giving reasonable cause for apprehension of personal injury among other innocent inhabitants, and the use of provocative sectarian and political slogans.'[17] Also in Derry on 19/20 April in the same year, the same report commented, 'we were presented with a considerable body of evidence to establish further acts of grave misconduct among members of the RUC, including on this occasion also serious allegations of assault occasioning personal injury and of malicious damage to property. We regret to say that there appears to us to be an ample *prima facie* evidence to support such charges.' The Cameron Report and the later Scarman Report, which also criticised the RUC, were careful to accompany their condemnations with reminders of police shortages in manpower and the prevalent disorders, stressing that the vast majority of policemen behaved with propriety and restraint. The Black Paper, however, accompanies its accusations of police misconduct during riots with other charges —leniency towards UDA parades, granting of fire arms certificates predominantly to Protestants, partisan execution of duties —to create a picture of a politically directed police force which has been the tool of Unionist administrations. What is an indisputable fact is that many from the Catholic minority saw the RUC as a hostile force, like the young man from the Bogside quoted in the Black Paper who declared that he would rather be hit on the head by an army baton than by a police baton because the former was impersonal.

If Catholics were antagonistic towards the RUC, they regarded the Ulster Special Constabulary with particular hatred. Leonie Dobbie wrote in 1971, 'The history of the Ulster Special Constabulary (or 'B' Specials) stems not so much from the Special Constables in Ireland than from that of the Ulster Volunteer Force.'[18] The UVF had been formed in 1912 to resist the possibility of Home Rule in Ireland, but was not an official body and could not officially carry arms. As a result of Unionist pressure, three auxiliary forces to the police were formed in 1920—the 'A', 'B' and 'C' Specials—and their purpose was to assist the RUC in the anti-IRA campaign then going on. The 'A' and 'C' Specials were eventually dropped, but the 'B' Specials were 'retained against the risk of further outbreaks of subversive activities'.[19] The number involved varied periodically from 25,000 in the early 1920s down to 8,285 in 1969. There were no medical or educational tests for members, and it was an exclusively Protestant force.

The slack recruitment procedures and training methods, not to mention the anti-Catholic bias in membership soon earned the 'B' Specials a reputation which they never lost. To many Catholics, even as late as the 1970s, the 'B' Specials were indelibly associated with deaths in Newry and Belfast in 1922. Their association with violence was also revealed by the investigations of the Cameron Commission, which found that 'B' Specials were among the members of the extremist Ulster Constitution Defence Committee which had ambushed the Civil Rights marchers at Burntollet in January 1969. In between these two periods the main duties of the 'B' Specials was the guarding of installations and manning of road blocks, especially during IRA campaigns. Both the Cameron and Hunt reports comment on the fact that the 'B' Specials, 'training and equipment . . . (are) primarily of a military nature and not designed for the ordinary police role,'[20] and certainly their control by the Stormont government appears to violate the Government of Ireland act, which reserved defence matters for the Westminster government. The Unionist MP Henry Clark was one who took this view. He acknowledged that the United Kingdom's only land frontier was in Ireland, but went on to add, 'Even this fact hardly justified the constitutional anomaly by which the provincial government in Northern Ireland raised, paid and controlled, without reference to the Ministry of Defence, the forces necessary to deal with quite serious guerrilla attacks across the border and against installations in Ulster.'[21]

Almost every responsible investigator of police conduct during the Civil Rights period—the Cameron, Scarman and Hunt reports, James Callaghan and Max Hastings—commented on the poor quality of the leadership in the force, although all of them remarked favourably on the actions of the great majority of policemen in the province. The most notable instance of the force's failure was the fact that parts of the province were not policed at all. James Callaghan rejected the argument that this situation had resulted from the troubles: 'For two years or more before 1969, parts of Belfast and Londonderry had remained almost outside the law and under their own so-called jurisdiction.'[22] He might have added that the last police station in the Bogside had been closed down when William Craig was Minister of Home Affairs. There can be little doubt that this inability to police some of the Catholic areas stemmed from the security functions which the RUC carried out in addition to their normal policing duties. The point is well illustrated by a report on the RUC which James Callaghan, the Home Secretary, commissioned in 1969. This report, compiled by Douglas Osmond and Robert Mark, found that many police stations could not perform a proper service for the community because they were permanently locked and barred for security purposes. Their final verdict was, 'At the first hint of trouble, normal police behaviour was suppressed and they became a para-military force.'[23]

Many policemen were aware of the defects in the force, and the Central Representative Body of the RUC actually welcomed reforms when they came. These reforms were initiated by the Hunt Report, published in 1969. This report made a total of forty-seven recommendations and five suggestions. The most important of these were the decision to establish a civilian police force with no military role, and the disbandment of the Ulster Special Constabulary and its replacement by an Ulster Defence Regiment. In addition to these it recommended an independent complaints tribunal and the formation of a representative Police Authority which would take over the management and policy side of policing from the Minister of Home Affairs.

The Hunt Report and the legislation which subsequently implemented most of its recommendations demonstrate the necessity of good timing as well as good substance in the introduction of reforms. Received initially with approval by the Catholic minority community, the euphoria soon passed.

62

The mounting IRA campaign forced Catholic policemen to leave Catholic areas of Belfast and Derry to protect their lives and those of their families; the increasingly military nature of the situation resulted in the police returning to the old security role; Catholic suspicions and distrust of the force revived. A survey conducted in a Catholic area of Belfast in 1973 showed that attitudes towards the police had hardly been touched by the Hunt reforms.[24] Only fifty-two from a total of 264 interviewees gave 'general support' to the RUC as the police organisation in Andersonstown, and fifty of these only gave this support with considerable conditions attached, either that it should be unarmed or 50% Catholic. As regards the police service which people actually preferred, only eleven opted for the RUC, ten of these with conditions. Instead a considerable majority preferred some form of community policing, although the form advocated varied considerably. Questions about the administration of justice produced a similar pattern; there was wide dissatisfaction with the existing courts, and 211 from 264 interviewees generally supported a community court system.

The Administration of Justice

The strong imbalance between Catholics and non-Catholics on judges' and magistrates' benches has been marked since the establishment of the state.

Table 4   Judicial Posts 1969[25]

	Non-Catholic	Catholic
High Court judges	6	1
County court judges	4	1
Resident magistrates	9	3
Commission for National Insurance	3	0
Clerks of town and peace	6	0
Under sheriffs	6	0
Crown solicitors	8	0
Clerks of Petty Sessions	26	1
TOTAL	68	6

But it was not only the religious imbalance which afforded annoyance; of more concern was the suspicion that many judicial posts were awarded as political patronage rather than as recognition of legal eminence. The control of many of these appointments, including those of resident magistrates, lay with the Ministry of Home Affairs and the Attorney General. Kevin Boyle, an academic lawyer and early civil rights leader, alleged that, as a consequence of this, there was 'an almost invisible connection between politicians and the bench'[26] in 8% of judicial appointments. Fr Denis Faul made the Catholic minority's case before the European sub-committee of the United States House of Representatives in 1972 :

> Twenty-one judges have been appointed to the High Court since 1921. Fifteen have been connected with the Unionist party. One out of three judges in the Court of Appeals is an ex-Attorney General—a political appointee. Of the five county court judges, two are ex-Unionist MPs. On the Resident Magistrate Bench there is an ex-Unionist MP, one ex-delegate to the Ulster Unionist Council, one ex-Unionist Senator, one defeated Unionist candidate and one former legal adviser to the Ministry of Home Affairs. Recently a Catholic, Turlough O'Donnell, has been appointed a High Court judge and another, John Higgins, a County Court judge. This may improve the situation.[27]

The regulations governing the selection of juries operated in practice against the Catholic minority for precisely the same reasons that the local government franchise did. Although there were no educational qualifications required for jury service, until December 1974 the jury list was confined to ratepayers, among whom Catholics were a marked minority. More serious however were the allegations of bias in the sentencing of convicted criminals, which have become considerably louder with the increase in civil disorder charges since 1968, and here the maintenance of order and the administration of justice become closely interwoven. As Edmund Curran has remarked, 'the charge of bias in the courts is not so much levelled against the judiciary as against the police.'[28] This refers to both the arrest of rioters and the charges against them. The arrest of forty Catholic women in February 1971 outside the Magistrate's court in Belfast during a riot in which Protestant women were also involved, provoked complaints to the Police Authority by a group of lawyers. This growing concern among lawyers 'rests more on alleged bias by the police force (mainly voiced by Catholic solicitors) and inconsistency of sentences handed out by magistrates (a criticism shared by both Protestants and Catholics)'.[29] The complaint by the Catholic lawyers is that the police charged Catholic rioters with riotous behaviour, which carried a minimum sentence of six months' imprisonment, and Protestant rioters with disorderly behaviour, for which the sentence might be a fine or even a suspended sentence. Two examples of this alleged leniency were frequently quoted. In the Shankill Road riots of July 1970 twenty-one Protestants were charged with riotous behaviour, and nineteen were subsequently reduced to disorderly behaviour; and in the other main Protestant riot on the Newtownards Road in Easter 1971 there were similar reductions of charges. Some support to these claims was provided by the publication in 1973 of *Justice in Northern Ireland*, by Tom Hadden and Paddy Hillyard, the first academic investigation into the administration of justice in Northern Ireland. It was based on a small sample survey of the operations of Magistrates' courts during early 1972, and on an analysis of all cases heard at the Belfast City Commission between January and June 1973; so it concerned the post-Hunt period and one of serious civil disorder. The conclusion of the authors was :

> There is a small but cumulative measure of (perhaps unconscious) sympathy with Protestants and Loyalists. This applies particularly to the decision to prosecute and the selection or withdrawal of charges by the police and the prosecuting authorities. It also applies to some jury verdicts.[30]

It is clear that the disputes about the courts have not yet ended.

Employment and Public Service

The government in Northern Ireland, like any other government, has the power to direct the distribution of jobs at two different levels. In the first place it has at its disposal many appointments to specific posts, such as Civil Service posts and positions on public bodies; secondly, by legislative and administrative initiatives it can to some extent control the distribution of jobs within the province, and influence whether industrialists are encouraged to invest in one area rather than another.

There have been allegations of discrimination in both spheres. The dispensing of direct patronage became an issue in the 1930s over such a minor affair as the appointment of porters to the parliament buildings at Stormont; much more serious, of course, is the charge that there is discrimination in appointments to the Civil Service and to public bodies. In July 1973 David Donnison, Director of the Centre for Environmental Studies, claimed that a study of 477 Northern Ireland Civil Servants from the grade of deputy to assistant principal upwards revealed that 95% of these officials were Protestants.[81] Earlier studies in 1927 and 1959 both produced figures of 94%. Barritt and Carter in fact claimed that among the very top positions—permanent, second and assistant secretaries—the percentage of Protestants had actually risen from 89% to 96% between 1927 and 1959.[82] A press notice from the Northern Ireland Office alleged that Professor Donnison's figures were incorrect, and claimed the 15% of the senior grades mentioned were Catholics, adding 'moreover, not all the remaining 85% were Protestants'.[83] Even accepting the lower figure there is clearly a serious disparity between Catholics and Protestants in the higher ranks of the Northern Ireland Civil Service.

The same pattern appears in appointments to public bodies. In 1969 the Campaign for Social Justice published figures on the membership of public boards which were never contradicted.[84] The twenty-one boards quoted—which included such politically innocuous bodies as the Electricity Board, the Hospitals Authority, the Tourist Board and the Youth and Sports Council—contained forty-nine Catholics from a total of 332 members. None of the boards had a Catholic majority, the best Catholic representation being $33\frac{1}{3}$%—one member from the three on the 1969 Commission to review Stormont's parliamentary boundaries. The Campaign for Social Justice also claimed in 1967 that there were only 31 Catholics among the 387 specialist doctors employed by the Ministry of Home Affairs.[85]

The government's indirect control of resources was much greater than its direct control. One of the major population trends in Northern Ireland, especially since the Second World War, has been the relative decline of those parts which lie to the west of the River Bann. Since this is largely an agricultural area, such a decline is not unparalleled in Europe over the same period. What has caused concern is the government's failure to arrest the decline, and the record of official decisions which had the effect of accelerating it.

1924. Male unemployment exceeded 25% in Derry city and the county surveyor's office was removed from Derry city to Coleraine.

1945–51. Seventy-seven firms were established in the province with government support before the first came to Derry in 1951.

1963. The Benson Report on railways led to the removal of the west's only railway line, and cut Derry off from Strabane, Omagh and Dungannon.

1964. The Matthew Report sited Northern Ireland's 'new town' at Craigavon, further attracting population to the east.

1965. The anti-submarine training school in Derry was closed, adding 600 to an unemployment figure already approaching 20%.

1965. The Lockwood Report rejected Derry's claim for Northern Ireland's second university despite the existence of a University College in the city. It was awarded to Coleraine, whose 12,000 population was less than a quarter the size to Derry's.

1965. The Wilson plan, which designated growth areas for Northern Ireland, concentrated them heavily in the east.

1966. Derry's naval base, another major source of employment, was closed.

In addition to these specific decisions, the western part of the province seemed to be missing out on Northern Ireland's post-war economic boom, at least up until 1968. This boom was at least partly due to an expansionist programme launched by the Northern Ireland government to encourage the entry of new firms into the province. Industrial development acts were passed in 1945, 1953 and 1966 which offered considerable financial assistance to firms which established factories in Northern Ireland. (The 1966 act for example, offered 45% of the cost of plant, machinery and buildings.) Advance factories were built and kept available for employers. The programme was successful; by 1968, 240 new firms, employing 60,000 workers, had come to the province and were supplying a third of the province's work force. But the pattern of the new employment was uneven. Between 1945 and 1963 70% of the new firms were located within twenty-five miles of Belfast, and less than 10% had moved west of the Bann.[36] While there is no doubt that the more developed eastern counties had more attractions to industrialists than the remoter western counties, the government cannot escape blame for the relative decline of the western areas. Of the 111 advance factories which the Ministry of Commerce had built by 1964 only sixteen were built in the three western counties—and the siting of all these factories was determined by the choice of the ministry, not by that of industrialists. It is true that the record improved considerably in the late 1960s, possibly as a result of publicity caused by civil unrest, and about half the jobs created between 1968 and 1971 went to the west. But the unemployment figures of towns east and west of the Bann show clearly that the neglect of the west has left its mark.

It is at this point that allegations of sectarian bias are made about the government's policy towards the west. The Unionist heartlands are concentrated in Counties Antrim and Down and in Belfast, where the population is more than 70% Protestant. When partition came, Counties Fermanagh, Derry and Tyrone had narrow Catholic majorities; despite higher Catholic birthrates, the Catholic percentages in these counties have not subsequently risen. In County Derry, indeed, it has declined from 58% to 43%. The reason for this is that the great majority of emigrants are Catholics, a result of their generally lower economic status. Brendan Walsh, in a study of Irish demography, remarked that 'in Northern Ireland the net emigration rate, 1951–61, was very much higher among Roman Catholics than other denominations—more than twice as high for males, and almost three times as high for females. Even more pronounced differentials are recorded at the county level for Fermanagh, and

68

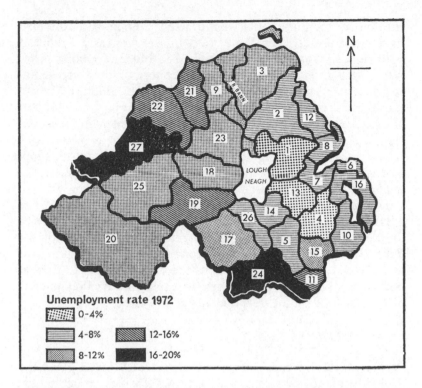

Unemployment rate 1972
- 0–4%
- 4–8%
- 8–12%
- 12–16%
- 16–20%

Distribution of unemployment in Northern Ireland (by local office areas)[37]

key

areas east of the River Bann

1. Antrim	3·6	7. Belfast	6·1	13. Lisburn	3·8
2. Ballymena	5·2	8. Carrickfergus	6·4	14. Lurgan	6·4
3. Ballymoney	10·4	9. Coleraine	8·5	15. Newcastle	9·0
4. Ballynahinch	3·5	10. Downpatrick	6·5	16. Newtownards	5·2
5. Banbridge	4·6	11. Kilkeel	14·6		
6. Bangor	5·3	12. Larne	5·2		

areas west of the River Bann

17. Armagh	8·6	21. Limavady	13·3	25. Omagh	11·0
18. Cookstown	10·4	22. L'Derry	13·3	26. Portadown	5·7
19. Dungannon	13·8	23. Magherafelt	8·0	27. Strabane	16·7
20. Enniskillen	10·9	24. Newry	16·1		

all figures (from the Ministry of Commerce) are for mid-1972*

* although the figures in this table relate only to mid-1972, they represent a consistent pattern in recent years

for Antrim the differential was reversed.'[38] Some anti-Unionists have consequently seen the neglect of the west as a deliberate political decision to counterbalance the higher Catholic birth-rate in the province, and quote in support of their arguments speeches like that of Mr E.C. Ferguson, the Unionist MP for Enniskillen, to the Annual Unionist Convention in 1948; 'the Nationalist majority in the county (i.e., Fermanagh) notwith-standing a reduction of 336 in the year, stands at 3,604 . . . I would ask the meeting to authorise their executive to adopt whatever plans, and take whatever steps, however drastic, to wipe out this Nationalist majority.'[39] But Mr Ferguson was not a member of the government, and it is impossible to speculate what its motives were. It is worth remembering that many of the decisions taken in the 1960s about the regions west of the Bann were as bitterly and strongly resisted by Derry Unionists as by Derry Nationalists. But, whatever the motives, a heavy portion of the blame for the west's neglect and decline must be placed squarely on the governments at Stormont.

Local Government
Jobs and Houses
Paragraph 129 of the Cameron Report, which investigated the civil disturbance between 1968 and 1969, begins, 'much of the evidence of grievance and complaint which we heard, when analysed, was found, as might be expected, to be concentrated upon two major issues—housing and employment. "Jobs" and "Houses" are things that matter and touch the life of the ordi-nary man more than issues of "one man, one vote" and the gerrymandering of ward boundaries.'[40] Not surprisingly most of the criticism of such practices, both before and after the report, came from committed and active bodies like the Campaign for Social Justice in Northern Ireland and the Fermanagh Civil Rights Association; although their data has never been con-vincingly challenged, their opponents have sometimes dismissed them as political propagandists. The Cameron Commission, however, was clearly an impartial body, and the importance of its report is that it confirmed many of the trends which had been highlighted by other bodies.

The maladministration of local government is discussed in Chapter 12 of the Cameron Report which, as has already been indicated, concentrates on employment, housing and, to a lesser degree, on gerrymandering. The report quoted a number of instances of bias by local authorities in their employment policies :

We are satisfied that all these Unionist-controlled councils have used and use their power to make appointments in a way which benefited Protestants. In the figures available for October 1968 only thirty per cent of Londonderry Corporation's administrative, clerical and technical employees were Catholics. Out of the ten best-paid posts only one was held by a Catholic. In Dungannon Urban District none of the Council's administrative clerical and technical employees was a Catholic.

In County Fermanagh no senior council posts (and relatively few others) were held by Catholics : this was rationalised by reference to 'proven loyalty' as a necessary test for local authority appointments. In that county, among about seventy-five drivers of school buses, at most seven were Catholics. This would appear to be a very clear case of sectarian and political discrimination. Armagh Urban District employed very few Catholics in its salaried posts, but did not appear to discriminate at lower levels. Omagh Urban District showed no clearcut pattern of discrimination, though we have seen what would appear to be undoubted evidence of employment discrimination by Tyrone County Council.

It is fair to note that Newry Urban District, which is controlled by non-Unionists, employed very few Protestants. But two wrongs do not make a right; Protestants who are in the minority in the Newry area, by contrast to the other areas we have specified, do not have a serious unemployment problem, and in Newry there are relatively few Protestants, whereas in the other towns Catholics make up a substantial part of the population.[41]

It is clear from the Cameron Report that many of the Unionist witnesses before the Commission were prepared to admit that both gerrymandering and bias in favour of Protestant employees had taken place. In the debates which followed, a frequent defence against these charges was that only a limited number of local authorities were examined by the Cameron

71

Commission, that they were not typical, and that the situation did not apply elsewhere. Two points need to be made in this respect: the first is that it would clearly be unnecessary to gerrymander in many council areas, where there are large majorities one way or the other; the second is that, since no evidence has been produced to substantiate the claim that, for example, other Unionist-controlled councils do not discriminate in employment, claims that they do or do not are equally baseless. In fact, what evidence does exist apart from that described in the Cameron Report largely tends to etch more deeply the claims that discrimination by local authorities was widespread, and to lend them further support.

The Fermanagh Civil Rights Association and the Campaign for Social Justice in Northern Ireland have both published pamphlets which demonstrate bias by some local authorities in the appointment of their employees.[42] *Fermanagh Facts*, which was produced by the former body is particularly impressive in its thoroughness, and supports its claims of gerrymandering and bias in employment with detailed and comprehensive data. All the full-time employees of Fermanagh County council in April 1969, excluding those working in schools, are examined in relation to their religion. Out of a total of 370, only thirty-two were Catholics. Aidan Corrigan claimed a similar pattern for County Tyrone and Lurgan borough, but did not quote the basis for his statistics.[43]

The same general pattern was confirmed by the *Sunday Times* Insight team's observations about Derry; it remarked that discrimination there was not confined to the number of people employed, but also applied to the quality and salaries of the jobs concerned. 'In 1966 the heads of all city departments (i.e. in Derry city) were Protestants. Of 177 salaried employees 145—earning £124,424—were Protestants, and only thirty-two —earning £20,420—were Catholics.'[44] Such discrimination was not confined to the west of the province as has sometimes been claimed. In 1971 a Belfast city councillor produced the employment figures for the Electricity Department of the Corporation :[45]

72

Table 5   Belfast Corporation Electricity Department Employees

	Protestant	Catholic
Motor Inspectors	91	4
Installation department	995	24
Street lighting	20	1
Garage	64	1
Mains	148	27
Cooker service	28	4
Total	1,346	61

Only 26% of Belfast's population are Catholics, so it is not surprising to find a majority of Protestants on the local authority payroll, but it would be difficult to argue that the holding by Protestants of 95·7% of the jobs in a corporation department was either fair or the result of chance.

The Cameron Report was particularly concerned with the effects of unfair housing allocation and was 'strongly of the opinion that these complaints must be placed very high in the list of deeply felt and justified grievances'.[46] The Commissioners confined their investigations to those towns where there had been major disorders—the city of Derry, Armagh, Newry and Dungannon. In all these areas there had been Catholic complaints about gerrymandering and about the allocation of houses for the maintenance of political control rather than on the grounds of social need. The report found 'that the complaint is abundantly justified. In each of the areas with Unionist majorities on their council, the majority was far greater than the adult population balance would justify. In Londonderry County Borough, Armagh Urban District, Omagh Urban District and County Fermanagh a Catholic majority was converted into a large Unionist majority on the council'. The report went on to discuss the case of Derry City Council, which is described earlier in this chapter. There, as in Omagh and Dungannon, the Unionist majority was preserved by confining Catholic families who were rehoused to wards where the anti-Unionist majority was already large. Furthermore, the report went on, 'we have no doubt also, in the light of the mass of evidence

73

put before us, that in these Unionist-controlled areas it was fairly frequent for housing policy to be operated so that houses allocated to Catholics tended, as in Dungannon Urban District, to go to rehouse slum dwellers, whereas Protestant allocations tended to go more frequently to new families.' An interesting footnote is Cameron's claim that both Unionist and non-Unionist councillors were happy to accept the system as they found it, on the grounds that it strengthened and consolidated their majorities by concentrating their supporters in particular areas.

Although the discriminatory pattern described by Cameron is confirmed by other studies, notably by an investigation of housing in Northern Ireland by four researchers at the New University of Ulster, it has been challenged by J.G. Calvert, a former head of the Northern Ireland Housing Trust.[47] Calvert demonstrated that, in aggregate, Catholics are more likely to be living in council houses than Protestants, although they only comprise one third of the population. This observation needs to be tempered by the reminder that not only are Catholics generally less prosperous than Protestants (and therefore less likely to own their own houses), but that Catholic families tend to be larger and consequently merit housing priority. Richard Rose, whose survey also failed to find blanket discrimination against Catholics in housing, examined these two variables. He found that the proportion of Catholics in subsidised housing was actually slightly higher than Protestants—by 4%; there was, however, a 12% difference against Catholics in the proportion of families with more than six children.[48] Nevertheless, apart from data on the practice of particular local authorities, there has never been a general investigation of housing allocation which considered all local councils in Northern Ireland. It is also important to note that the incidence of segregated housing in many parts of Northern Ireland is due in part to the unusual clusters in which Catholics and Protestants congregate in particular villages and parts of towns. This would not explain, however, the disparity of allocation in large areas which contain both Catholic and Protestant tenants, whether they live in segregated clusters or not. It seems reasonable to argue that the gerrymandering practices of some councils have done much to increase residential segregation. Austin Currie pointed to such a case in the Stormont parliament in 1965, 'the Council built 194 houses in the East Ward of Dungannon urban district and it allocated every single one of these 194 houses to a Unionist, to a Protestant. Not one Catholic managed to slip through the net, which shows how thoroughly the religious affiliations of the applicants were gone into.'[49]

Most of the investigations into both discrimination in employment and the allocation of houses by public bodies have arisen from the grievances of the Catholic minority. Cameron was at pains to make the point that both sides indulged in the same practices; the difference, of course, was that the Protestant majority had more opportunity to carry them out effectively: 'It is only fair to point out that certain authorities which were controlled by Catholic majorities pursued precisely analogous policies. To this day, for example, Newry Urban Council as already stated employs very few non-Catholics.'[50] Many Unionists would accept that some abuses detailed by the Cameron report actually did take place, but that they are not representative of the general situation. Two studies are sometimes quoted in defence of this view. The first is the survey conducted by Professor Richard Rose in the late 1960s which 'found very little sign of grievance directed specifically against local council activities';[51] and the second is to be found in the reports of the Commissioner for Complaints. This office, which was established in 1969 to hear complaints about maladministration by public bodies, received very few complaints of discrimination— only 6% of the total complaints accepted for investigation in 1970 and even less in 1971.[52] However, the Commissioner's brief only permits him to investigate individual grievances and prohibits him from general investigations against particular local authorities; consequently, none of the general grievances indicated above could have been examined by his office, even if it had been in existence earlier.

Evaluation

Much of the data concerning alleged discrimination by the state and state institutions in Northern Ireland has been provided by political pressure groups. The quality has been very uneven; conflicting evidence is sometimes ignored, sources are often omitted and particular anecdotes used to claim general points. Indeed, some of the reports and pamphlets produced by such pressure groups are more interesting for their reflection of popular attitudes than for their findings. This is not to argue that all evidence produced by pressure groups is unreliable—some of the evidence supplied to the Cameron Commission by such bodies as the Fermanagh Civil Rights Association is of the greatest importance and will withstand close scrutiny—but that a lot of it is.

Nor have academics helped very much to clarify the situation. Until the mid-1960s there had been an almost complete failure by academics in Northern Ireland to examine the central social division in their own community. One among many examples of this relates to allegations of discrimination in employment, perhaps the most persistent and frequently voiced complaint by the minority group in Northern Ireland. Certainly research into this problem would meet with peculiar difficulties but it is remarkable that there has never been an attempt by academics to investigate the extent and manner of job discrimination and to throw some light on such a central issue.

This combination of a shortage of serious academic investigations and a prevalence of pamphlets, papers and broadsheets produced by political pressure groups does cause problems when it comes to assessing the available data. In some instances official reports, notably Cameron's, offer a valuable collection of evidence and an impartial evaluation of it. Another useful aid to researchers is the reaction or failure to react of bodies accused of bias; thus, when David Donnison alleged that Catholics held only 5% of senior civil service posts in Northern Ireland it is both important and useful to consider the reply of the Northern Ireland Office to this charge, because it presented new data. The problem then becomes one of considering whether Donnison's estimate of 5% or the Northern Ireland Office's figure of 15% is correct; but one can be reasonably sure that the correct figure falls somewhere around these two estimates. Given all this, one can only approach the mass of material on discrimination with two major guidelines : the first is to suspect the motive of all researchers whether they be academic or polemical; and the second is to examine all the available evidence, from whatever source, and to measure it against other available data.

Using these standards, there is no doubt that some of the

allegations of discrimination against the Unionist governments are not supported by evidence and that others have been exaggerated. Two instances of the former allegations are the charges that extensive gerrymandering has been used to secure Unionist dominance at Stormont and Westminster, and that there has been discrimination specifically against Catholics in the western parts of the province. With the single possible exception of County Fermanagh, the first claim has not been sustained by any evidence; and, while it is possible to construct a strong case of governmental neglect of the area west of the Bann, and especially Derry city, no evidence has been produced to show that this was directed specifically against Catholic areas; indeed, if such neglect was discriminatory, one would expect to have seen it exercised more precisely against certain parts of the west rather than operate in a general way.

Apart from allegations which are not substantiated by evidence, there has been exaggeration in some cases where discrimination has been shown to exist. For example, Hadden and Hillyard investigated the question of prejudice in the administration of justice and found that the charge was justified. Their judgement was that the courts' sympathy with Protestants and Loyalists was 'small but cumulative', and not perhaps as extensive as has often been claimed.

The tendency to exaggerate the extent of discrimination practised by official bodies is not surprising. Where a broad pattern of bias operates, it is natural for people to explain abnormalities in terms of discrimination even if much more obvious explanations apply. In the first fifty years of the Northern Ireland state there is considerable evidence of just such a broad pattern of bias. This has been most closely examined in relation to local authorities, and there is overwhelming evidence that some local authorities practised discriminatory employment policy, and allocated the houses under their control in a sectarian fashion and for the electoral advantage of the dominant party. Practices also occurred at the Stormont level which demonstrate a deliberate bias against members of the minority community. There is a body of evidence that emergency powers were operated in a discriminatory fashion, and that both the administration of justice and the use of the police force were subjected to political pressures. Perhaps the clearest instances of all, however, are those relating to public employees and appointments to public bodies. Whether it applied to the employment of dustmen by Fermanagh County Council, to promotion in the civil service or to judicial appointments, there is a consistent and irrefutable pattern of deliberate discrimination against Catholics.

Equally as important as the existence of discrimination by official agencies is the effect that this has had on the minority in Northern Ireland. Boehringer's survey of attitudes towards the police in Andersonstown, the general Catholic suspicion which greets any governmental initiative in education and the general lack of confidence in the efficiency of reforms when they were introduced all point not only to Catholic resentment of governmental actions in the past, but to a growing cynicism towards the possibility of liberal reforms. Hadden and Hillyard are among a number of commentators who have pointed out the relationship between the frustration felt by some Catholics at their failure to achieve civil rights through the courts and the civil rights campaign, and the emergence of the Provisional IRA with their policy of physical force. This development cannot be fully explained by a refusal on the part of government to introduce changes; the reforms introduced in Northern Ireland between 1969 and 1974, although not meeting all the demands of the early civil rights campaigns were on a completely unprecedented level and created a new situation where many of the old malpractices were no longer possible. The franchise abnormalities were removed; housing allocation was taken away from the councils and centralised in a Housing Executive; Derry City Council was replaced by a popular commission; the appointment of a Commissioner for Complaints and Parliamentary Commissioner provided watchdogs against further abuses, although the possibility of job discrimination by local authorities remains until he or someone else has the power to initiate general investigations.

But these reforms failed in their objective of satisfying Catholic demands. The reasons for this failure are varied: the realisation that they were conceded reluctantly, the piecemeal manner of their introduction and the failure to tackle discrimination in employment all combined with a basic distrust of all governmental initiatives to ensure that the alienation of

78

the minority continued, virtually unaffected.

One of the lessons illustrated by this failure is that the timing and manner of reforms are as important as their content. It is quite conceivable that the alienation of the minority would continue, even if all their grievances were remedied, unless they also have the right to contribute meaningfully to the process by which reforms are determined. But even if this situation can be reached, another difficulty remains which will not be easily resolved. Whether or not every legitimate grievance is settled in the future, a backlog of Catholic discontent will surely remain until some way is found of remedying the existing shortage of Catholics in top public positions. If natural promotion procedures are followed, it will be many years before Catholics can work their way through the ranks and be represented at the top in approximate proportion to their numbers in the population. To discriminate in favour of Catholic applicants is as unfair as to discriminate against them. Northern Ireland appears doomed to the legacy of discrimination for many years to come.

CHAPTER IV

Orange, green and grey:
Political parties

In some areas a Nationalist is as certain of winning an election as a Unionist is in others. No amount of party organisation is going to win votes outside of these areas. There is no floating vote on the constitutional issue.
J.L. McCracken, 1967

The main criticism that one would direct against the operation of the party system in Northern Ireland is not that it fails to permit of nice shades of distinction in public opinion nor yet that it fosters a bellicose spirit, but that it subordinates every vital issue, whether of social or economic policy, to the dead hand of sectarian strife.
Nicholas Mansergh, 1936

IT is in the nature of political parties to reflect the divisions and conflicts within the state. In most cases, however, rival interests construct machinery whereby the more serious differences might be resolved. Political activity in Northern Ireland has been remarkable, not only for failing to build such machinery, but for not even attempting to do so. The central political division in Northern Ireland concerned the fundamental question of whether or not the citizens accepted the state's legality and were willing to be directed by its government. Both sides recognised the permanence of the division; consequently political activities and beliefs were petrified, and permanent Unionist rule was ensured. One question posed by this problem is how far political parties, by accepting polarised positions, contributed towards the polarisation of an already divided society; another is the degree to which it is possible to operate liberal democratic procedures in a situation where there is a significant minority which disputes the state's right to exist. The conduct of

Northern Ireland's political parties helps to indicate part of the answers.

Unionist Parties 1921–69

The origins of the Ulster Unionist party are to be found in an odd coalition of diverse interests which were determined to oppose the passage of a Home Rule bill for Ireland during the 1880s;[1] their antagonism to this proposal was sufficiently great to overcome their many other differences. Some of the elements which comprised this loose coalition were to control the reins of unionism in Ulster for the next ninety years : the Orange Institution, outlawed earlier in the century, re-emerged during the 1880s to marshal popular opinion against 'home rule'; the landed gentry were represented by the Duke of Abercorn; William Ewart and Sir James Corry personified Ulster's two main industries, linen and shipbuilding; James Henderson, owner of the *Belfast Newsletter*, established that newspaper's long association with unionism; and 'Roaring' Hugh Hanna, the Belfast revivalist, supplied the inevitable voice of fundamental Protestantism. The continuing dominance of political life in Northern Ireland by such unlikely bed-fellows was largely due to the structures and policies of the Ulster Unionist party.

Party Structure

Possibly the most remarkable aspect of the Unionist Party's 50-years monopoly of power was its success in maintaining support which defied class divisions. The regularity of working-class loyalty continued despite the party's poor record in policy areas affecting living standards and conditions. Openly antagonistic to trade unionism, devoid of urgency in the fields of housing and planning, suspicious of the welfare state, the Unionist party still effortlessly secured the votes of the Shankill and Newtownards Roads. This outstanding record of cloth-cap toryism was due in no small part to the Unionist party machinery and the Orange Order. It is still in these two areas that the first straws in any wind of change can usually be seen.

It was the formation of the Ulster Unionist Council in 1905 which converted the haphazard collection of unionist interests into an effective and disciplined force. It still controls the party machinery and policy, and has altered little since its early days, only expanding reluctantly to admit more pressure groups. As well as elected representatives, the council included such members as Northern Ireland peers, their wives and co-opted members. In 1970 almost 1,000 people were entitled to membership, although the structure of the council was again altered in 1974.

The largest, and perhaps the most active, group within the membership were the 306 members nominated by the affiliated divisional associations. As with similar amorphous groups whose members are only united in a central principle, the Unionist party is not a rigidly centralised organisation. Indeed very considerable powers, including those of defining their own memberships and selecting parliamentary candidates, are firmly in the control of local associations. This has sometimes caused conflict; in 1969, for example, it provided the back door through which loyalist opponents of Terence O'Neill attempted to swing the party. The subsequent attempt by the standing committee of the Ulster Unionist Council and the new Prime Minister, James Chichester-Clark, to impose more central controls were not successful: subsequently, in 1973, the same conflict between constituency associations and party headquarters was again resumed when Brian Faulkner, then premier, insisted on Official Unionist candidates signing a policy pledge. The refusal of some associations to do so resulted in the return of dissident Unpledged Unionists to the Northern Ireland Assembly.

Apart from the divisional and women's associations, the Loyal Orange Institution of Ireland has the strongest representation on the Council, sending 122 members from the County Lodges, and 10 from the Association of Loyal Orange Women. The Institution was founded in its present form[2] in 1795 as an exclusively Protestant body pledged to defend 'civil and religious liberty'. After a chequered history it emerged during the 1880s as the chief vehicle for Protestant grassroots opposition to the Home Rule campaign. Its main political significance dates from then.

There are currently about 1,500 Orange lodges in Northern Ireland. Richard Rose reckoned that there was a total of 90,000 members, or 32% of Northern Ireland's Protestant male adults, and that it was stronger in rural areas;[3] John Harbinson, however estimated that the figure was as high as 125,000–130,000.[4] The Institution's structure is hierarchical, with local lodges, district lodges, county or provincial lodges, Grand Lodge and Central Council, the officers of each lodge sending delegates to the next body on the ladder. Each lodge has a chaplain whose influence on the lodge, given the religious aims of the organisation, is considerable. To many clergymen the Order represents a means of providing political influence without actually joining a political party.

Membership of the Orange Order mirrors almost exactly the social mix of Protestant Northern Ireland. Membership cuts right across class barriers, and the top tier represents the ultimate synthesis of Protestant political, religious, economic and aristocratic influence; Orange politicians, clergymen, factory-owners and landlords have controlled the institutions of the state and determined policy. To ordinary members the Order probably provided a better means of political communication than the party. Orange members of parliament benefited as well; the local or district lodge provided an accurate sounding board of grassroots loyalist opinion. It is this mixture of different elites at the top, and the broad popular support at the bottom, that gives the Orange Institution its considerable political influence.

The Orange Order's relationship with the Unionist party was close, and demonstrated by the remarkably high proportion of Unionist representatives who were also members of the Institution.[5] Between 1921 and 1969 a total of fifty-four Unionist members of the Northern Ireland parliament reached Cabinet rank, only three of whom were not in the Institution; of the remaining ninety-five backbenchers, eighty-seven were members; all Unionists elected to the Northern Ireland Senate between 1921 and 1968 belonged to the Institution, as did fifty-four of the fifty-six Unionist MPs elected to the Westminster parliament—the other two were women. The influence of the Orange Institution was as much a matter of discipline as of numbers. Orangemen were not allowed to forget their first loyalty, and those who did were ostracised. Members have been expelled for attending funerals of Catholic friends; Phelim O'Neill, a Unionist MP, was expelled from the Order for entering a Catholic church. It is significant that Robert Simpson felt it necessary to resign from the Order when he was appointed Minister of Community Relations, the implication being that his duties would involve activities inconsistent with Orange principles. Indeed the influence of the Institution on the party was so marked and openly acknowledged that Lord Craigavon was able to say in 1934, not to an Orange meeting, but to the Northern Ireland House of Commons, 'I am very proud indeed to be Grand Master of the Orange Institution of the loyal county of Down. I have filled the offices for many years and I prize them far more than I do being Prime Minister. I have always said I am an Orangeman first and a politician and a member of this parliament afterwards . . . all I boast is that we are a Protestant parliament and a Protestant state.'[6]

It would have been surprising if an organisation with such influence over Unionist party members did not have a considerable effect on party policy. While the Institution's high membership among Unionist representatives could be relied upon to ensure that Orange principles would be safeguarded on most occasions, the Order did not hesitate to use its strength when it disapproved of government policy. These occasions were infrequent, and almost always involved what the Order regarded as concessions to Catholics or an erosion of Protestant influence. When the Unionist government implemented an Education act in 1923 which appeared to diminish the position of the Protestant churches in schools, it was the Order rather than the churches which secured its amendment. Again, it was the Order which opposed every attempt to open Unionist party membership to Catholics, as Sir Clarence Graham suggested in 1959. Both of these issues were significant; the Orange Institution saw its political role as that of watchdog against any moves to weaken the Protestant basis of the Unionist party.

For all this, the real nature of the relationship between the Orange Institution and the Unionist party is too subtle to be measured either by statistics or by overt political pressure. It was an integral part of Protestant Ulster's social system. Orange platforms on their annual festival on 12 July advocate political solidarity as often as religious application. The Orange halls which comprise the bulk of public meeting places in the province are central to Unionist party organisation; Unionist constituency associations often meet there; Unionist candidates

84

are selected in them and use them as campaign headquarters. Indeed the entire machinery of the Orange Institution is fundamental to the party's structure, and it is impossible to disagree with the view expressed by Lawrence Orr, Orangeman and member of the Westminster parliament, in 1970, 'Without the Orange Order there would have been no Unionist party and no union. If the Orange Order and the Unionist party were to be separated, the Unionist party would cease to exist as such.'[7]

Policies

In the field of policy making, the unity of disparate elements which comprised Unionism had its weaknesses as well as its strength. When the combined voice of the Unionist party was agreed on an issue, its harmony was remarkable and its volume loud; the problem was that the range of agreed notes was narrow and restricted. In effect, agreement was confined to their attitude towards the constitutional *status quo* and the general necessity of preserving hegemony over the Nationalist minority. The justification for maintaining this control was the mass treason of the minority. Firmly united in this attitude, virtually any means of control—job discrimination, gerrymandering, etc. —could be justified, at any rate during the first forty years of the Northern Ireland state. Thus in 1934 Sir Basil Brooke, then Minister of Agriculture and later Prime Minister, advised 'those people who are loyalists not to employ Roman Catholics, ninety-nine per cent of whom are disloyal.'[8]

This simple equation of Catholics and rebels justified their exclusion from any share of power, political or otherwise. The electorate was encouraged to regard the constitutional issue as the fundamental one, and questions about housing, welfare and education (except where sectarian control was involved) were rarely issues during elections. Barritt and Carter demonstrated this electioneering gambit by quoting editorials from the *Newsletter* (the Unionist morning paper) at every election since 1921, all of which hammered home the constitutional issue.[9] In terms of parliamentary control, it was completely successful. For at least the first forty years of the state, worry about Nationalist or Republican opposition was not a factor which had any influence on Unionist policy.

Freed from the burden of having to consider Nationalist

wishes, the party's only problem was piloting the ship of state down the narrow channel on which the various components of unionism agreed. Since the common bond—that of maintaining their own supremacy within their own state—was essentially defensive, almost any legislation outside this channel was potentially dangerous. In such circumstances, one would not expect to find a dynamic programme of social reform, and one would not be disappointed. Unforced initiatives were rare, and the guiding principle was that the less the government governed the better. Hence Lord Brookeborough was to claim that one day a week was quite sufficient for the discharge of his duties as Minister of Agriculture. Even when Prime Minister, he spent the whole winter in Australia and New Zealand, going each way by ship.[10] It was hardly surprising that the years between 1921 and the late 1940s were characterised by social decline and legislative stagnancy.

The introduction of the welfare state in Britain after the Second World War changed all this. Since the principle of parity of social services between Britain and Northern Ireland had been agreed in the 1920s, the implementation of all the British social reforms in Northern Ireland was automatic. This created two problems for the Unionist party. In the first place, the social benefits of the welfare state—especially an Education act which provided free secondary education for all—were of greater relative value to the less prosperous citizens; in the case of Northern Ireland, this meant the Catholics. More important, it introduced social legislation of a type bitterly opposed by the more traditional anti-socialist Unionists, and this applied strain to party unity. In retrospect the social reforms of the late 1940s were important in encouraging the emergence of a more liberal element within the party. No doubt these liberal Unionists were primarily motivated by a desire for social justice, but there were also more practical considerations. Some realised that one of the fruits of the 1947 Education act would be the emergence of an educated and more articulate Catholic middle class which would be a good deal less willing to accept their exclusion from positions of economic and political power in the state. Indeed, they argued, this presented a challenge to the party. It was at least possible that many of these new Catholics would be quite happy to settle for a reformed Ulster state rather than strive for a united Ireland.

If the liberal Unionists felt that the tide of opinion had turned in their favour, they reckoned without the strength of the party's traditional structures. Unionism is essentially a defensive movement—a union of groups aimed at preventing rather than constructing. So the apparent disappearance of the threat to the constitutional settlement which followed the rejection and defeat of the IRA campaign of the late 1950s, far from allowing the party to abandon sectarianism and to attempt the attraction of Catholic support, in the end crumbled the cement holding it together. If it is true that external threats created internal cohesion, it is equally true that the weakening of the threats removed the bond which had united the party's diffuse supporters. Many Unionists believed that the new liberalism was a greater danger than any number of IRA campaigns. In 1959 they were provided with an opportunity to show their strength.

In November of that year Sir Clarence Graham, chairman of the standing committee of the Ulster Unionist Council, declared that he could see no reason why a Catholic should not be selected as a Unionist candidate for parliament. His support by Brian Maginess, the Attorney-General, gave the suggestion extra weight. Maginess said, 'Toleration is not a sign of weakness, but proof of strength. This will require some change of thinking on the part of many, and it will need on the part of some a less provocative form of speech. It will require considerable words instead of clichés, reasoned arguments instead of slogans.'[11] The reaction was speedy. Just over a week later, Sir George Clark, Grand Master of the Grand Orange Lodge of Ireland, delivered the verdict of the Order. 'It is difficult to see how a Roman Catholic, with the vast differences in our religious outlooks, could be either acceptable within the Unionist party as a member or, for that matter, bring himself unconditionally to support its ideals.'[12] The party soon fell into line and Lord Brookeborough, the Prime Minister, told a meeting of Young Unionists at Lisbellaw, 'There is no use blinking the fact that political differences in Northern Ireland closely follow religious differences. It may not be impossible, but it certainly is not easy for any person to discard the political conceptions, the influence and impressions acquired from religious and educational instruction by those whose aims are openly declared to be an all-Ireland Republic.'[13] The question was not formally resolved. No resolutions were passed by the Ulster Unionist Council either excluding or welcoming Catholic membership of the party. In effect, the joint exclusion by the heads of the Orange Order and the state were taken as the rule, and an attempt in 1969 by a young Catholic to secure Unionist nomination in Newry, a Catholic area which had been traditionally anti-Unionist, was unsuccessful.

For all his talk of bridge-building, Captain O'Neill also found the question of Catholic membership of Unionism too hot to handle. It was not until November 1969, when the party was in disarray, that Major James Chichester-Clark gave official approval: 'I want to make it very clear indeed that, in the name of the party, I welcome those Roman Catholics who wish to be associated with unionism and support its principles—not just as voters, but as active members with, of course, an equal right with all other party members to be considered for party office and all that flows from it.'[14]

Despite the party's rejection of Sir Clarence Graham's proposals in 1959, the early 1960s represented the crest of the liberal unionist wave. This was largely due to the initiative of Terence O'Neill, who succeeded Lord Brookeborough as premier in 1963. In 1965 he paid the first visit by a Northern Ireland premier to a Catholic school; in the same year he invited the Irish Republic's Prime Minister to visit him in Stormont, and returned the visit to Dublin. These were gestures rather than reforms, and it was not until pressure was applied by the Civil Rights movement that practical changes followed. Captain O'Neill later admitted this: 'Any liberal-minded person must admit that the Civil Rights movement brought about reforms which would otherwise have taken years to wring from a reluctant government.'[15] When the reform package of December 1968 did come, to be followed by the dismissal of Mr William Craig, it was too little too late for the minority, and too much too soon for elements within the party. To Catholics, the reforms were seen as minimum concessions rather than rights, and this seemed to be confirmed by a radio interview in which Captain O'Neill said: 'A militant Protestant . . . cannot understand, in fact, that if you treat Roman Catholics with due consideration and kindness, they will live like Protestants in spite of the authoritative nature of their church.'[16] This seemed to many Catholics to be still the language of condescension.

Unionist Threats to Unionist Unity

Despite constant Unionist vigilance against the fragmentation of the party, unity was difficult to maintain. The recalcitrant groups of unionists who persistently broke with the official party and opposed it in elections generally belonged to one of three categories, two were spasmodic and transitory, but some manifestation of the third was always present. In the first place there were unionist parties which campaigned for specific legislative targets. One of these threatened to emerge from the United Education Committee, formed in 1925 from the three Protestant Churches and the Orange Order to secure amendments to the 1923 Education act. Similarly in 1929 three Local Option candidates sought changes in the licensing laws, obtaining an average poll of 28·5% in their constituencies. The abolition of Proportional Representation as the method of electing MPs was introduced in 1929 specifically to make such fragmentation of the party vote more difficult. It succeeded. Eight MPs elected in 1925 (the last PR election) were not solely identified with the Border issue; in 1929 this had been reduced to four.[17]

The second category of independent Unionists wished to see the implementation of more enterprising policies, especially in the social and economic fields. Such were the Independent Unionists, who won four seats in 1925, and W.J. Stewart's Progressive Unionists who contested twelve constituencies in 1938, mainly ones where they hoped to win enough Nationalist votes to secure election. They were defeated in all twelve despite collecting 30·9% of the votes cast in these constituencies. In both cases the party machine had little difficulty in exploiting Protestant fears about the reliability of the breakaway parties' attitudes towards the constitution and about their betrayal of unionist unity.

The most consistent pressure from independent groups has come from the loyalist right wing. The Belfast Protestant Association of 1902 set the pattern here, and was followed by a number of successors. Some of these sat as Independents and opposed social reform, such as the group of Independent Union‑ ists who secured seats in the 1920s. In 1938 a loyalist Independent Unionist Association contested six seats and was more successful than the moderate Progressive Unionists, winning seats in Shankill and Woodvale. But it was the changes in Unionist policy introduced by Terence O'Neill in the 1960s that produced the Protestant Unionist party which under Ian Paisley attracted growing support in their campaign against change.[18]

The Protestant Unionist party had emerged from a group known as Ulster Protestant Action which had been formed to resist ecumenism in the province; in 1971 it changed its name to the Democratic Unionist party. From its formation the party's strident anti-Catholicism and traditional unionism, personified in its uncompromising leader, provided a focus for those Protestants who were opposed to the mood of religious and political tolerance which appeared to be emerging during the 1960s. It represented the old unchanging values, and opposed both political and religious leaders who wished to change these. The Prime Minister, Terence O'Neill, was a favourite target for Protestant Unionist demonstrations, and in 1966 Paisley was jailed for his part in a demonstration at the General Assembly of the Presbyterian Church in Belfast. Paisley's charisma and fundamental message were not new to Ulster. But he added to them a real understanding of the media, organising and fund-raising abilities and a willingness to enter directly into active politics. The first five Protestant Unionist candidates stood in the 1969 Northern Ireland General Election and averaged 28% of their polls. In 1970 they secured two Stormont seats, and Paisley followed this up by winning the North Antrim seat in the Westminster election of the same year. They won nine seats in the 1973 Assembly election.

Harbinson points out that the growth of the Democratic Unionist party was due to more than its anti-Republicanism, which many of its followers regard as synonymous with anti-Catholicism.[19] In addition, it is a movement with strong working-class support which has attacked government and local authorities on their housing, public health and general economic records. There is little doubt, however, that Paisley's personality, his sectarianism and his defence of traditional unionist values were the main reasons for its popularity.

All of these Unionist parties, although occasionally hysterical, were committed to parliamentary tactics. But there was also a tradition of extra-parliamentary groups which were prepared to adopt more direct methods to defend unionist supremacy. One was the Ulster Protestant League, established in 1931 when unemployment was running at 30% in Northern Ireland, which advocated a policy of total discrimination against Catholics. Another was the Ulster Volunteer Force (UVF) which supported more violent tactics. In fact, little is known about this militant loyalist body, except that it appears to have emerged in 1966 as a reaction against the Republican celebrations in Belfast of the fiftieth anniversary of the Easter Rising.[20] On 19 May the body issued a press statement: 'From this day we declare war against the IRA and its splinter groups. Known IRA men will be executed mercilessly and without hesitation.'[21] In that year three UVF members were sentenced to life imprisonment for the murder of a Catholic barman, and the UVF was named as an unlawful assembly under the Special Powers act. Since then the organisation has claimed responsibility for the destruction of a number of electrical and water installations in March and April 1969; in 1972 they claimed a number of cross-border raids into the Republic and in 1975 that they had killed six opponents. It is frankly difficult to assess the UVF. Owen Dudley Edwards wrote, 'It is clear that the UVF and some of its alias organisations played a critical part in the coming of the pogrom to Belfast in August 1969.'[22] On the contrary, on the evidence available, it is as invalid to claim this as it is to claim that the IRA played a similar role within the Civil Rights movement prior to 1969/1970. Both statements are frequently made, but no evidence has been produced in either case. It was estimated in 1973 to have 300–500 active members, not very well equipped, and to be funded 'almost exclusively from criminal activities and protection rackets'[23] but the real truth is that the UVF's security has been so tight that very little reliable information about it can be found.

Anti-Partitionist Parties 1921–1969

Opposition to the partition of Ireland has adopted both parliamentary and violent methods. These approaches did not suddenly emerge in 1920 with the Government of Ireland act, but were the heritage of the Home Rule struggle of the previous century. The Northern Ireland parliamentary Nationalist Party was the successor of the party started by Charles Stewart Parnell in 1879 to campaign in Westminster for Irish Home Rule. The only difference was that by 1921 twenty-six of Ireland's thirty-two counties had achieved Home Rule, and the issue centred on the six remaining counties of Northern Ireland. The other tradition in Irish nationalism—the physical force tradition—had a longer pedigree and the initial morale booster that it had actually produced results in the south. The exclusion of the Northern Ireland counties from the new Free State acted as a stimulus to northern republicans, but it posed strategic problems for the IRA. After the Civil War in the south, their support diminished. Many supporters who were prepared to fight for an independent Ireland were less enthusiastic after they had achieved most of their objective. For the remainder, the problem of conducting a campaign, military or political, in what would be mainly hostile territory posed strategic problems which proved difficult to solve.

Republicans

Normal political involvement by the Republicans was seriously compromised by the refusal of Sinn Fein (the Republican political wing) to recognise the existence of the Northern state or its institutions. On the other hand, general elections proved tempting opportunities for gauging their support in the community. The dilemma was resolved by occasionally proposing candidates who, if elected, abstained from taking their parliamentary seats. In the first elections for the new Northern Ireland parliament, for example, they won six of the twelve anti-partitionist seats, although they lost four of these to the Nationalists in the 1925 election. Again in the 1955 Westminster elections, for no apparent reason except the vagaries of the current Republican leadership, they contested twelve seats, winning two. Since the function of these candidates was to measure entrenched support, campaigning was minimal and no effort was made to win support across the sectarian divide.

The refusal of the Republicans to adopt a consistent political role did not only arise from their attitude towards the state. Equally important was the state's refusal to allow them par-

92

ticipation in normal political exchange. The 1934 Representation of the People act insisted that candidates declare their intention to sit if elected; in 1962 the Electoral Law act forced candidates to 'recognise the lawful authority of the parliament of Northern Ireland'. The Flags and Emblems (Display) act (1954) forbade the display of flags or emblems which 'may occasion a breach of the peace' and was widely recognised as a measure against republican election emblems. All these measures were directed at the electoral ambitions of Sinn Fein and the republican movement and encouraged the republicans to emphasise their military strategy.

While a united Ireland was the main aim of the IRA movement as a whole, it afforded shelter to a considerable variety of interests. The southern part of Ireland had always viewed unification more romantically than the north. Within the north, there were considerably different shades of republicanism between the cities and the country areas, and between Derry and Belfast; there have always been and still are recognisably different emphases even between different parts of Belfast; but the most fundamental differences were probably those between north and south. The primary function of the northern IRA, which is strongly influenced by the Belfast and Derry battalions, has been an essentially practical one, that of protecting Catholic areas against possible invasion.[24] Ideological objectives, such as a united Ireland or a socialist Ireland, took second place to their primary defensive role. It was for this reason that the IRA in Belfast retained considerable potential support during the 1920s and 1930s when sectarian troubles were common, and that this support was eroded by the comparative peacefulness of the next two decades. Since the basis of the movement was sectarian, it is hardly surprising that the IRA made no serious effort to canvass widespread support from Protestants.

The 1956–62 IRA campaign showed that the Catholics in the north no longer felt a need for the traditional IRA protection. The impetus for the campaign came substantially from the south and from the rural parts of Ulster. Although the disarray of the organisation in the city of Belfast was one reason for Catholic non-involvement, perhaps a stronger one was that there was no apparent advantage for Catholics in a campaign. The violence never really spread to Belfast, and it slowly died away in the rest of the province. The IRA statement in 1962 acknowledging the defeat of the campaign was a significant one: 'Foremost among the factors motivating this course of action has been the attitude of the general public whose minds have deliberately been distracted from the supreme issue facing the Irish people—the unity and freedom of Ireland.'[25]

The 1956–62 campaign produced radical changes in republican strategy. Over the next few years there was a deliberate and discernible shift towards social issues—housing, trade unionism, etc.—and a corresponding move from the discredited physical force approach. It was this fundamental change in emphasis toward an increasingly socialist ideology which dictated the IRA attitude towards the Civil Rights movement in 1968; it also led to the ceding of IRA weapons in Belfast. This new departure, which may have represented a shrewd reading of social developments, presented for the first time the possibility of attracting non-Catholic support.

August 1969 changed this completely. Many of the more traditional IRA leaders, especially in the more vulnerable Catholic parts of Belfast, had been worried by what they regarded as increasing complacency and unpreparedness; they had been squeezed out by the more progressive elements. But the invasion of the Falls Road and the subsequent destruction and death confirmed their deepest suspicions and raised a spectre which many were beginning to think had at last been successfully laid.

The fears of the 1920s and 1930s were resurrected almost overnight, as was the protective role which the IRA had deliberately rejected in the years of the new departure. It is unlikely that the opposition to the IRA's moves towards socialism would ever have amounted to more than murmurings without the invasion of the Falls. In the event, the violence of August 1969 precipitated a reaction against both the policies and leadership of the Republican organisation, and the emergence of the Provisional IRA and Sinn Fein. Although the Official (or 'Red') Republican movement kept some supporters in Belfast, Derry and a few country areas, it was the Provisional (or 'Green') IRA which became the major influence in the North. The aberration from traditional republicanism towards a more

94

fluid, socially-based movement, had only succeeded for about five years.

Parliamentary Opposition

Though the strategic problems facing the IRA and the Nationalist party were different, they were united in their refusal to accept the legality of the state. The IRA demonstrated its opposition by waging war on the state whenever possible. To the Nationalists, however, the situation posed a fundamental dilemma. Should they adopt the purist attitude that the state, being illegal, should be completely shunned or should they work from within the new state to secure its failure? The former policy meant abandoning the decision-making arena completely to the Unionists, and the latter implied a *de facto* acceptance of structures which they were determined to destroy. The history of Nationalism for the next fifty years is one of ineptitude rising from their failure to resolve this dilemma.

The ineffectiveness of the Nationalists was due in part to the nature of Northern Ireland politics, but more to the party's own indolence and political short-sightedness. Its organisation, strategy and policies all reveal an acceptance of a permanent minority position, and either unwillingness or inability to do anything about it.

The organisation of the party had always been informal. Although in theory there had been a party machinery since 1928, there had never been a full-time party official. Organisation in the 1920s and 1930s amounted to a combination of traditional support and the skills of Joe Devlin, the Nationalist leader. In the nationalist country areas, support was generally secure. Polarised and conservative, it was unlikely to diminish as long as the Nationalists had a monopoly of the anti-partitionist platform. If it occasionally strayed towards Sinn Fein, this was usually because no Nationalist candidate was standing; it was an aberration rather than a pattern. The towns, especially Belfast, were more difficult to control. Here the party's undoubted conservatism ('Green Tories' was a frequent name applied to Nationalists) and lack of interest in social policies were considerable drawbacks; but they were counter-balanced by the dominating personality of Joe Devlin. Irish Nationalism had always preferred charisma to organisation.

Joseph Devlin is one of Northern Ireland's nationalist folk heroes. Rising from the working classes in Belfast to a position of eminence in the Irish Parliamentary Party, he became Nationalist leader after partition. He also controlled the Nationalist members on Belfast City Council. In effect, Joe Devlin was the acknowledged spokesman for the political minority in Belfast, supported by organised Catholicism. The Church approved his conservatism and anti-socialism, and the *Irish News*, the daily newspaper favoured by Catholics, supplied the role of an almost official party organ; the Ancient Order of Hibernians, which attempted to function as a Catholic equivalent of the Orange Order, had particularly close links with him and in turn provided a connection with Irish America where the movement was quite strong. With such backing, what need was there to construct a party organisation? Indeed, it would provide a possible forum for rivals. The problems arose when there was no leader strong enough or skilled enough to mould together the different components of nationalism. Personal relationships were the cement of the party; the trouble was that, when they became strained, the party floundered. It was for this reason that attempts to create a united front of anti-partitionists continually collapsed as a result of personal squabbles.

Such attempts frequently disturbed the placid history of the Nationalist party. In 1928 The National League was formed for this purpose and in 1936 the Irish Union Association. Yet another initiative was attempted after the war by James Mc-Sparran and 1959 saw the creation of National Unity. None of these was successful. As long as political activity was stratified and stagnant, the Nationalist party only required its traditional allies.

Nationalist politics were no more dynamic than Nationalist organisation. Having spurned the use of force, the party also rejected the alternative strategy of trying to attract support across the sectarian divide. They failed to follow the logical consequences of their return to parliament in 1926, and to assume a normal opposition role. Instead they opted for the long-term hope of an eventual majority from the higher birth rate of Catholics. In the interim period their main activity was

96

that of highlighting abuses and voicing minority complaints on an *ad hoc* basis.

These strategies of birthrate politics and watchdog for abuses were equally unsuccessful. The birthrate advantages were countered by the high Catholic emigration rate and the watchdog role was ineffective because of the Nationalists' inability to apply pressure for the redressing of grievances. Furthermore their public stance relieved them of the necessity of presenting themselves as an alternative government and consequently devising alternative policies. Opposition politics became almost entirely destructive; social stances were particularised and negative; and the party rapidly lost the philosophical background and dynamism which it had exhibited in pre-partition years.

The first apparent realisation that their political road was a dead-end coincided with the post-war Labour government. Its declaration that 'in no event will Northern Ireland or any part thereof cease to be part of the United Kingdom without the consent of the Parliament of Northern Ireland'[26] appeared to put eventual unification even further away; the social benefits of the welfare state introduced a wide new area of legislation affecting citizens that required deeper involvement by opposition MPs in parliament. The problems posed by this new factor were not solved in the 1950s, but were reinforced by the failure of the 1956–62 IRA campaign. There was increasing evidence that some members of the minority were relegating Irish unification to a far distant future, or even oblivion, and demanding immediate reform within Northern Ireland. The comparative success of the Northern Ireland Labour Party in 1958, and the formation of National Unity in 1959 which only desired unity through the 'consent of the people of Northern Ireland' were obvious indications that there was need for change. Under the cautious leadership of Eddie McAteer the party slowly began to involve itself more in political exchanges. At a conference in Maghery in 1964 the Nationalists issued a statement of party policy on a wide front for the first time. In 1965, following the O'Neill-Lemass talks, the Nationalists took the traumatic step of becoming the official opposition at Stormont. One year later the party's first annual conference was held, to be soon followed by a party manifesto. The way seemed clear for the establishment of a more normal political situation.

But the changes had come too late. The social factors which had nudged the Nationalists towards a new strategy had also produced a number of changes in the attitudes of Northern Ireland Catholics. A generation had emerged which did not remember the sectarian troubles of the 1930s, which was better educated and whose aspirations were too complex and varied to find satisfaction in the Nationalist party. Some of these Catholics looked for a more satisfying and dynamic form of nationalism with National Unity; others, especially in Belfast, looked to the Connolly socialism of the Republican Labour Party; some joined the Northern Ireland Labour Party, perhaps the first time that significant numbers of Catholics tried to satisfy their aspirations within a party which had clearly rejected the idea of a united Ireland. Indeed the radical change which took place in the 1960s was that almost all opposition parties in Northern Ireland came quietly to accept—if sometimes only conditionally—the existence of the state. Combined with the IRA debacle, it was the rejection of revolution in favour of internal reforms.

While these new trends rendered the Nationalists increasingly irrelevant, their support in the country areas was still considerable and they still held a majority of opposition seats. It was the emergence of the Civil Rights campaign which really created serious problems for them. The Civil Rights campaign created a common front for the aspirations of many Catholics, whether their political allegiances lay with the Northern Ireland Labour party, Republican Labour, modern Nationalists or even the IRA of the new departure. The Nationalist party suspected the new phenomenon and could not cope with it. At its 1968 conference, a motion favouring civil disobedience was shelved. The 1969 general election was to show how severely the Nationalists had misjudged the temper of the time.

The Centre
So far none of the political parties which were based on policies other than sectarian ones have succeeded in building up wide support in Northern Ireland. The Liberals never recovered from the Home Rule struggle, when they alienated Protestant opinion and lost their Catholic supporters to the more direct appeal of Sinn Fein and to the Nationalists. They only held

one Stormont seat and, ironically enough, lost it as a result of parliamentary reform when the four University seats were abolished. Their main contributions to political life in Northern Ireland was in producing outstanding personalities like Rev. J.B. Armour and Sheelagh Murnaghan; their main—virtually their only—forum since 1969 has been the annual British Liberal party conference.

The Northern Ireland Labour Party

The Northern Ireland Labour party (NILP) was more success-ful.[27] The first attempt to establish a coalition of socialist groups in Ireland took place in Belfast in the 1890s, at the same time as similar moves took place in Britain. From the start their unity was jeopardised by conflicting attitudes towards the national question. It was James Connolly who best presented the Irish mixture of socialism and nationalism as an alternative to the British version. He wrote while in jail, 'The Socialists will not understand why I am here. They forget that I am an Irishman.'[28] This peculiarly Irish form of socialism has since taken many different forms, and is still strong today. It is one of the main reasons why the Northern Ireland Labour party was not more successful than it has been.

The party won its first seats in the Northern Ireland Parliament in 1925. Its insistence on maintaining a non-sectarian line, leaving partition as an open question, was easier said than done, although the purpose was clear enough. If the question of the border could be avoided, Labour supporters argued, it would be possible to campaign on the real social and economic problems which bedevilled the province. This policy was not successful. There was constant pressure on the party to make a stand either for or against the constitution. In 1937, for example, a motion proposing co-operation with the workers in the south 'to achieve the unity of Ireland' was defeated by 90 votes to 20. The two figures who dominated the party during the 1930s, H. Midgely and J. Beattie, personified the party's problems.

Both were NILP members of parliament at Stormont, but Midgely favoured closer connections with Britain and the Commonwealth while Beattie campaigned for Irish unity. Beattie's love-hate relationship with the party saw his expulsion

99

on two occasions during the 1930s, and his election as party leader in 1942. Midgely left the party on Beattie's election as leader. His attempt to establish a rival Commonwealth Labour Party failed, and Midgely eventually became a Unionist.

The split was, of course, much more fundamental than a personality duel between Midgely and Beattie. It was one matter to declare that both partitionists and anti-partitionists could remain within the NILP but quite another to maintain party unity in elections. The plain fact was that the electorate, encouraged by the two main parties, saw partition as the main issue and NILP candidates were forced to accept this. The result was that Labour candidates presented quite different platforms during the same election, depending on the constituency which they were contesting. Ambivalence on the constitutional issue meant that a Labour party continued to exist, but the price was continual electoral failure.

It was the declaration of the Irish Republic in 1949 that provided the catalyst which forced the choice. In the party conference of that year, the NILP opted for the British connection. In the election which followed, all the NILP candidates were defeated, but the feeling was that the bogey had been laid at last and there was a chance that a real socialist party could be constructed on a firm foundation.

In the next ten years there appeared to be signs that this might happen. Although some loyalists were still suspicious and some Catholics alienated by the 1949 declaration, support for Labour policies soon became evident. The surprise was that Catholic support began to return in the late 1950s, coinciding with the failure of the IRA campaign.

The NILP won four seats in the elections of that year, and became the official opposition at Stormont. In the next election in 1962 these seats were held, but no new ones acquired. But the momentum was not maintained, and these years represented the apogee of the party. In 1965, although they only polled 10,519 votes less than in 1962, they lost two of their seats.

There appears to have been two main reasons for this decline. The first was an internal split on tactics. One wing of the party, represented by David Bleakley and W.R. Boyd, thought that the party should concentrate on consolidating support among the Protestant working class; the other, led by Charles Brett and Sam Napier, wanted to make a more direct appeal to the new Catholic voters who appeared to be drifting towards the party. This indecision could not have come at a more inopportune time, with a party apparently poised for a major breakthrough.

The other reason for Labour's collapse was the emergence of the unforeseen—a Unionist party under Terence O'Neill which caught the mood of moderates, and the support of the new British Labour government. The electoral losses in 1965 were to pro-O'Neill Unionists, and the message was driven home in 1967 when the NILP suffered a crushing defeat in the local government elections.

Demoralisation set in. 'From May 1967 onwards', Graham wrote in 1972, 'the Party was virtually directionless'.[29] Policy towards the new Civil Rights campaign was divided and weak. In May 1969 they endorsed it, but voted against involvement. In protest, Paddy Devlin, one of their two MPs, left the party, soon to join the Social Democratic and Labour Party. Eamonn McCann, one of the more radical civil rights leaders, was expelled from the party.

The history of the Northern Ireland Labour party is a cautionary tale demonstrating the difficulty of attempting to win support for non-sectarian policies. There were three clear chapters in the story. Before 1949 the NILP tried to win support by ignoring the issue which the electorate considered central—the existence of the state. Between 1949 and the mid-1960s, that problem was tackled and the party began to benefit from the improvement in community relations then prevalent. From then on it lost its initiative, prevaricated and was caught up by events.

The NILP had electoral successes, but these successes were almost exclusively in constituencies in which only one of the two main parties was competing. Thus Protestant workers were prepared to vote Labour rather than Nationalist, but not to prefer them to Unionists. The reverse was equally true. Catholics supported Labour only when no anti-partitionist was standing. Thus in 1969 Catholics who had supported NILP in 1965 preferred candidates who were associated with the Civil Rights campaign—those who were later to unite in the Social Democratic and Labour party. The formation of the Alliance party in 1971 dealt yet another blow to the NILP, since it too courted the scanty moderate vote in Northern Ireland. It was the NILP which suffered from this situation in the 1973 Assembly elections. From a total of seventy-eight seats, it was only able to secure the election of one candidate.

The Alliance Party

The Alliance party was a new phenomenon in Northern Ireland.[30] The policies of the NILP were based on class rather than religious differences, so its non-sectarianism was incidental rather than fundamental. But the Alliance party was the first Irish political organisation which professed non-sectarianism, or rather cross-sectarianism, as its *raison d'être*. The genesis of Alliance's eventual support was the moderation of the mid-1960s, which at first operated as liberal wings within the more conventional parties. It was the growth of Protestant extremism and IRA violence which produced a new party. In 1969 the New Ulster Movement was launched. It regarded itself as a non-party ginger group and professed traditional liberal values. During the Northern Ireland election of that year, it saw the main struggle as between liberal and traditional Unionism and campaigned on behalf of those unionist candidates who supported Terence O'Neill. It did not support more radical candidates. like the Civil Rights Independents and the People's Democracy. Subsequent to the election the New Ulster Movement began to doubt the viability of working within any of the traditional parties and in January 1970 it set up a committee, known as 'the Group', to investigate the possibility of forming a new party. Vacillation continued, however, and it took a good, if unsuccessful, campaign by a young liberal candidate without an organisation in the south Antrim by-election of April 1971 to persuade people that a new party might be viable.

In the same month the Alliance party was formed largely from Unionist and Liberal refugees and uncommitted people, and began to build up constituency organisations. It acquired its first MPs in 1972 without requiring an election; three MPs defected to the party—two from the Unionist party and one from the Nationalists. But the Alliance party's hopes of a dramatic and speedy success were soon dashed. Its first experi-

102

ence at the polls in the local government elections only produced 14% of the total poll, a level of support confirmed by the party's performance in the elections for the Northern Ireland Assembly's seventy-eight seats one month later. Despite some anticipation of a moderate majority emerging to vote for the parties of the centre, the Northern Ireland Labour party and the Alliance party only mustered nine seats between them, eight going to Alliance. Ulster politics remained stubbornly soft-centred.

The Civil Rights Campaign

It was not difficult for a close observer of the Northern Ireland political scene in the mid-1960s to forecast the rapid growth of Catholic dissatisfaction. As early as 1965 John Macrae, who had conducted an early sociological study of a number of Northern Ireland towns, was able to write, 'Many people exhibit a mere hopeless antagonism to the present situation, but there are signs that this is changing to a more active self-respect. It is not ridiculous to envisage a Catholic civil rights movement in the not too far distant future.'[31] The use of the word 'Catholic' is important. The rejection of republicanism in the late 1950s had channelled Catholic aspirations into a six rather than a thirty-two-county context, and they were dissatisfied with what they saw. The reluctance of the new liberal Unionism to provide much more than gestures was apparently matched by the unwillingness of the Nationalists to seize the initiative in demanding real reforms. The formation of the Northern Ireland Civil Rights Association (NICRA) in February 1967 was equally a reaction to Unionist intransigence and Nationalist ineptitude.

The aims of the new organisation, though comprehensive and far-reaching, were hardly revolutionary—universal franchise, impartial electoral boundaries, anti-discriminatory legislation, a points system for housing, the disbandment of the 'B' Specials, the repeals of the Special Powers act and Public Order bill. They were firmly rooted in an atmosphere of liberal democracy.

It is completely mistaken to regard NICRA as a revolutionary body. Eamonn McCann's description of the Derry Citizens' Defence Committee, an important ally of NICRA, as 'middle-

103

aged, middle-class and middle-of-the-road' may have been over-generalised, but the leaders of the new movement—Austin Currie, the McCluskeys in Dungannon and John Hume in Derry —were not notable for their radicalism.[32] The strategies of NICRA borrowed heavily from pacifist non-violent techniques which had been tested elsewhere, especially in North America—sit-ins, processions, songs and publications—all conducted in full view of television cameras and pressmen. The combination of liberal objectives and pacifist techniques initially attracted much Protestant sympathy and some Protestant support.

In discussions about the development of the Civil Rights campaign, the significance of two pressure groups in particular is often mentioned. These are the IRA and the People's Democracy (PD). Perhaps the most persistent of the many myths about NICRA is that the IRA infiltrated the organisation and influenced its policies from the start. It is true that Cathal Goulding, Chief of Staff of the IRA, attended the August 1966 Maghera conference which was instrumental in establishing the Civil Rights campaign in 1967, but the IRA appears to have played little part in the deliberations and its interest appeared to be confined to any benefits the movement's success might bring to the republican movement. They merely sent observers to the 1968 Dungannon march; as Max Hastings put it, they appeared to be simply 'gratifying their liking for a finger in every pie'.[33] As for the development of NICRA during its first two years there is no evidence at all that the IRA either captured the leadership or directed the policy of NICRA. Whatever happened subsequently, nothing has emerged since the writing of the Cameron Report to contradict its judgement that in 1968 'There is no sign that they (the IRA) are in any sense dominant or in a position to direct the policy of the Civil Rights Association.'[34]

The People's Democracy had a much more radical influence on NICRA than any republican combination.[35] It made significant contributions towards the provision of both leaders and policies. Eamonn McCann, Bernadette Devlin and Michael Farrell attempted to direct the People's Democracy and, through it, NICRA towards a more radical socialist stance than any of its other leaders. The initial Civil Rights programme was

104

regarded as aiming at a bourgeois settlement which would not solve basic conflicts. The radicalisation of PD was rapid. By the end of 1969 there was an influential group within the PD which saw its objectives as the overthrow of the state, to be replaced, not by a republican Ireland, but by a socialist state. This group's control of PD was irregular, and PD's influence on the Civil Rights campaign was only considerable between October 1968 and mid-1969. Nevertheless this radical group brought about a major shift in the Civil Rights campaign.

The conflict between radicals and liberals within NICRA came to a head in late 1968. In November the campaign had achieved some of its initial liberal aims—an Ombudsman had been appointed, and Derry City Council replaced by a Commission; William Craig, a particular enemy of the Association, had been dismissed from the government. There was cause for hoping that more reforms would follow and NICRA agreed to hold off their campaign to allow these. It was at this point that PD decided to march from Belfast to Derry on New Year's Day 1969. Some PD leaders, like Kevin Boyle and Bernadette Devlin, were worried about the plan, and so was NICRA. Even after the event, Max Hastings wrote: 'The political thinking which inspired the 1 January march was very naïve, whatever the justice of the cause they sought to promote.'[36] Judged by the criteria of the Civil Rights movement, this would have been true, but these criteria no longer applied. By January 1969 the objectives of the PD had become radically different to those of NICRA.

The events of the march are well known and need not be recounted here.[37] The ambush by Loyalist extremists at Burntollet in effect marked the end of the breathing-space conceded to the government by NICRA, and the end of the campaign of non-violence. In the short term the significance of the incident was not apparent, but as 1969 passed it became clear that Burntollet marked the major turning point in the Civil Rights campaign. Demonstrations increased in violence; both Protestant support and general sympathy dissolved; disillusioned liberals and pacifists left the movement, many of them shocked by the fact that the reaction to the civil rights campaign had produced even greater community polarisation. The movement continued and still continues. The support and influence of PD diminished

105

as its policies became increasingly radical and it began to move towards a rapprochement with Republicanism. NICRA, having lost much of its liberal leadership, found itself outbid by more republican factions, especially after the rekindling of violence in Belfast in August 1969. With seven people killed and more than 3,000 rendered homeless, many of the people in the Catholic ghettos demanded more secure guarantees than those promised from political pressure. The Provisional IRA was born. For the interim at least, the horror of August 1969 marked the end of the liberal dream.

The Political Effects of the Campaign

The effect of the civil rights campaign on the established political parties was substantial. The pressure for change produced an equally strong determination to resist it. The main vehicle for this resistance outside the Unionist party was Ian Paisley's Protestant Unionist party, which had bitterly opposed O'Neill since 1964. But Paisley was anathema to many conventional Unionists who were equally opposed to concessions. It was not long before opposition appeared from within the official party. William Craig had many of the necessary qualifications to attract such support. His early opposition as Minister of Home Affairs to the early civil rights campaign was seen by some Unionists as justified by events. When Captain O'Neill dismissed him from the Cabinet in 1969 the extent of Unionism's split soon became apparent. Within months O'Neill had been forced to resign and was replaced by what was regarded as a stop-gap premiership under James Chichester-Clark; but the concessions continued, increasingly under pressure from Westminster, and the party split hardened. Developments between 1970 and 1973 were largely an extension of the events of the previous two years, and may be described diagrammatically. In 1970 there were three main interest groups in Unionism, none of which was tightly organised.

1. PARTY UNITY GROUP : This central group was primarily concerned with party unity rather than with policy. Its members played active behind-the-scene roles.
2. TRADITIONAL UNIONISTS : Many hardline unionists began to look for support outside the party's structures. The emerg-

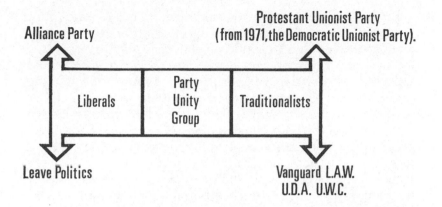

Alliance Party

Protestant Unionist Party
(from 1971, the Democratic Unionist Party).

Liberals | Party Unity Group | Traditionalists

Leave Politics

Vanguard L.A.W.
U.D.A. U.W.C.

ence of grassroots organisations like the Loyalist Association of Workers (LAW), the paramilitary Ulster Defence Association (UDA) and William Craig's Vanguard movement were regarded as pressure groups which might be used to move the party back to its old policies and practices. When Craig expanded Vanguard into a political party—the Vanguard Unionist Progressive party (VUPP)—closely linked to the UDA and LAW—a formidable combination was created which appealed to some right-wing Unionist party members who were not prepared to overcome their antagonism to Paisley. Both Vanguard and Paisley's Democratic Unionist party believed that the only way to restore loyalist dominance was for Unionists to leave their party and place their trust in new organisations; but there were many traditional Unionists who were not prepared to make this break and who were determined to alter Unionist policies from within. They did not have to wait long for success.

3. LIBERAL UNIONISTS: The moderates too tended to look outside the party for support. Phelim O'Neill and Robert McConnell, disturbed by the right-ward trend, actually joined the new Alliance Party; a much greater number retired from politics—Robert Porter, Richard Ferguson, Robin Baillie, even James Chichester-Clark and Terence O'Neill. Those who remained found themselves increasingly isolated as the Provisional IRA campaign further hardened Protestant opinion, and some were to join Brian Faulkner's new party when it was formed in 1974.

From 1973 the struggle between these groups for control of the party came to a head. Following the elections to the newly established Northern Ireland Assembly, the Unionist party, now led by Brian Faulkner, joined with the Social Democratic and Labour party and the Alliance party to form a power-sharing executive, and this came into office in 1974. Although it was the first government in Northern Ireland to contain elected representatives of both communities, its main significance was probably its effect on consolidating right-wing Unionism. It was to be expected that Craig's Vanguard party and Paisley's Democratic Unionist party, the two unionist groupings outside the party fold, would co-operate in their opposition to the new Executive; but it soon became clear that Faulkner could not even rely on the support of his own party. In January the Ulster Unionist Council rejected his support of power-sharing and his acceptance of the need for an 'Irish dimension' in any attempt to solve the Northern Ireland problem. This rejection had two important consequences. The first was the coming together of the official Unionist party and the other two main loyalist parties, and their agreement not to oppose each other in the forthcoming elections to the Westminster parliament in February 1974; instead the three parties agreed on the selection of one common candidate in each constituency, and the chosen candidates stood under the party banner of the United Ulster Unionist Council (UUUC), which was created for that purpose. The second major consequence was the isolation of Brian Faulkner, still supported by some Unionist MPs as Chief Minister in the power-sharing Executive despite the Ulster Unionist Council's rejection of this policy. In May 1974 Faulkner and his Unionist supporters broke from the party and formed the Unionist party of Northern Ireland (UPNI). But their remaining period in office, along with their allies in the SDLP and Alliance party, was shortlived. In the next month a successful general strike by loyalist workers, called by the newly-formed Ulster Workers' Council (UWC) forced the Executive to resign. Direct rule from Westminster was restored.[88]

On the Nationalist side, the effect of the Civil Rights movement was even greater. Its formation provided a focus for many nominal Nationalists; more important, it attracted people into politics who had previously seen party structures as irrelevant.

Most of these supporters were Catholics, and many of them were young. Because political decisions were being determined on the streets rather than in parliament, the Civil Rights pressure group acquired the sort of following usually associated with political parties. The 1969 Stormont election showed the extent of this development. NICRA did not participate by proposing candidates, but the PD candidates, without electoral experience or machinery, polled remarkably highly, only one of its eight candidates losing a deposit. Furthermore, Independent candidates closely associated with the civil rights campaign won seats, John Hume defeating Eddie McAteer, leader of the Nationalist party. 'The real casualty of the election was the Nationalist party which lost three of its nine seats to Independent candidates.'[39] It was soon to lose all the other six.

The formation of the Social Democratic and Labour party in August 1970 was a direct result of the Civil Rights campaign.[40] The six MPs who united in the new party had differing backgrounds, but all had been associated with the campaign. Two of the six were Nationalists, Patrick O'Hanlon and Austin Currie, the man whose squatting in a house in Dungannon had launched the civil rights movement in its first demonstration; Gerry Fitt had been leader of the Republican Labour party; Paddy Devlin had left the Northern Ireland Labour party because it had refused to become actively involved in the campaign; the other two, John Hume and Ivan Cooper, had sprung into prominence through the campaign itself. Thus all three parties which had shared Catholic support prior to 1969—Nationalists, Republican Labour and NILP—lost MPs to the new party. It was announced that the policy of the SDLP should be radical, socialist and aimed at a united Ireland. Although designed as a mixed-religious party, its support was and is massively Catholic and suggestions that it represents Catholic opinion have never been denied by the SDLP.

A much more dramatic challenge to conventional nationalism was the emergence of the Provisional IRA. Rising from the ashes of August 1969 its original purpose was the defence of the Catholic areas. The arrival of British troops in Ulster established a scenario familiar to republican mythology, and they embarked upon an offensive bombing campaign in October 1970. The narrative and analysis of this campaign have yet to be written,[41] but two of its immediate effects are indisputable. It has further polarised attitudes in Northern Ireland; and it was instrumental in provoking a violent counter-reaction from loyalist para-military bodies. In such an atmosphere intimidation and murder flourished; the loyalist and nationalist communities moved further towards polarisation.

By 1974 it was possible to appreciate the extent to which the civil rights campaign had shaken traditional political structures, and how little it had affected general political allegiances. The Nationalist party had lost all the nine seats which it had won in the 1965 Stormont elections; but the SDLP had taken over the old Nationalist support, winning nineteen of the eighty Assembly seats in 1973. The Northern Ireland Labour party and Alliance party were competing for the scanty centre voters, only managing a total of nine seats. The Unionist party, apparently decimated in 1970, was working in harness with Paisley's DUP and Craig's VUPP. On the face of things much had changed. Many of the party names were new. But in terms of political loyalties the pattern differed little from that which had existed before the civil rights campaign.

Evaluation

It is not unusual for political parties to follow directions established when independence was granted, especially if the state was conceived in violence. The trouble was that in Northern Ireland no working relationship was established between the two major parties.

This was partly due to the unusual structure of politics in the province. In most liberal democracies, politics is a battle for control of the floating centre vote. There is little political advantage to be gained in Britain, for example, for either the Labour or Conservative parties to aim their electoral messages at, respectively, their extreme left and extreme right wings. On the contrary, governments and oppositions are determined by whichever of the two main parties capture the centre voters. Consequently the policies of the major parties tend to be determined by moderate rather than extreme views. This situation is reversed in Northern Ireland. Every election since the formation of the state has demonstrated that the political centre is electorally irrelevant—the best performance of cross-sectarian

110

parties was just under 30% of the poll in 1962, but this was more than double their support in elections before and since that date.[42] The main problem for both the Unionist and Nationalist parties was not the winning of such support; it was ensuring the allegiance of their extremist wings. The policies which were rewarded by success at the polls were those which emphasised basic loyalties and the need for sectarian solidarity.

The two parties were bitterly opposed to each other, of course, but their strategies had much in common. Each was firmly rooted in their attitudes towards partition; they were equally opposed to any form of socialism; both settled for a division of parliamentary seats, and both accepted the permanence of sectarianism. Although their exchanges were bitter and virulent, each was content to have the other as its main enemy. The permanence of the battle lines between them is recorded in the number of uncontested seats in Stormont elections. Apart from the first election in 1921 for the Northern Ireland parliament and the 1973 election for the Assembly, a substantial number of the fifty-two seats were uncontested.

Table 6   Unopposed returns at Northern Ireland general elections, 1921–1969:[43] Total seats 52

Election	'21	'25	'29	'33	'38	'45	'49	'53	'58	'62	'65	'69
Unopposed returns	—	12	22	33	21	20	20	25	27	24	23	7

The fact that up to 63·5% of the seats were unopposed (in 1933) is comment on the mutual acceptance of the *status quo*. Unofficial unionist parties and the Northern Ireland Labour party were more serious threats to Unionism than the Nationalists, because they were competing with the Unionists for the same support; similarly the Republican Labour party, the Peoples Democracy and the Social Democratic and Labour party were the most serious threat to Nationalists. Brian Faulkner's remark that the NILP was 'not in the true traditions of Northern Ireland'—almost a reprimand for infringing accepted rules—would have received a hearty echo from some Nationalists. The situation was neatly summarised in 1967 by Professor McCracken : 'In some areas a Nationalist is as certain

111

of winning an election as a Unionist is in others. No amount of party organisation is going to win votes outside of these areas. There is no floating vote on the constitutional issue.'[44]

Nor was there a floating vote on many other issues. So comprehensive was the split in parliament that party votes applied to almost every branch of legislation. Few issues were trivial enough to create cross-party alignments. The only instance in the Northern Ireland parliament's entire history of the government supporting an opposition bill was the passage of the Wild Bird act of 1931, a measure which even the most ingenious argument could not make controversial. Stormont was an arena of conflict, not compromise. The Northern Ireland Labour party was the only group which attempted to apply pragmatic criteria to legislation, judging matters on their merits; but their strength was never great and their influence was minimal.

Even the catalyst of the civil rights movement could not dent this tacit alliance. It produced, not political fragmentation, but two political fragmentations; the structures of the old Unionist and Nationalist parties were severely rocked, but not sufficiently for new political combinations to be formed from support across the sectarian divide. Certainly attempts to establish non-sectarian parties are more likely to succeed when the traditional establishments are reeling, but more than 50 years of habit are difficult to eradicate. It is difficult to avoid the judgement that the major parties, by their failure to accept the need for some sort of mutual accommodation, encouraged hardline attitudes and laid a foundation of intransigence which will not be easily destroyed.

CHAPTER V

Saints and scholars:
Churches and schools

The obstacle to co-operation between the churches lies in the pews.
G. Lee and R. Taylor, 1971

Given the present state of our knowledge, a judicious conservative conclusion would be that it is certain that the schools of Northern Ireland are almost entirely segregated, that it is highly probable that the segregated schools do nothing to neutralise hostile and prejudicial attitudes between religious groups, and that it is probable (but by no means proven) that the segregated school system exacerbates inter-group frictions.
Donald Akenson, 1973

RELIGION and education have been closely linked in Ireland, even from before the sixth century when Irish eminence in both fields earned her the title, 'the island of saints and scholars'. The violence of the early 1970s once again focused attention, but of a more critical nature, on churches and schools. This time the interest was related to the role of both institutions in the Northern Ireland conflict.

Certainly there are superficial indications of a religious component in the province's community divisions: the opposing groups refer to themselves and are referred to as Catholics and Protestants; a number of clergymen have played dominant parts in politics; the great annual ceremony of unionists on the Twelfth of July is nominally a religious gathering. Despite this, the major churches deny that the community conflict in Northern Ireland has a doctrinal basis.

In education, too, the fact that the great majority of Catholic and Protestant children attend denominational schools has led many people to the assumption that there is a likely relationship

113

between educational divisions and sectarianism. How extensive is educational separation? How different are the curricular and extracurricular emphasés within the two school systems? Does the separation reinforce community differences?

These are the questions which will be considered in this chapter.

Churches

In May 1973 the leaders of the four main churches in Ireland published a joint letter which included the following paragraph:

> The conflict is not primarily religious in character. It is based rather on political and social issues with deep historical roots. Undoubtedly, again for reasons that are largely historical, the political and social divisions have religious overtones. But this is far from saying that the conflict between extremists here is anything remotely resembling a religious war.[1]

They must have been somewhat surprised by the number of letters which were sent to the local press contesting this view, not only from the professional evangelical letter-writing lobby, but from well-accredited moderates like Brian Walker, chairman of the New Ulster Movement. He quoted a long series of events to demonstrate the religious basis of the conflict – Pope Adrian IV's grant of Ireland to England, Cromwell's campaign, the Penal Laws, the Protestant bishops signing the 1912 Covenant, the *Ne Temere* decree, the activities of the Rev. Ian Paisley, and the construction of a Protestant state in Northern Ireland. He went on to write, 'If all the people of Ireland were Christian—or Protestant—or Catholic—do our Church leaders really imagine that we would still have killed almost eight hundred people because of endemic socio-economic problems?'[2]

Whichever of the two points of view is correct, there is no denying the importance of organised religion in Northern Ireland. The 1971 census returns may not give an entirely accurate breakdown of religious allegiances in the province. For the first time the question about religious denominations was optional, and there was also a campaign by some anti-Unionist groups against answering it. Nevertheless the main denominational outlines are clear enough. Disregarding the

114

9·4% of the population who did not answer the question, about 35% of the respondents were Catholic, almost 30% Presbyterian and less than 25% Church of Ireland; the real Catholic percentage was probably larger, as most non-respondents were almost certainly Catholics. But the most significant figure of all is that, from a population of 1,519,640, only 510 were atheists and 1,200 agnostics. As Richard Rose pointed out, 'Northern Ireland ranks second among western nations in church attendance; only the Republic of Ireland is ahead of it.'[3] In 1970 a survey conducted by the Independent Television Authority found that 76% of the population felt that religion affected their lives 'a great deal', compared with 46% who gave the same answer in Britain; 75% in Northern Ireland, as opposed to 50% in Britain, described themselves as either very religious or fairly religious.[4]

Table 7   Main religious denominations in Northern Ireland, 1961 and 1971[5]

	1961	1971
Roman Catholic	497,547	477,919
Presbyterian	413,113	405,719
Church of Ireland	344,800	334,318
Methodist	71,865	71,235
Others	69,299	87,938
No Response	28,418	142,511
Total	1,425,042	1,519,640

Roman Catholics

It is almost a truism to say that the Catholic Church in Ireland is among the most conservative and powerful in Europe. Its conservatism springs from the general caution of a largely rural society and from an internal structure which rewards conformity; its power from the devotion of its followers and from the influence of its clergy. For these reasons its political power, when it chose to publicly use it, has been considerable. Its growing association with nationalism during the second half of the nineteenth century and its part in weaning that movement away from the Protestant adulterer Parnell had profound effects on the Home Rule movement and on Protestant opposition to it. Protestant fears of influence by the Catholic hierarchy in any independent Irish state was pithily summed up in the slogan 'Home rule is Rome rule'—a religious rather than a political sentiment—fears which appeared to be confirmed by the famous *Ne Temere* decree in 1908, whereby the hierarchy forbade Catholics to marry non-Catholics; when rare exceptions were allowed, they were only with the condition that all the children should be raised as Catholics, a ruling which ran counter to the nineteenth century Irish practice that children of mixed marriages should follow the religion of their father. Owen Dudley Edwards described the *Ne Temere* decree as 'the proclamation of religious apartheid'.[6]

The *Ne Temere* decree, for all the criticism which it has attracted, could be regarded as the Church disciplining its own members. What worries a lot of Protestants is the extent to which Catholic values were integrated into the constitution and legislation of the Irish Republic, thereby affecting all citizens. There are many examples : the 'special position' of the Catholic Church guaranteed in the constitution; the provision in the constitution that 'no law shall be enacted providing for the dissolution of marriage'; the illegality of contraceptives and the strict censorship of books and plays. The hierarchy's opposition to the 'Mother and Child' bill in 1950 because it offended Catholic social teaching led to drastic changes in the bill and the resignation of the Minister responsible. Even the judiciary appeared to lend support to Catholic dogma. In 1950 the Tilson judgement established that agreements made about the religion of children of mixed marriages in accordance with the *Ne Temere* decree would in future be enforceable in law. To many people these and other similar instances appeared to confirm the state's acceptance of the claim made in 1935 by Dr Lucey, the Bishop of Cork, that the Catholic hierarchy 'were the final arbiters of right and wrong even in political matters. In other spheres the state might for its own good reasons ignore the advice of the experts, but in faith and morals it might not.'[7] More recently Cardinal Conway said :

I believe that a written constitution is the most solemn document any people can draw up, and I think that the document

116

should reflect the character of the society which has framed it, and Irish society, Catholic and Protestant, is not a secular society. It is a deeply religious society, and I think that any constitution ought to reflect the basic values of that society.[8]

Many Protestants believe that the Catholic Church is trying to have its cake and eat it, supporting religious influences in the largely Catholic south, but opposing it in the predominantly Protestant north. Indeed the power of the Catholic Church in the Irish Republic is a fundamental factor in the case which most Northern Ireland Protestants would make against Irish unification; they believe that this power works to the disadvantage of their co-religionists in the south, and their argument was supported in 1971 by Dr Noel Brown, the Minister of Health in the Irish Republic who had resigned upon the defeat of his Mother and Child bill in 1951 :

> The Church used the state; the state used the Church. This, in my view, led to the setting up of the sectarian society of the north because of their fear of becoming part of a theocratic society in which Catholic law and moral teaching became state law. For that reason it has resulted in the real, genuine, and to me perfectly understandable fear of Faulkner, the Unionists, Paisley and the rest, of joining in a united Ireland.[9]

The Catholic Church in Ireland does not recognise the existence of the border in either its organisation or its politics. The Church of Ireland is also organised on an all-Ireland basis. In 1921 Cardinal Logue declared that 'our countrymen spurn . . . the sham settlement devised by the British government'[10] and his opposition to the Northern Ireland state was echoed by many of his successors. Apart from separate schools the Catholic Church also maintained the Mater Infirmorum Hospital in Belfast as an independent hospital which practised Catholic medical ethics, until agreement was eventually reached with the state in 1971. In other areas too, accommodations were reached despite basic antagonisms. Relations with the Ministry of Education, for example, were usually friendly. In 1963 the hierarchy appointed a Catholic chaplain to the Northern Ireland parliament at Stormont. Nevertheless many Protestants regard the Catholic Church as obstinately opposed to the will of the majority in Northern Ireland, as adopting a frankly political role in association with nationalist politicians and as professing doctrines which are actively impairing the freedom and values of Protestants in Southern Ireland.

Protestants

'Any discussion of religious groups in Belfast is dominated by the fact that the population is sharply divided into Protestants and Catholics. Differences between denominations within Protestantism tend to be overlooked or dismissed; comparisons and contrasts are constantly framed in terms of the two major groups.'[11] The evidence available indicates that Emrys Jones' observation about the insignificance of differences between Protestant churches may be oversimplified. Rosemary Harris and Thomas Kirk found considerable strains and divisions between the three main Protestant denominations in 'Ballybeg' and Lurgan, and in the latter case it was at least partly based on ecclesiastical grounds—both on the unwillingness of Anglicans to recognise the validity of Presbyterian and Methodist orders, and on the closer adherence of the other two churches to what Kirk called 'doctrine, and in particular to an elevation of many Old Testament laws such as Sabbath Day observance.'[12] Such jealousies and suspicions may well be remnants of earlier differences; the seventeenth and eighteenth centuries can show many examples of hostility between the Church of Ireland and the Presbyterians. They fought each other during the Civil and Cromwellian wars; the former sponsored a code of penal laws against the latter; Presbyterians had provided the main leaders of the republican United Irishmen movement in the late eighteenth century. Such rivalry does not easily disappear, but the external factor which did most to remove it, according to Megahey, was a growing awareness of 'a powerful and hostile Catholic Church' in the last half of the nineteenth century. Conscious of the minority position of Protestants in Ireland, 'the Protestant denominations as a whole shared a common mind, and the laity in particular . . . were Protestants first and members of their own church after that'.[13]

For many years Protestant clergymen have played an active role in Irish politics. This particularly applies to fundamental-

118

ist evangelical pastors who have stood firmly against Catholicism and in favour of the British connection and Protestant values. Ian Paisley is the latest manifestation of a familiar Ulster phenomenon which earlier had produced the Rev. Henry Cooke (the Black Man) who had swung the Presbyterians away from their eighteenth-century liberalism, and the Rev. Hugh Hanna (Roaring Hugh), one of the most prominent influences in starting the anti-Home Rule campaign. Paisley's adroit use of the media and his direct political role do not disguise his sturdy seventeenth-century puritanism. The message, the rhetoric and the style remain unchanged. It is remarkable that, despite the publicity which attends Paisley's religious utterances, his Free Presbyterian Church had only 7,337 members in 1971 —0·5% of Northern Ireland's population.[14]

The last thing one could say about Mr Paisley is that he is typical of Northern Ireland clergymen, but his views and activities offer more than a hint of parody of the whole Northern Ireland ecclesiastical scene. All the major Protestant churches have produced clergymen who were also public representatives, although their influence cannot be measured by a simple head count. Protestant ministers, both directly and by their association at ground level with the Orange Order, have been closely associated with the Northern Ireland government and with the Unionist party, although the political influence on the governing of the province has always been a matter for speculation. That this influence was considerable, and that it was used towards the creation of a sectional society was accepted in a 1969 report to the General Assembly of the Presbyterian Church in Ireland:

Other problems arise as consequences of churches seeking to impose their own particular principles or convictions on the general community by legislation or controls rather than by persuasion. This might apply, for instance, to our views on Sunday observance . . . or our views on drinking and gambling. On the Roman Catholic side it might apply to marriage regulations, relating to birth control, divorce and mixed marriages; to separate schooling; and to the dominance by Hierarchy and by priest in the control of social institutions.[15]

Certainly a number of Protestant principles and convictions have been translated into official restraints at both central and

119

local levels, but it is in the field of educational policy that the Protestant churches have most obviously and successfully sought to impose their views 'by legislation or controls rather than by persuasion'. These areas however are merely some of the measurable and identifiable instances of a general Protestant ethos which permeates Northern Ireland life and establishes its standards. Martin Wallace put it like this :

While Protestants and Catholics live partly separate lives in Northern Ireland, the state to some extent imposes a Protestant ethos on the Catholic minority. In such matters as Sunday observance and liquor licensing laws, it is the more puritanical Protestant outlook which prevails; the Protestant churches are influential in this respect, but there is a wider Protestant feeling that a stand must be taken against Catholic values. At different levels of society, this instinctive attitude has always proved an obstacle to dealing justly and dispassionately with Catholic grievances.[16]

This argument could be amplified by quoting instances of local councils closing down playgrounds and swings in Belfast and Craigavon and picture houses in seaside towns, on the sabbath. It is more revealing, however, to consider the degree to which the imposition of Protestant values merely reflects the relationship between a majority and a minority, or if it reflects a basic and irreconcilable difference in values between the two creeds. Until comparatively recently, few people were prepared to concede that the conflict had anything to do with religious differences. Most shared the view of Boserup that 'the conflict in Northern Ireland is not a religious conflict at all; it is not even a conflict between Catholics and Protestants, and its appearance of being a modern version of St Bartholomew's Massacre is just that—an appearance.'[17] This however ignores the fact that many participants in the conflict, especially on the Protestant side, perceive themselves to be in opposition to a church rather than to its members. This view has been expressed most often by fundamentalist Protestants. It is typified in its extreme form by an article in the *Christian Advocate* in 1886 which attempted to argue from sociological evidence that the Church of Rome encouraged vice. The evidence quoted was the murder rates in a number of Protestant and Catholic countries.

120

Thus the murder rates in England, Holland and Russia were respectively 1 per 187,000, 1 per 168,000 and 1 per 100,000. Residents in the Catholic heartlands of Rome and Naples would have been alarmed to discover that in their cases the rates shot down to 1 per 2,750 and 1 per 750. This was attributed solely to the teachings of the Roman Church.[18] Anyone who believes that such arguments were only used in the last century should look through the files of the *Protestant Telegraph* or the *Ulster Protestant*. More significantly, he would discover similar information in issues of the UDA news sheets and other loyalist broadsheets; many of Northern Ireland's political publications see no incongruity in featuring religious propaganda.

No single issue has more clearly demonstrated the extent of Protestant fears of the Catholic Church than the debate on ecumenism. The ecumenical movement, advocated by the World Council of Churches and by the Catholic Church since the pontificate of John XXIII, has as its ultimate aim the reunification of all the Christian churches. To fundamentalist Protestants this amounted to a betrayal of the Reformation and surrender to the Church of Rome. As Ian Paisley put it, 'the aim of both movements (i.e. Protestant and Catholic ecumenism) is a Super One-World Church. Rome of course already sees herself as that Church and works in ecumenism for the inclusion of "the separated brethren".'[19] Louis Gardner, one of the most convincing loyalist propagandists, pointed out the local implications: 'The main danger of Irish ecumenism, apart from its doctrinal humbug, is that since it can never unite two disparate religio-cultural systems it can advance only at the expense of one or the other.'[20] It was this belief which directed Paisley's energies during the 1960s more against Romanism than nationalism, as a chronicle of his protest demonstrations testifies:[21]

1959 Against the view of the liberal Methodist theologian, Dr Soper
1962 Against Protestant observers attending the Second Vatican Council
1966 Against the 'Romeward trend' of the Presbyterian General Assembly
1966 Against Archbishop Ramsey's visit to Pope John XXIII
1968 Against Cardinal Heenan's (Catholic Archbishop of

121

Westminster) invitation as guest speaker at Westminster Abbey
1969 Against a Catholic observer attending the General Assembly of the Church of Scotland

The fight against closer relations with the Catholic Church has not always been confined to 'extreme' Protestants. The 1950 Presbyterian General Assembly declared: 'One root of the Catholic-Protestant conflict, especially here where numbers are sometimes nearly equal, is the fact that the Roman Catholic Church is a world-wide religious organisation that seeks to gain control of the institutions of mankind and of public life generally; it is not merely a church, it is a political organisation.'[22]

If some Protestant churches tend to see their differences more in doctrinal terms, all the major churches have accepted some degree of culpability for the deep sectarian divide in Northern Ireland. In February 1972, for example, an editorial in the *Clergy Review*, a middle-of-the-road Catholic monthly, warned against turning too readily to economic reasons for an explanation of the troubles. It added, 'religion is most certainly a powerful contributory factor in the appalling antagonisms unleashed in Northern Ireland.'[23] The 1969 report to the Presbyterian General Assembly also pointed to the failure of churchmen to speak out plainly against evils in society which they know to exist: 'Those who hoped for an uneasy peace by preserving the status quo or by a gradual improvement in relationships without seriously disturbing the established pattern, do not seem to have realised the passions which have been welling up in situations to which they have become uncritically accustomed. There has been, for too long, a conspiracy of silence, or of crying "Peace! Peace!" where there was no peace.' One reason for the conspiracy of silence may lie in the conservatism of many congregations, some of whom have removed ministers who were considered too liberal. The writer of the weekly Churches column in the *Belfast Telegraph* quoted an eminent Presbyterian clergyman as saying, 'I know several of my brother ministers who had to leave congregations because they spoke out courageously about housing conditions, voting rights and discrimination.'[24]

Whatever differences and antagonisms there may be between

Catholic and Protestant churches in Northern Ireland, they share many similarities—a high participation in religious activities, doctrinal conservatism, the importance of their clergymen as social leaders. Important components of Irish Catholicism can only be explained as a reaction to Irish Protestantism, and vice versa. Like political parties, part of what they believe is principled and immutable, and part is dictated by the beliefs and behaviour of those whom they see as their opponents. The extent of this mutual dependency raises the interesting if unanswerable question as to how church attendance and membership would be affected if the political component could be removed. But one point is becoming increasingly indisputable. If people's perceptions of problems, as distinct from the problems themselves, are what count, there is a basic religious component in the Northern Irish conflict.

Schools
The history of Irish education is unremarkable except for occasional pioneering experiments and the regularity with which crises accompanied any attempt to alter existing educational practice. What is remarkable is how frequently the crises have been the result of the same dispute—the extent to which the churches should control the schools. The most constant thread running throughout the saga is the deep-rooted suspicion of Catholics towards state control of their schools.

The Development of Separation
The roots of this suspicion are easy to find. In 1537 Henry VIII instructed his Anglican bishops in Ireland to ensure that each clergyman 'keep or cause to be kept . . . a school for to learn English'.[25] The resulting schools, whose main objects were to propagate an alien tongue and an alien church, represented a political and religious challenge to the Catholic Irish. It was a challenge which failed because of the apathy of Anglican ministers and the opposition of Catholic parents. The private trusts and societies which began to establish schools in Ireland during the seventeenth century had similar aims and were more efficient in securing them. Erasmus Smith, for example, who stated : 'My aim was to propagate the Protestant faith according to the Scriptures, avoiding all superstition'[26] established a

trust which controlled 144 elementary schools by the middle of the nineteenth century.

The Charity schools, which were also established by the Church of Ireland, were a good deal more specific in their objectives. Archbishop Boulter of Armagh approvingly described the Charity schools as places where children 'are now instructed in the principles of the religion of the church of England, are taught to read the scriptures in the English tongue, and learn everything which a good Protestant schoolmaster instils into their heads'.[27]

Education also figured prominently among these repressive anti-Catholic acts which were passed after the Williamite wars in the seventeenth century. Catholics were forbidden to keep schools, to teach in Protestant schools or to employ tutors to teach their children at home. They were excluded from university education, and it became illegal to send their children abroad for education. In effect, Catholic parents were presented with the legal alternatives of education in Protestant schools or no education, and both were rejected. The Celto-Catholic culture which the Penal Laws were designed to subvert continued to flourish illegally. Mass was celebrated and schools were conducted in the open country, with lookouts to warn against the authorities. By the end of the eighteenth century the greater part of Catholic education was being conducted in these Hedge Schools, and observers like Arthur Young described 'many a ditch full of scholars' which they met on their travels.[28]

The same period saw the enunciation of 'a principle which, if not exactly new, was nevertheless completely at variance with official policy in Ireland since the Reformation'.[29] This was the principle of toleration. From 1794 Maynooth College for the education of Catholic clergy was grant-aided by the Irish government; the 1812 report of the Commissioners enquiring into Irish education insisted that 'no attempt shall be made to influence or disturb the peculiar religious tenets of any sect or description of Christians'.[30] The objects of the Kildare Place Society, formed in the previous year to encourage education, also reflected the new approach. It set out 'to afford the same educational advantages to all classes of professing Christians, without interfering with the peculiar religious opinions of any'.[31] When the government announced its intention to estab-

124

lish a National system of education in 1831, it was natural that the principle of religious non-intervention would be incorporated in it.

Considerable effort was made to consult the Catholic hierarchy about the proposed National system, and they eventually agreed to support it, although enthusiasm was by no means universal. The reactions of the Protestant churches were much stronger. By 1839 the Anglicans had founded the Church Education Society to continue denominational schools outside the system, and by 1859 it controlled 1,700 schools containing 80,000 children. Many Presbyterian schools too found the terms unacceptable—especially the Board's insistence that other clergymen, including Catholic priests, should have free access to their schools—and only entered the system after considerable concessions (including the abandonment of free access) had been granted in 1840. As time went by the opposition among the Catholic bishops came more obviously into the open. The concessions to the Presbyterians increased Catholic suspicions and strengthened the influence of hardliners like Archbishop MacHale of Tuam. By 1859 the minimum demands of the hierarchy were 'a Catholic education, on Catholic principles, with Catholic masters and the use of Catholic books'.[32] So the unfortunate Commissioners were attacked from every angle. 'Their only relief', as Balfour drily remarked, 'seems to have been an occasional change of assailants.'[33] By the 1870s the National schools were de facto denominational establishments, and remained so until the system came to an end fifty years later. The first great experiment had failed. The 1920s were not the most auspicious time for beginning the second.

The Ministry of Education of the new state of Northern Ireland was established in June 1921. It was clear that a radical examination of the system of education was required, not only because the old system operated on an all-Ireland basis, but because it was obviously not effective. In 1924 it was estimated that 15,000 elementary school places were urgently needed in Belfast alone.[34] A committee was set up in September 1927 under Sir Robert Lynn to examine the existing structure and to make recommendations for changes. The recommendations of the Lynn Committee were forthright and unspectacular, and were largely accepted by the government. The one area where

125

the Minister of Education, Lord Londonderry, ignored the Lynn report was the field of religious instruction, and the controversy which followed dominated Northern Ireland's internal politics until 1930.

Briefly, Lynn's recommendation was that there should be denominational religious instruction in schools. Instead, the 1923 Education act forbade the new local education authorities to provide religious instruction (although they were permitted to allow facilities for it outside school hours). In addition, the authorities were not permitted to consider a teacher's religion when considering him for employment. Londonderry was in fact again attempting to introduce 'mixed education' where Catholic and Protestant children attended the same schools. His motive was primarily social. When the proposed 'godless schools' were attacked in the House, he argued strongly that his main purpose was, not to provide secular education, but to safeguard the educational systems from denominationalism which could only produce 'division when union is so essential to the well-being of the province'.[35]

His arguments cut little ice. With a rare ecumenical spirit, all the churches opposed the act. The Catholic hierarchy announced that 'the proposed schools are impossible for our children'.[36] Apart from their opposition to the absence of religious instruction in the schools, they strongly opposed the handing over of control to local authorities which would often be dominated by Unionists. However, it is probable that, given the political climate of the time, they would have rejected any proposal made by the Northern Ireland government. For the first few years of the new state's existence Catholics refused to have anything to do with it, anticipating its early collapse. Already they had refused to sit on or give evidence to the Lynn Committee; consequently no Catholic voice was heard in its report. Nationalist and Sinn Fein MPs were boycotting the parliament, so the bill passed through its various stages without Catholic amendments. The minority community was slow to see the effects of this boycott and when the Nationalist party at last took its seats in 1925, the educational system had already been established and no Catholic had participated in its construction. The Lynn committee had attempted 'to keep in mind and to make allowances for the Roman Catholic viewpoint.'[37]

126

The problem was that, even with the best will in the world, the Catholic case was only interpreted by Protestant spokesmen. The Catholic opposition to the Bill never approached the fury of the Protestant churches. Satisfied with the Lynn Committee report—it was signed by the five Protestant clergymen on the committee—they were furious at Londonderry's subsequent alterations. It seemed to them that they were being called to sacrifice their schools for an unattainable ideal. S.E. Long accurately caught their sense of disillusionment:

> The 1923 Education bill caused an uproar among the Protestant people who saw in it a betrayal of what they had fought for in the Home Rule crisis—the opportunity of ensuring that their children be brought up as Protestants. The Protestant churches and the Orange Order felt betrayed. They had believed that their interests had been secured in the 1920 Government of Ireland act. Now they were told that there would be no Bible instruction in schools and no guarantee that Protestant teachers would teach in Protestant schools.[38]

The campaign against the bill was not long delayed. In 1924 the Presbyterians and Anglicans formed the United Education Committee. They were soon joined by the Methodists and by the Orange Order. The rallying calls were 'The Bible is in danger' and 'Protestant teachers for Protestant children'. By 1925 they had succeeded in making the act unworkable. Of the 1,996 elementary schools in Northern Ireland in that year, two had been provided by the state and only ten had been transferred by the churches. The remaining 1,984 were still under independent control. So the government had to give in. The threat of unionist disunity in the year of the Boundary Commission report and a general election meant that political priorities exceeded educational ones. The Prime Minister, James Craig (later Lord Craigavon) went over the head of his Minister of Education and a new Education act was passed deleting the offending terms in the 1923 act and permitting 'simple Bible instruction' in the schools.

The dispute did not end there. Disputes broke out between the Protestant churches and some of the local education authorities over the terms of transfer. The United Education Committee revived its campaign and by 1930 had secured the passage of a new Education act. Lord Craigavon made no attempt to disguise its purpose. 'You need not have any fears about our educational programme for the future,' he said. 'It will be absolutely certain that in no circumstances whatever will Protestant children ever be in any way interfered with by Roman Catholics, any more than Protestants wish to interfere with Roman Catholic children.'[39] The second mixed-school experiment had been abandoned. It has not been revived since.

So the failure of Catholics to act as a pressure group and Protestant efficiency in securing alterations in the 1923 act produced a situation where the Catholics found the state schools system uncongenial and remained outside it. Catholics considered that the 50% grants which they received in the 1930 act were entirely inadequate and a successful campaign in 1947 pushed the grant figure up to 65%. But although the 1947 Education act introduced wide changes, denominational education continued. In 1968 a further compromise was reached. The maintenance of those Catholic schools which accepted it was now paid entirely from taxation, and building grants were raised to 80%. In return, a third of the seats on the management committees of Catholic schools were nominated by the local education authority. During the debate preceding this agreement, Dr Philbin, bishop of Down and Connor, represented traditional Catholic suspicion of the state's motives :

> We have to take account of the strongly-supported campaign against the existence of our schools in recent years, and to ask ourselves whether the present move is not seen as a first step towards their disappearance. No educational considerations appear to have been operative in (this) respect of the proposed changes. The motives have been political and belong to the darker areas of politics, in which religious prejudice is paramount.[40]

A similar distrust was expressed in the news sheet of the Campaign for Social Justice in Northern Ireland, which went on to point out what the editors saw as the extra importance of Catholic schools in a sectarian society :

> One of the few opportunities there are for educated Catholics lies in being teachers within the Catholic school system. One

has only to think of how Unionists discriminate in the local councils, Electricity Board, Belfast Shipyard and the Stormont Civil Service, to quote a few examples, to realise that it would be madness to lose control of the one large field of opportunity remaining in Catholic hands.[41]

Despite this suspicion, there was some signs in the late 1960s that some members of the Catholic hierarchy were softening their attitudes. Cardinal Conway expressed cautious willingness to discuss mixed-religion sixth-form colleges; extra-curricular co-operation between Catholic and state schools greatly increased; the 1968 compromise and the acceptance of 'four-and-two committees by the church produced a harmonious relationship. There were signs that the Catholic laity showed a stronger desire for co-operation than their clergy, and in 1970 a curious incident occurred which in some ways demonstrated the new atmosphere.

During the summer of that year large numbers of Protestants fled from the New Barnsley estate in west Belfast as a result of the violence in the area. The Catholic families who moved in found it convenient to send their children to the existing state school, and did so. Their requests for a Religious Instruction teacher was rejected by the church and they were instructed to withdraw their children or the sacraments would be withheld from them. The parents refused and, at their own expense, employed a Religious Instruction teacher. Two days before their Confirmation ceremony, the Church gave in and the first ever Catholic RI teacher was seconded to a state school. However, any hopes that the Vere Forster Case may have established a precedent were not realised, and in 1974 Dr Philbin was still prepared to refuse the sacraments to children who attended state schools. As a result a number of parents formed an organisation called All Children Together (ACT). Its campaign to integrate Catholic and Protestant children in schools has involved them in a running dispute with the bishop.

The Effects of Division[42]
When Barritt and Carter conducted their sociological survey into Northern Ireland in 1961, they found that 41% of the school population was Catholic, as opposed to 35% of the total population. 'As far as can be discovered', they added, 'at least

98% (and probably more) of all Catholic primary school children attend Catholic schools.'[43] A similar picture emerges for the two main branches of post-primary education. In 1971 there were 174 secondary intermediate schools in Northern Ireland, exactly half of which are state schools, and half Catholic voluntary schools. As this indicates, there is almost complete duplication of services in this field. In grammar school education the edges are rather more blurred and some schools like Rainey Endowed in Magherafelt and Dalriada in Ballymoney have both Catholics and Protestants on their staffs and among their pupils. Where this happens, it is usually because there is no Catholic grammar school in the area. Children of all religions attend technical intermediate schools, but in January 1972 this amounted to a total of only 119 pupils. Northern Ireland's two universities and her new Polytechnic, as well as some other branches of further education, are attended by both Catholics and Protestants. Of the 5,831 full-time students at Queen's University Belfast in 1972, 91·4% were from Northern Ireland, as were 69·3% of the 1,637 students at the New University of Ulster.[44] These account for the bulk of Northern Ireland's university requirements and provide a common forum or cockpit, but the Colleges of Education are divided according to religion.

Despite slight improvements since the 1960s, most of them dictated by general educational trends, Catholic and Protestant teachers still operate within systems which have little contact with each other. The failure of Lord Londonderry to establish a non-sectarian college at Stranmillis means that more than two-thirds of teachers trained in Northern Ireland were trained exclusively with fellow-students of their own religion.[45] Up-to-date figures are not available, but in 1960 Barritt and Carter found that there were only two Catholics among the 995 student teachers at Stranmillis; none of the 509 students at St Mary's and St Joseph's Training Colleges were Protestant. When these students qualified the great majority had no choice but to remain within the schools for which they had been trained. Teachers' unions, conspicuous almost everywhere for internal dissensions, have in Northern Ireland the added complication of religious polarisation. In 1919 a number of loyalist teachers from Northern Ireland became increasingly dissatisfied with

130

the growing relationship between the Irish National Teachers' Organisation (INTO) and Irish Nationalism. They broke off and formed the Ulster Teachers' Union (UTU). Its first president informed the 1920 UTU conference that 'they were loyal before they were teachers, and loyal they would remain'. The appointment in 1934 of an anti-partitionist MP, John Beattie, as Northern secretary of the INTO underlined the political separation of the unions and further hastened their drift towards religious polarisation. 'As a result', wrote Erskine Holmes, 'the elementary school teachers came to reflect the division in the community in the north of Ireland, for the bulk of the membership of the INTO was Catholic and the UTU was Protestant'.[46] Since these two unions far outstripped all their competitors, at least until the 1960s, trade unionism did not provide the cross-sectarian educational forum which it might have done.

All of this amounts to a fairly comprehensive sectarian divide in elementary and secondary education as well as in the training of most teachers. But it is the effects of such a division in a society which is polarised in many other aspects which has caused concern and interest. The more serious questions relate to standards of educational achievements in Catholic and state schools, differences in content and emphasis in curriculum, and the effects of separate education on the social attitudes of children.

The charges that conditions and facilities in Catholic schools are inferior to those in state schools are based on the assumption that any general system of education which depends on voluntary contributions, even in part, will not be able to afford the same facilities as one entirely financed by the state. Many observers believe that this applies to Northern Ireland, although the matter has never been properly investigated. What can be said is that the Catholic community has had to find considerable amounts of money to maintain its own schools, including from 20% to 33% of their capital expenditure. In 1968 the Catholic bishops estimated that in the twenty-one years since the Education act, Northern Ireland's Catholics had contributed 'something in the region of £20 million in present-day money towards the erection and maintenance of their schools'.[47] However the question has often been asked whether even such a large expenditure was sufficient, particularly in respect of the provision of a large enough number of grammar school places for Catholics. Some parts of the province, especially those with small Catholic populations like North Antrim, the region around Portadown, and North Down, lack Catholic grammar schools for boys. In the Portrush-Portstewart area, for example, boys who wished to attend a Catholic grammar school had to travel fifty miles to Garren Tower, a boarding school. The decisions by the Catholic authorities to admit boys to Portstewart convent has greatly improved matters, but the extra financial burdens involved in boarding school education was sometimes very considerable and it appears a not unlikely proposition that some potential grammar school pupils may have been deprived of grammar school education.

All of this would certainly lead one to suspect that Catholic educational performance would be inferior, but the existing evidence does not support this. David Kennedy quoted the fact that a substantial proportion of Queen's University's eleven major foundation scholarships go annually to Catholic schools, although this must be balanced by the consideration that some Protestant grammar schools are more inclined to enter their best students for British universities;[48] nevertheless, eight of the eleven 1968 scholarships went to Catholic schools. A 1962 dissertation which conducted a survey of 60 grammar school students also found no significant differences between the educational performances of the Catholic and Protestant children.[49] In fact no evidence substantiates the ocasionally expressed view that Catholic schools are academically less successful than state schools.

But there is evidence of considerable differences of emphasis between the curricula studied by Catholic and Protestant secondary schoolchildren. This is demonstrated by a look at the percentage of Catholic students in different departments at Queen's University Belfast, which clearly reflects curricular and cultural priorities in their schools. In 1971 32·2% of the undergraduates were Catholics, exactly 10% more than a decade before. Disproportionately high numbers were attracted to the Law (39·3%) and Economics/Social Studies (47·7%) departments; on the other hand only 23·3% of the Medicine and Dentistry Departments were Catholics and only 12·4% of the Agriculture Department.[50] Furthermore, the fact that the Irish language is

132

taught in almost every Catholic secondary school, but only in one Protestant grammar school, clearly reflects a difference of cultural outlooks. These different values and emphases cause greater concern in the subjects which relate more directly to the formation of attitudes and values among pupils—subjects like History, Geography, Civics, Literature and Cultural Studies and of course, Religious Instruction.

The reservations which many educationalists have about the teaching of political history to young children are supported by a survey conducted in 1969 by Alan Robinson in Derry.[51] Robinson found that perceptions about the industrial geography of the city were similar among Catholics and Protestant school children; for example, they similarly described its most important industries. But when it came to matters which had a political flavour, the picture was rather different. For instance, 62% of the Catholic children named either Bishop Farren or John Hume as Derry's most important citizen, while 70·9% of the Protestant children named Northern Ireland's prime minister or the city's mayor; when asked to name the capital of the country in which Derry is situated, more than half the Catholic children named Dublin and more than two-thirds of the Prot- estant children Belfast. Robinson comments that, since the his- tory of one community has been the antithesis of the other, the evidence of such divisions should not cause surprise; but more worrying is the failure of education to affect the myths. A comparison between the answers of primary and secondary school children to Robinson's questionnaire appears to indicate that, at best, prejudices are not diminished by education and, at worst, they are in fact strengthened. The existence of separate schools and of teacher bias, which Robinson alleges, may not be responsible for introducing myths which are already established before the child started attending school, but help to perpetuate and reinforce them.

Jack Magee's excellent paper on *The Teaching of Irish His- tory* describes the process by which these different traditions of history became incorporated into school curricula. Southern schools tended to propagate a nationalist mythology which had emerged in the late nineteenth century. In the north, apart from in Catholic schools, 'Irish history was taught only where it impinged in a significant way on the history of Great Britain. . . .

133

The impression generally was that Ulster children could be educated as if they were living in Chelmsford or Bristol or Haverford West.'[52] These traditions were also reflected in text-books. Lorna Hadkins, researching in 1971, found extensive bias in history textbooks used in Northern Ireland schools; she quotes in particular the deliberate use of emotionalism in some 'nationalist' textbooks as well as what she called 'a strange blindness towards the rest of Ireland' in 'unionist' ones.[53] Although the quality of textbooks has improved considerably in recent years[54] many people are still concerned about the effect of propagating two hostile cultural traditions. Apart from de-priving children of half their heritage, there is the danger of encouraging them to view some of their neighbours as alien and hostile. James Russell found in his 1972 survey that the only school subject which had a close relationship with political attitudes was history, although he added that 'extra-curricular knowledge of history may be gained from books not generally used in schools—traditions, poetry, songs, and from political and religious pamphlets portraying discordant versions of par-ticular events.'[55]

Although subjects like History and Civics may be presented differently to Protestant and Catholic children, at least the pupils deal with similar material. In other subjects the contents of the curricula may be quite different. John Greer's investi-gation of Religious Instruction demonstrated one notable gap in most Religious Instruction courses. Although Hinduism, Buddhism and other religions are studied in Religious education classes, little reference is made to 'the problem of comparative religion which lies at the root of so many social problems in Ireland, the Protestant-Roman Catholic division'.[56] His ques-tionnaire of 1,631 sixth form pupils revealed 'no evidence of any serious attempt to study these problems', and he stressed the need for an informed and objective study of contemporary community relations.

Nor is it that pupils do not enjoy an acquaintance with the other culture when the opportunity arises. A case in point was a project carried out by graduate students with sixth formers in Methodist College, a large voluntary grammar school in Belfast. The project concerned Anglo-Irish culture, and covered a wide range of interests, including literature, language, placenames, music, folklore and social issues. When the project began, only 22% of the sixth-form students felt deprived by their lack of contact with Irish culture: when it ended, 90% felt that more Anglo-Irish culture should be taught in schools. The subsequent comments of the pupils were remarkable for their surprise at the inherent interest of Irish culture. A typical evaluation was:

I enjoyed being able to express views on Gaelic culture without political involvement, and learning the derivation of placenames. I think I am more aware of Gaelic culture now, which before was something associated with politics. I think most Protestants fear Gaelic culture as a political instrument to push them towards a United Ireland.[57]

The differences in curricular emphasis and content are supplemented to a degree by different extra-curricular activities. Virtually no Catholic secondary school in Northern Ireland officially plays rugby or cricket; traditional Catholic games like Gaelic football, hurling or handball are not played in state schools. Some games of course are widely played, like soccer; but even here Catholics and Protestant children rarely play on the same field except in some districts outside Belfast. When extra-curricular contact does take place across the sectarian divide, it tends to be confined to grammar schools, and to less popular activities such as basketball, swimming, debating and athletics. Even in these areas of contact, the schools almost invariably meet on a competitive basis. Part of the blame for this must rest with the schools' authorities, which have done little to encourage real co-operation in the sharing of facilities or the conduct of joint projects. The situation has further deteriorated since the outbreak of violence in 1968. The Ministry of Education (NI) Report for 1971 commented: 'Out-of-school activities are threatened when they involve cross-town travel after school; and evening youth centres in secondary schools are in difficulty.'[58] The cross-religious contact between pupils, never extensive, is one of the less sung casualties of civil disorder.

The real question, however, is whether the cumulative effect of so many differences, perhaps insignificant in themselves, amount to the transmission of different cultural heritages to Protestant and Catholic children. Is there a failure to appreciate or even to consider those cultural values which are considered important to the other group? In this respect it is also important to consider, not only the subjects which appear on the school timetable, but the hidden values which are transmitted by the school—whether a school team is called Pearse's or Carson's, the presence of religious artefacts, the flag flying above the front door, the recitation of prayers before classes, the formation of an officers' cadet corps. All these details help to reinforce the standards and cultural values which the schools have adopted, and to emphasise the differences between schools attended by Protestants and Catholic children. John Boyd the poet described the profoundly different atmosphere between the Catholic school he visited and the Protestant school he had attended as a boy :[59]

> And now this week of June
> is ended; and now I've left this school
> of pale children with strange names,
> children who may see some harmony
> in this place I call native;
> But I am conscious of the bond and break
> between us

Evaluation

It would be surprising if the churches did not have considerable influence in Northern Ireland, where church attendance is so high. Nevertheless, when considering their relationship to the province's community tensions, it is avoiding the issue to debate whether or not the conflict is a religious one. Clearly on some issues, like ecumenism, and with some individuals, like Ian Paisley, there is an overlap between political and religious stances, but it would be difficult to argue that the community divisions in Northern Ireland are rooted in doctrinal differences. A more serious charge is that all the major Irish churches have used their influence, where possible, to enforce a sectarian ethos on the general community. In the Republic of Ireland, where most citizens are Catholics, the Catholic church has used its influence to secure the state's sanction for church teaching on contraception, divorce and mixed marriages, thereby abusing the rights of the Protestant minority. In Northern Ireland the Protestant churches have similarly imposed denominational values on the Catholic minority by campaigning for restrictive gambling and licensing laws, by their insistence on sabbatarianism and by permitting discriminatory practices by governments and local authorities to pass without protest. Indeed, by their direct involvement with the political activities of the Orange Order and Unionist party, many clergymen have involved themselves and their churches in the creation of a sectarian state.

This emphasis by all the major churches on their denominational differences rather than their common Christianity is nowhere better illustrated than in their attitudes towards education. From the sixteenth to the nineteenth centuries the Church of Ireland became involved in the building and management of schools with the prime purpose of proselytising Catholic children; during the nineteenth century, the educational policy of the Catholic church swung towards active segregation of Catholic children from those of other religions, where it still remains; the legislative concessions by the Northern Ireland government to pressure from the Protestant churches in the 1920s ensured that state schools in Northern Ireland, became, in fact, Protestant schools. The only difference, some Catholics argued, was that they were fully financed from public funds, whereas Catholic schools are not. Although educational policy in Northern Ireland has been influenced by a number of factors and not least by what happened in Britain, there is no doubt that the major reason why most Catholic and Protestant children are educated separately is that all the major churches had demanded that it should be so. It might similarly be claimed that the churches are the main obstacle to educational change in that sphere.

Educational division, like all administrative divisions, tends to harden with time. Nevertheless, any assessment of the current extent of segregation must begin by pointing out the considerable variations from one part of the province to another, especially between urban and rural areas; polarisation between the two school systems is less marked in the country areas outside Belfast and Derry, in terms of pupil contact, inter-school activities and extra-curricular co-operation. Despite this qualification, however, the overall divisions are extensive. The vast majority of Northern Ireland's pupils, apart from those in some branches of further education, are being taught alongside their co-religionists by teachers of their own religion and have minimal educational contact with children from the other main religious group. The cultural heritage with which the school encourages them to identify is significantly different for Protestants and Catholics, and the differences manifest themselves in the contents of curricula, the loyalties and values which are assumed and the extra-curricular activities offered by the school. All these are, each to a greater or lesser degree, measurable. What is more difficult to assess are the more fundamental questions—those relating to the connection between segregated schooling and sectarian attitudes.

There have been very few attempts to investigate the problem. It is surprising, for example, that no one has ever tested, in the Northern Ireland context, the very premise on which Catholic schools are based—that they produce better Catholics. One relevant study into social attitudes was completed by John Salters in 1970, which found that Catholic children were more tolerant and no less civic minded than Protestant children.[60] A smaller study by Vincent P. McCormack produced similar findings, claiming that the Catholic children involved in the project were 'less authoritarian and more tenderminded than the Protestant'.[61] The scope and nature of both studies, however, make it impossible to judge whether or not the schools had any influence on these attitudes, and their findings are somewhat contradicted by James Russell's research, which found a greater likelihood among Catholic children to exhibit negative attitudes towards government. So it is not possible to claim, on the existing scanty evidence, either that segregated schooling has contributed towards the maintenance of a segregated community, or that it has not. What can be claimed is that, not only have the schools failed to contribute towards the creation of better community relations, many of them have refused to even acknowledge the existence of a community problem.

The prevalence of overt violence in Northern Ireland since 1969 has focused attention on the influence of the schools, but the quality of the debate has failed to measure up to the concern expressed by many educationalists. The trouble is that both defenders of the present system and those who advocate integration have confronted each other from uncompromising and unsubstantiated positions—the former arguing that the schools have no responsibility in the conflict, and the latter that integration could be introduced by a stroke of the legislative pen. Neither position is defensible. For the denominationalists the most common argument—that denominational schooling is clearly unrelated to the maintenance of conflict since it operates peacefully in other countries—ignores the fact that, in the case of Northern Ireland, separate schooling confirms and endorses the province's central community split, fosters its mythologies and does nothing to encourage their erosion—factors which do not often apply elsewhere. The stroke-of-a-pen argument is just as spurious; if the history of Irish schooling has any lesson, it is that any attempt forcibly to integrate schools would be unlikely to have any more success than the earlier attempts in 1831 and 1923.[62]

Paradoxically, consideration of the available evidence should point segregationists and integrationists in the same direction. In the former case, few advocates of denominational schooling would reject the premise that, in a divided society, there is an extra onus on educators to ensure that there is great contact between Protestant and Catholic children. To integrationists the existing evidence may indicate the extent of some of the more detrimental effects of separation, but it equally demonstrates both the impossibility of speedy change and the lack of public knowledge on the issue. Recognition of these factors would relegate integration to a long-term objective and concentrate energies on the immediate tasks of creating more opportunities for contact within the existing systems and encouraging an informed public debate. Most educationalists then, whether advocates of denominational or integrated schooling, would accept the need for a number of immediate initiatives—greater sharing of school facilities, teacher exchanges, joint projects, extra-curricular contacts which are based on co-operative as well as competitive activities, the creation of joint teaching materials, closer liaison at teacher and College of Education levels. An acceptance of such initiatives within the existing educational framework, far from implying an abandonment of the ideal of integration, really represents for integrationists the most likely strategy for achieving their aims. For those who oppose integration, they are worthy aims in themselves.

CHAPTER VI

Segregation by choice:
Social organisation

It is a matter of common observation that in every context the average Ulsterman's first reaction in joining any collection of people is to assess their political affiliations.
Rosemary Harris, 1972

They mingle with a consciousness of the differences between them.
J.C. Beckett, 1967

WHETHER or not the divisions between Northern Ireland's two communities are sufficiently radical as to constitute separate cultures cannot be debated solely in terms of segregated housing, education, religions or political parties; other societies exhibit similar institutional differences but still can claim a common identity. Consequently one must also consider the extent to which segregation infiltrates those aspects of community life which are private rather than public. In the case of housing, for instance, enforced separation is only part of the reason for segregated estates. It is clear that many Catholics and Protestants, who could live in integrated communities if they wished, have made a deliberate choice to live among their own co-religionists. It might be presumed that the reverse is also true—that is, that Catholics and Protestants who live together have opted for integrated living—and no doubt this applies in many cases. Nevertheless, this premise can be applied generally only if it can be demonstrated that social organisation and activities within the 'mixed' areas have a cohesion similar to the community cohesion which exists in one-religion areas. To put it another way, the question posed is whether people in these areas conduct their social relationships and activities around their geographical unit or whether they seek most of their social contacts among their co-religionists. Are there religious links in Northern Ireland society sufficiently strong to cut across and supersede any bonds caused by mere geographical proximity? The intention in this chapter is to look at what might be termed voluntary segregation, as distinct from that imposed or encouraged by institutions. How far have people in Northern Ireland deliberately arranged their activities on a segregated basis? Do they employ their co-religionists, play different sports, and join different organisations? Is the divide sufficiently comprehensive to justify the claim that there are two separate cultures in Northern Ireland? In all such considerations the principal sources of information are the news media, and a consideration of their record and influence in a divided community is an appropriate starting point.

The Media

One of the apocryphal stories about Northern Ireland's two morning newspapers concerns the coverage of a local story by the unionist *Belfast Newsletter* and the nationalist *Irish News*. A child fell into the crocodile pool at Belfast zoo and a bystander, reacting quickly, jumped in, punched the reptile on the snout and pulled the child out. The *Newsletter* headlined the story, 'Protestant rescues boy'; the *Irish News* headline was, 'Protestant attacks dumb animal'.

The willingness of the two Belfast morning newspapers to interpret, and even to select, news in the light of what is likely to interest a sectarian readership is not surprising. As Richard Rose remarked, 'religious differences are an incentive for newspapers to concentrate their readership appeal, and both Belfast morning newspapers do this'.[1] It has been estimated that 87% of the *Belfast Newsletter*'s readership is Protestant, and 93% of the *Irish News*'s Catholic.[2] Neither makes a serious effort to win readers from its rival and, although virtually no systematic research has been conducted into their presentation of news, a number of commentators have charged both papers with bias.

The *Newsletter* has always been virtually an official organ of the Unionist party, only faltering on those occasions when it was difficult to determine which party faction was official. This commitment has sometimes led to an over-eagerness to accept hearsay evidence, rumours and speculations when they hap-

141

pened to coincide with the *Newsletter*'s prejudices. Two examples demonstrate the pitfalls in this practice. When William Whitelaw arrived in Northern Ireland as Secretary of State in 1972, the *Newsletter* informed its readers that he was a Roman Catholic, and a member of a leading Roman Catholic family. Earlier, on 7 August 1970, its sensational lead story was headlined 'Reign of terror in Coalisland', and told how Catholic mobs had taken over the town and terrorised Protestants. Both stories excited Protestant fears, both were complete fabrications and, typically, no apology or withdrawal was printed in the subsequent issue.

The motto of the *Irish News*, 'Pro fide et patria', proclaims its willingness to entertain anti-unionist views, from those of Provisional Sinn Fein to those of the SDLP, and to supplement these with coverage aimed at an exclusively Catholic readership. As Simon Winchester, the *Guardian*'s correspondent, described it, 'Its six pages were dotted with sacred mottoes and supplications; its news pages were crammed with accounts of confirmation ceremonies and fleadhs'.[3]

Neither the *Newsletter* nor the *Irish News*, especially the latter, have much time for feature articles; both their correspondence pages are virulently political; editorials proclaim official party lines; most important, the main news stories in one are often ignored or only briefly mentioned in the other. To

Table 8 Newspapers:
Average issue readership in Northern Ireland[4]

Place of Publication	Daily Newspapers		Sunday Newspapers	
Northern Ireland	Belfast Newsletter	358,000	Sunday News	298,000
	Irish News	224,000		
	Belfast Telegraph	627,000		
Britain	Eight newspapers (total)	641,000	Nine newspapers (total)	1,568,000
Irish Republic	Three newspapers (total)	92,000	Two newspapers (total)	303,000

an uninitiated reader, they might well be describing two different countries. But, as Gay Firth observed, 'they do not balance, let alone cancel each other out; you can't add them up and divide by two'.[5]

The influence of the *Irish News* and the *Newsletter* must be considered in proper context. In the first place they are not the only regular newspapers produced locally; thirty or so regional weekly newspapers are also published in Northern Ireland and are usually based on the larger urban centres, Ballymena boasting three. The great bulk of information in these papers relates to the immediate vicinity and, while bias can readily be found, their political content is largely confined to straight reporting of speeches by local politicians. In addition to these, the evening *Belfast Telegraph*, which has a larger circulation than both local morning newspapers, and the *Sunday News*, Ulster's only Sunday newspaper, have succeeded in establishing a cross-sectarian readership. The *Belfast Telegraph* in particular has taken a definite liberal stance since the early 1960s and has attacked both political extremes. Its readership is 68% Protestant, which reflects the religious breakdown of the province fairly closely. It has on occasions been accused of partiality by both sides, but there is no doubt that the *Belfast Telegraph* approaches its task with responsibility and, along with *Fortnight* magazine and the Dublin-based *Irish Times*, offers the most objective and astute coverage of events in Northern Ireland.

It is not widely appreciated that English-based newspapers and magazines have a much wider readership in Northern Ireland than most local publications. British morning newspapers, for example, have about 60,000 more readers than their Ulster competitors; British and Irish publishing houses produce 87% of the Sunday newspapers read in the province; excluding provincial weekly newspapers, almost all of the remaining general weekly publications, 1,461,000 copies, and about 82% of the monthly magazines read in Northern Ireland are produced outside the province; so are all the women's magazines (750,000 copies).[6]

These factors may point to a limited influence on the part of the *Newsletter* and the *Irish News*, but it is important to remember the quantity and quality of Irish coverage by the British press. With some exceptions, notably the *Guardian, Times,*

Sunday Times and *Observer*, their approach is often superficial, emotive and impressionistic. It is fair to ask why so many British newspapers ignored the situation in the province before 1968, and why so many have been attracted over since then. Such evidence as there is suggests that the appeal of the story lay, not in the issues being debated, but in the possibility of the debate becoming violent. An analysis by Mary Davies of newspaper coverage following the 1968 marches by NICRA at Dungannon on 26 August and at Derry on 5 October revealed that coverage by British newspapers increased by 400%–500% from the first march to the second.[7] Since the issues in each case were the same, she suggested that the increased interest of the British media is largely explained by the greater possibility of violence in Derry. Eamonn McCann described the naïve and simplistic approach of the reporters who were sent over at that time : 'Immediately after 5 October 1968 dozens of journalists descended on Northern Ireland. At one point the *Mirror* had twelve people in Derry. Few of these had any detailed knowledge of the situation. Some, mindful of the May days in France that year, spent much of their time trying to identify a local Danny the Red. Others would wander into the Bogside and ask if they could be introduced to someone who had been discriminated against.'[8]

Apart from these more conventional publications, the unprecedented proliferation of political newspapers and news sheets since 1968 will offer fruitful hunting grounds for future researchers; but it is almost impossible to assess their current circulation or influence. One difficulty is the frequency with which such publications go out of print, only to emerge again shortly afterwards with a new title and editor. There are some permanencies however. On the republican side the Official IRA's *United Irishman* has been in print since 1931 and the Provisionals' Northern newspaper, *Republican News*, which was started in 1970, had a circulation of 17,000 copies each week within two years.[9] Ian Paisley's *Protestant Telegraph* has been beating the loyalist drum since 1966 and has since been joined by the *UDA News, Loyalist News, Orange Cross* and others. Apart from these regular publications there is a varied and incalculable host of duplicated news sheets published by Republican clubs, UDA branches, Sinn Fein cumainn and, it sometimes seems, almost every group which can beg, borrow or steal a duplicator. All are heavily political in tone, and many are openly violent in their views.

The new awareness in both republican and loyalist circles of the importance of media outlets was also demonstrated in 1969 by the emergence of a number of backstreet radio stations. These turned out to be even more ephemeral than the news sheets and soon stopped broadcasting. Nevertheless the growth of violence greatly increased the audiences who depended on radio and television for news. According to Richard Rose, 79% of the population made a point of listening to news and current affairs programmes; television and radio were regarded as their most reliable source of information by 55%, as opposed to 24% who favoured the press.[10] It is hardly surprising, therefore, that radio and television coverage of events in Northern Ireland have been subjected to careful scrutiny. Nor did the British Broadcasting Corporation (BBC) emerge unscathed from such examination. Professor Rex Cathcart, formerly Northern Ireland officer of the Independent Broadcasting Authority, quotes from the 1930 BBC Handbook to demonstrate the Corporation's earlier identification with Northern Ireland's Unionist government: 'Thus the broadcasting service reflects the sentiments of the people, who have always retained a lively sympathy with, and unswerving loyalty to, British ideals and British culture.'[11] George Beadle, the BBC's second station director in the province, went further and suggested to his London superiors that 'our position here will be strengthened immediately if we can persuade the Northern Ireland government to look upon us as their mouthpiece'[12]—advice wisely rejected by Reith, the Director General. Cathcart suggests that the Northern Ireland BBC's move to an independent position was a slow and reluctant one. Nevertheless few would now accuse the BBC or Independent Television Authority (ITA) of sectarian bias; the charges of partiality levelled against them in recent years have been different in kind to those aimed at local newspapers. In the case of newspapers the charges have concerned sectarianism, selective and careless reporting and bias; the complaints about television have been about alleged instant interviews after violent events, rigorous questioning of official spokesmen, providing a forum for extremist views and demoralising the army.

One of the few investigations conducted into television coverage of Northern Ireland was a minor survey carried out by Jay C. Blumer, of the Centre for Television Research in Leeds. He suggested the charges of bias were baseless. Furthermore, he pointed out, 'the critics are asking only one question about Ulster coverage : not if it is accurate, if it deals with the important developments, if it is clarifying, or even if it is fair, but simply—is it demoralising?'[13] In such an atmosphere, the danger is that radio and television reporters will be pressurised to select their material in such a way as to avoid this sort of criticism.

Private Employment

Another aspect of Northern Ireland's community problem which has attracted more speculation than serious study is discrimination in private employment. The reason for this is clear enough; it is virtually impossible in Northern Ireland to find reliable statistics about the work forces within private commercial and industrial concerns. Most firms claim that they cannot provide such data since they do not ask the religion of potential employees—an apparently liberal attitude which is by no means a guarantee of impartiality, since discovering the religion of potential employees poses no problems for any employer who wishes to discriminate. As John Benn, Northern Ireland's first Commissioner for Complaints, wrote in his second annual report, 'It is to my mind unconvincing in the Northern Ireland situation for the head of a small office or other group of workers to claim not to know pretty accurately how many of his staff are Protestants and how many are Roman Catholics, and correspondingly for a chief officer to claim that he has no means of finding this out.'[14] Indeed, there are some who argue that, to prevent industrial discrimination, the religion of applicants *ought* to be recorded—a precept contrary to the usual conditions of anti-discriminating legislation which would, however, allow the investigation of claims. In the present circumstances researchers must devise methods of investigation which are unconventional and often unreliable.

Even if a convincing and well-argued case were made that discrimination was practised by some firms, it is by no means sure that any official condemnation would follow. The fact is

146

that discrimination in employment is not forbidden in Northern Ireland—even the terms of the British Race Relations Act do not apply in the province. This absence of the letter of the law is endorsed by the absence of its spirit. Northern Ireland has a long history of politicians both publicly endorsing and actively participating in discriminatory activities. Some of these are well known, like Sir Basil Brooke's (later Lord Brookeborough and Prime Minister) advice to the Fermanagh Orangemen in 1933 : 'There are a great number of Protestants and Orangemen who employ Roman Catholics. I feel I can speak freely on this subject as I have not an RC about my own place . . . I would appeal to Loyalists, therefore, whenever possible, to employ good Protestant lads and lasses.'[15] Rather more embarrassing was the publicity of a job vacancy in a local paper during a more liberal period—'Protestant girl required for housework. Apply to the Hon. Mrs Terence O'Neill, Glebe House, Ahoghill, Co. Antrim.'[16] These and other incidents are often quoted, because of the public position of the men involved, but they are really no more than open acknowledgements of a practice widely condoned and overtly encouraged by many employers in Northern Ireland.

One consequence of this practice is a relatively higher unemployment rate in Catholic areas of Northern Ireland. This is supported by a considerable amount of evidence. A recent study of social malaise in Belfast, for example, demonstrated the uneven distribution of unemployment in the city.[17] At the time of the study the city's overall unemployment rate was 6·6%, the four areas with worst unemployment were Ballymurphy-New Barnsley, Milltown-Turf Lodge, St Pauls and Lower Falls. These areas represent a roll-call of most of the Catholic working-class parts of the city and, incidentally, the regions of most serious social disturbances between 1969 and 1974. The pattern of abnormally high unemployment in Catholic areas was also confirmed by two studies carried out in West Belfast during 1972, St Agnes Parish showing a 14% unemployment rate and Turf Lodge estate 38%.[18]

Such evidence as there is indicates that there are also significant economic differences between Catholics and Protestants outside Belfast. The generally higher unemployment rates in the predominantly Catholic areas west of the Bann has already

147

been noted; and Rosemary Harris in her study of 'Ballybeg', a small village and its hinterland in southern Ulster, demonstrated on a smaller scale how Catholic small farmers owned the least productive land. Only 42% of the Catholic farmers in the area, as opposed to 78% of the Protestants, had their farms located in the more prosperous infield areas, the remainder farming in the more difficult hilly regions. Since there were considerable differences in the incomes of the Hill farmers and the Infield farmers, Harris had no doubt that 'there was a significant overall difference in the average incomes of Catholic and Protestant'.[19] Thomas Kirk's study of Lurgan revealed a similar pattern, with Catholic farms predominating in the inferior land between Lurgan and Lough Neagh. Kirk also observed 'the relatively high proportion of Presbyterians among employers and managers and professional workers' and 'the low percentage of Catholics in the employers and managers and professional groups and conversely, the high proportion in all the manual groups'.[20]

In Belfast the conservatism of economic structures applies particularly to the traditional shipbuilding, textiles and engineering industries, but the real difficulty lies in assessing its extent. Occasionally there have been official estimates, as when trade union officials were quoted as estimating the proportion of Protestant to Catholic engineering workers in Belfast at nine to one.[21] More precise religious breakdowns for individual firms are more difficult to find, although in 1971 Kathleen Boehringer compiled a list of some firms which discriminated against Catholics—Harland & Wolff, shipbuilders, 500 Catholics out of 9,000 manual workers; Mackies, engineers, 120 out of 8,500; Sirocco engineering works, no Catholics in their 400-strong work force; Ormeau bakery, perhaps four out of 300. The trouble, as in every similar investigation, is that none of these statistics are substantiated. Indeed, Boehringer herself conceded that the figures 'have either appeared in newspapers or have been let slip by ex-employees . . . or have been vouchsafed by "common knowledge"'.[22] Nevertheless, although the figures may not be precisely accurate, the consistency with which similar claims have been made and allowed to pass unchallenged over the last fifty years argues strongly for the general picture they paint. Not that the traffic is entirely one-way: there are virtu-

148

ally no Protestants employed in the deep-sea docks in Belfast, and the licensing and bookmaking trades are largely Catholic. But, as Barritt and Booth put it, 'where discrimination exists, Catholics come off worse, if only because more firms are owned or controlled by Protestants'.[23]

Although it has not yet been the subject of serious study, there is little doubt that the growth of a Catholic professional class in the 1950s and 1960s has reduced the disparity between the two religious communities and greatly increased job integration at middle class level. One indication of this is the rise of Catholic full-time undergraduates at Queen's University, Belfast from 13% in 1941 to 32% in 1971.[24] The tendency towards integration was also encouraged by many of the new manufacturing firms which were attracted by the government's industrial incentive schemes from the late 1940s. Many of these firms, especially the international ones, refused to acept the habits of segregation and discrimination practised by the more traditional industries.

One of the bodies which might have been expected to provide a lead in breaking down such divisions is the trade union movement. Union membership is unusually high in Northern Ireland. Indeed its labour force is the most unionised in Western Europe with more than 270,000 out of 477,300 workers (55%) union members.[25] Most belong to one of the sixty-five British-based unions in the province, but there are nineteen Northern Ireland unions and five based in the Irish Republic. On occasions some of these unions have taken strong stands against sectarianism, as when the Amalgamated Society of Carpenters and Joiners issued the following injunction to its members in 1920 :

In consequence of the serious disturbances in Belfast District, causing the expulsion of several hundred members of our society from the shipyards where they were peacefully earning their livelihood, you are hereby informed that you must not seek employment from, and remain in the employment of, the following firms :

Messrs Harland & Wolff, Shipbuilders,
Messrs Workman & Clarke,
Messrs McLaughlin & Harvey, Housebuilders,
Messrs Coombe, Barbour, Fairbairn and Lawson, Engineers,

149

Messrs Musgrave & Company Limited, Engineers,
Messrs Davidson & Company Limited,
Messrs The Sirocco Works, Belfast,
Messrs James Mackie & Company,

after 25 September 1920. Any member remaining in the employment of these firms after the above date will be expelled from our society.[26]

It is likely too that there would have been serious trouble for the few Catholic workers in the shipyards in August 1970 if the shop stewards had not assumed leadership and calmed matters down. Perhaps the most practical step taken by the unions as a body was the establishment in 1972 of a joint 'fire-fighting' service by the Northern Committee of the Irish Congress of Trade Unions (ICTU) and the Confederation of British Industry which was aimed at defusing sectarian dissension among employees; in 1973 it dealt with seventy incidents.[27] However, this was a rescue operation and avoided any attempt to investigate the reasons for the dissension.

Such steps by trade unions have been rare, and usually confined to periods of civil disorder. At other times some unions have accepted local practices and condoned sectarianism; the deep-sea docks, for example, are manned almost exclusively by Catholic members of the Irish Transport and General Workers' Union, while the cross-channel docks are in the hands of the largely Protestant Amalgamated Transport and General Workers' Union. Indeed dissension and threat of dissension between unions which were based in Ulster, Britain and Southern Ireland partly explain their early ineffectiveness. Even when the unions did come together in 1959, the Northern Committee of the Irish Congress of Trade Unions was ostracised by Lord Brookeborough's government at Stormont and refused official recognition until 1964. It is perhaps unrealistic to expect a full-scale onslaught on sectarianism amid such administrative chaos and misunderstanding, and the unions affiliated to the ICTU point proudly to the fact that Catholics and Protestants generally belong to the same unions. Of trade union members interviewed by Richard Rose, 82% believed that their union mixed the two communities.[28] The situation however has only been reached by carefully avoiding many of the contentious issues

150

which divide Northern Ireland society, and indeed almost any hint of political controversy. While this is to some extent understandable, it occasionally reaches ridiculous proportions, as, for example, when a speaker at the 1974 ICTU annual conference was criticised for advocating a socialist transport plan on the grounds that he had introduced a party issue. This nervous pragmatism on the part of the unions is in large part caused by the ICTU's fear of loyalist workers establishing a breakaway union movement. There has in fact been more than one attempt to do this, the most recent being the Loyalist Association of Workers, formed in 1970, and the Ulster Workers' Council (UWC) which emerged in 1974, brought the province to a standstill with a general strike[29] and caused the resignation of the power-sharing Executive. The ability of the UWC to marshal loyalist workers contrasted with the ICTU's attempts to get them back to work, and makes a union crusade against unfair practices even more unlikely. The paradox of Ulster trade unionism, then, is that it only continues to be a forum for workers of all religions for as long as it avoids the basic community split. They share the problems of amorous eunuchs, well-intentioned and willing to take action, but unable by their nature to produce fruitful results.

Social Habits

When studying the degree of polarisation in Northern Ireland, the most difficult aspect of it to chart is how differently Catholics and Protestants behave in their daily activities. This does not concern the major separations—education, housing, employment—but the trivia of everyday life. Do people play and support different sports, or enjoy different types of social activities? To what clubs do they belong? What newspapers do they read?

The leisure activities of the Ulsterman are largely dictated by the amenities available. Many of them revolve around the local pub and, while it might be true to talk about a tendency in many places for Catholics to favour Catholic pubs and vice versa, this is by no means general. Proximity appears to be a more potent consideration than religion in determining where one drinks. Dancing establishments on the other hand often draw most of their custom from a single religious group. This is partly due to housing segregation, and the fact that some dance halls serve a largely local neighbourhood. The determining factor is often the acute shortage of public halls, and the close links between them and religious organisations. Many Orange halls form the social centre for Protestants, especially in the smaller towns; and it has been observed by researchers like Kirk and Harris how the Catholic church often performs a similar function for its people. For example, Harris observed how the absence of a cinema in Ballybeg and the showing of films in the Catholic church hall caused considerable worry to some Protestant parents. One of the main reasons for the involvement of all the churches in social activities is to provide opportunities for young people of their religion to meet each other, and to reduce the possibility of mixed-religious relationships and marriages—a not unreasonable precaution in a society where mixed-married families sometimes live in conditions of considerable stress and isolation.

The sporting habits of Catholics and Protestants also show considerable differences. Most of these appear to spring from schooldays, especially regarding actual participation in sports. It is true in general terms that Catholics play and support Gaelic football, hurling and camogie, and Protestants rarely do; equally, few Catholics in Northern Ireland play or support hockey, rugby or cricket.

There is no doubt that the main reason for this separation is the close relationship between sport and politics in the province. On the Catholic side the Gaelic Athletic Association (GAA) which is the governing body for Gaelic football, hurling and camogie, was, from its foundation, closely linked with political and cultural nationalism. Until recently the GAA enforced a ban on their members attending or participating in 'foreign games'. Anyone in the British Armed Forces or the Royal Ulster Constabulary was not permitted to participate in the sports, and no serious effort has been made to interest non-nationalists in them. This spirit still remains. In 1972 the chairman of the County Antrim Camogie Convention, Mrs Nancy Murray, urged delegates to encourage the learning of the Irish language and Irish dancing and reminded them that their association embraced the 32 counties and recognised the Irish tricolour as the national flag. She went on : 'If we don't subscribe to a pro-

152

gramme which includes the eventual unification of our country, not stipulating how and when it is to be achieved, then don't be in the association as there is no room for hypocrites.'[30] Few Protestants play Gaelic games and few support them. Harris relates how the Protestants in Ballybeg would follow the interests of its Gaelic football team and enquire about its prowess; but they did not attend its matches, partly because Gaelic games are usually played on Sundays, and Protestants (in Northern Ireland at any rate) are stricter sabbatarians than Catholics.

There are no political implications in the playing of rugby, hockey or cricket, but few Catholics play these sports. The early association of these games with 'the Ascendancy' may help to explain this, and a more accurate analysis of the situation may reveal that social class is a greater determining factor than politics. It is true that very few Catholics play these games, but neither do many working-class Protestants. In the south of Ireland, where religious differences count for less, there is a clear-cut class division between these sports and some others.

Non-participatory interest in sport is also sometimes drawn along sectarian lines. Since the resignation of Belfast Celtic from the Irish League after a riot there has been no 'Catholic' football team in the Irish League, and many of its supporters switched allegiance to Glasgow Celtic. Boal found that 73% of the (Catholic) Clonard people supported Glasgow Celtic, and none of them supported Linfield (an Irish League team); in the neighbouring Shankill, 74% supported Linfield and none Glasgow Celtic.[31] The venue for Northern Ireland's international matches (except when civil unrest frightened away visiting teams) was Windsor Park, Linfield's home ground, and the fervent loyalist/unionist atmosphere at that ground discouraged Catholic support for them. The holding of Ireland's rugby international matches in Dublin (rugby, like many other sports including hockey, cricket, golf, swimming, is still organised on an all-Ireland basis) and the playing of the Irish national anthem has not noticeably alienated support from Ulster Protestants, who attend these matches in considerable numbers. Even with football, the Linfield-Glasgow Celtic divide is by no means universal. Many of the Irish League teams attract support from both Catholics and Protestants from the immediate vicinity, especially in towns outside Belfast like Ballymena and Coleraine. It is fair to add, however, that Belfast, where the most obvious sectarian support can be found, is the only urban area with more than one senior football team. Absence of the opportunity for sectarian support has meant that the senior Irish League teams often perform an integrative function.

Most sports are played by both religious communities. Both Catholics and Protestants regularly engage in boxing, swimming, water polo, soccer, athletics, squash, golf, basketball and darts, among others. In some of these sports, however, politics lurk close to the surface and great restraint is practised to prevent it emerging. In 1973, for example, a dispute broke out involving what national anthem should be played and what flag used by the all-Ireland hockey team in Spain. In the same year Ulster delegates walked out of a meeting of the central council of the Irish Amateur Boxing Association after a provocative political speech by one of the Southern delegates. Both disputes were ultimately resolved, but in each case there was talk about dissolving the all-Ireland organisation of these sports. It should also be recorded that, although both Catholics and Protestants participate in a number of sports, it does not necessarily follow that they always play with or against each other. Some amateur soccer leagues, for example, are organised by churches and therefore exclusive. The same applies even to some dart leagues, although they are based on pubs rather than churches. But it would be misleading to give the impression that segregated social habits are the norm throughout Northern Ireland; there is, for instance, a considerable degree of social and recreational mixing in most country areas and in small towns. Until a systematic examination is carried out into social segregation it will not be possible to gauge its extent with any accuracy.

Clubs and Organisations
'In general the social network of any individual is based overwhelmingly in most fields on ties with his co-religionists. This is partly because most formal organisations are connected in one way or another with groups that have a religious basis and most individuals have strong ties with such organisations.'[32]

Rosemary Harris' observations were based on her own investigations in Ballybeg. Most of the activities which were supported by Catholics in the village, like the film show and the Pioneer Association, were sponsored by the church. In other parts of the province, Catholic associations like the St Vincent de Paul society, the Legion of Mary and parish youth clubs have received considerable support. The Catholic church has also been closely associated with parish socials, whist drives and bingo games, which had the double benefit of providing opportunities for social intercourse and supplementing parish funds. By their very nature, these occasions are largely Catholic.

The most important voluntary organisations for Protestants are equally exclusive, and one of the most important of these is the Orange Order. Anders Boserup described it as a 'mixture of a non-denominational church, a local club, an interest organisation and a link to the ruling classes',[33] and its social function was at least as important as its political function. Dances and other social activities were held in Orange halls, especially in rural areas; naturally they are almost all exclusively patronised by Protestants, and loyalty to the lodge cuts across Protestant denominational barriers, just as the unique 'equality rule', which gives each lodge member an equal voice in discussion, cutting across class barriers. There is no equivalent Catholic organisation to the Orange Order, although the Ancient Order of Hibernians is supported in some country areas, and the Catholic church itself provides a social cohesion similar to that encouraged by the Orange Institution.

All these voluntary organisations have been openly sectarian, in that their *raison d'être* is the existence of a divided community. But there are also dozens of associations in the province which are unrelated to the central divide in society. Women's institutes, drama and arts societies, historical societies, Lions' clubs, Chambers of Commerce, youth clubs, young farmers' clubs and many others. Harris describes how, in a small community, even such organisations as these were sometimes seen in sectarian terms, bazaars, sales of work and sports days all being supported by half the community. A small study of voluntary organisations in Belfast carried out in 1970 confirmed that voluntary organisations in the city tended to reflect the divisions between the two communities—especially if they were working-

155

class organisations.[34] While the great majority of working-class youth clubs were single-religion, some had members from both communities; but in these clubs there was a tacitly accepted taboo on religious or political discussions, and members tended to associate with their co-religionists inside the club. In middle-class associations, on the other hand, it was quite common for a strong mutual interest to overcome sectarian divisions. Thus the Astronomical Society, Tyrone Society, choirs and drama groups attracted members from both communities, although in three branches of the Women's Institute (a non-sectarian body), one of them in a predominantly Catholic area, there was a total of only one Catholic member. These general findings are endorsed by a study of the religious distribution of Lurgan, a small town in County Armagh, carried out in 1967.[35] The researcher remarked on the existence of parallel establishments for the Protestant and Catholic communities. Thus there was a Protestant Mechanics' Institute and a Catholic Working Men's Club; the Irish National Foresters (Catholic) in some degree corresponded with the Masons (Protestant); there was a Catholic Gardening and Crafts club, a Catholic Young Men's Association and, of course, an Orange Lodge. There were even segregated Old People's homes. The two communities were served by two local newspapers. However, considerable recreational links existed as well, especially among the professional classes who frequented a non-sectarian art club, film society and local history society. Golf and tennis clubs also served a socially cohesive function.

Indeed the differences between the social habits of the working-class and middle-class populations in Northern Ireland are very marked. Many of the generalities about polarisation apply to the middle classes to a significantly less marked extent than to workers. Although there are considerable differences at working class level between Catholic and Protestant leisure practices, the sports and dances they patronise, and the clubs and associations to which they belong, this applies to a much lesser extent among middle-class people. They belong to similar clubs—although there are notable exceptions to this generalisation—are more likely to play and support the same activities, compete for the same jobs, read the same newspapers, and live in mixed areas. It is a moot point whether the differences in living styles

156

between the classes are more marked than those between the religions.

Community Groups

One of the most remarkable urban phenomena in Northern Ireland since 1968 has been what the Northern Ireland Community Relations Commission described in its second annual report as 'a spontaneous genesis of a host of small community groups'.[36] Within one and a half years of the Commission's formation in 1969 its fifteen Community Development Officers (CDOs) were giving support to 394 of these groups, most of which had been formed during this period. When it is remembered that the CDOs only operated in Derry, Dungannon and parts of Belfast, some impression can be gained of the dynamic upsurge of community action in the province.

It is no coincidence that this upsurge took place during a time of severe political crisis. The failure of the government and opposition to cope with both Catholic grievances and Protestant fears had already led to an alienation of both communities from existing political parties and from the administrative machinery at local and central government level. Dissatisfaction grew as the continuation of violence produced a complete breakdown in some areas and increased inefficiency in others. It became increasingly clear to some community groups that, if they were to improve the living conditions, they must take action themselves. The motivations for such action differed considerably from community to community, just as the perceived needs of each community differed from place to place. But the main community needs which the new groups attempted to satisfy were for protection, employment and social amenities.

As violence worsened from 1969 into the 1970s the greatest fear of many Catholic and Protestant communities was imminent attack from their rivals, and their most vocal demand was for protection. To many Catholics the invasion of the Lower Falls in August 1969 was a warning of what might take place in any Catholic community in Belfast. Age-long distrust of the police and the army led to the communities' determination to arrange their own protection. The immediate response was the formation of vigilante groups to patrol the streets; later the Provisional IRA emerged as well as other groups like the

Catholic Ex-Servicemen's Association, the Central Citizens' Defence Committee and the Derry Citizens' Action Committee. All of these groups, with varying degrees of intensity, were defensive in intention, and the formation of 'No-go' areas like 'Free Derry' and 'Free Andersonstown' were attempts to carry out a defensive role more effectively. The same desire for protection appeared in many Protestant areas in 1970 and 1971 with the intensification of the Provisional IRA bombing campaign. The formation of the UDA and other defence organisations arose from frustration at the failure of the police and army to protect their areas, and the UDA barricades of 1971 were conscious reactions to the 'No-go' Catholic areas. All these organisations were by definition sectarian, since their main purpose was opposition to the other religious community.

Although at first the new community groups were defensive in character, it was not long before they were perceived as means of tackling other problems. One of the most obvious of these problems was the abnormally high unemployment rates in some parts of Northern Ireland, which had persisted for many years. Self-help economic enterprises and co-operatives were already fairly familiar phenomena in Ireland, but these had been almost entirely rural and concerned with agricultural products. The new community determination produced a number of industrial self-help schemes in urban areas, with mixed success. Schemes like Tyrone Crystal in Dungannon and Ballymurphy Enterprises in Belfast provided social as well as economic benefits for their communities; the most ambitious of all, Whiterock Industrial Estates, acquired 12 acres and established a building company, training unit, candle factory, filling station and car repair shop—all despite considerable difficulties and shortage of funds.[37] This modest success encouraged the formation of similar community-based enterprises in Ardoyne and the Oldpark area of Belfast, as well as outside the city.

By far the greatest number of new community groups were tenants' and community associations concerned with lack of social amenities. Poor planning produced a rash of postwar housing estates around Belfast which were deficient in amenities. Many of them lacked any community meeting place; others had no facilities for young people. The living conditions in these estates further deteriorated as a result both of the troubles and of proposed redevelopments. Bad conditions became worse as a result of violence in the streets. The intimidation of people from their homes produced serious overcrowding; some estates had no street lighting at night—both the British army and paramilitary groups had destroyed the lights; services like house repairs, road maintenance and refuse collection gradually disappeared as repair men refused to enter the areas. At the same time massive redevelopment of the city threatened to destroy many of the old communities in the city, which had provided a form of security in troubled times. These factors merely exaggerated grievances which had existed previously, but were themselves accentuated by the inability of local authorities and government agencies effectively to improve matters. The result here, as in the other spheres outlined, was the eruption of a large number of tenants' associations, community organisations, ratepayers' associations and redevelopment associations. All of these operated as pressure groups and some of them achieved considerable successes, especially as their expertise increased. There are few public housing areas in Belfast and many other towns which do not have an elected local association dedicated to improving amenities in their neighbourhood.

It would be wrong to suggest that the different functions of these groups were quite separate from each other. In fact there was a considerable degree of interaction between them, and many community groups performed more than one role. Thus it was not unusual to find a tenants' association which was usually involved in campaigns for better amenities taking on a temporary vigilante function, or gearing itself to tackle intimidation. The dynamic which had produced vigilante patrols in 1969, 1970 and 1971 did not disappear when the patrols ended, and many made the fairly smooth transition to community groups. With so much activity on so many fronts at around the same time there were early fears that all these community groups would be taken over by, and eventually become front organisations for, military or para-military organisations. There have been occasions when this has happened, but it is likely that the greater influence has flown in the other direction, and that the militants have been forced to consider real needs and demands in the communities.

As a result of the defensive origins of some of these groups,

159

and because of the residential segregation between Catholics and Protestants which has been accelerated by intimidation, most of the new tenants' associations are either entirely Catholic or entirely Protestant. This was not universally true, but demographic patterns in Northern Ireland, and especially in Belfast, ensured that any association which was based on small communities was likely to be religiously homogeneous. Nevertheless it soon became clear to some of the tenants' organisations on both sides of the sectarian divide that the lack of amenities and services in their areas was common to them all. It also became clear that some of their objectives could not be achieved without co-operation between them. The struggle against the proposed redevelopment of Belfast, for example, which was opposed by many communities in the city, would clearly be unlikely to succeed if each area conducted an isolated campaign; similarly a campaign to increase government aid to community groups would greatly benefit from concerted action.

Consequently it is not surprising that, in some parts of Northern Ireland, local groups began to work together within community associations. The groups retained their local identity, but used the community association as an umbrella organisation when action was required on a broader front. By 1974 there were four community associations in Belfast, representing many local groups in the city, and one in Derry; the first steps had also been taken towards the formation of an association for rural groups. In 1974 a committee was established to propose means of forming a Northern Ireland federation of community groups.[38] This and all the other developments have taken place with the minimum of sectarian discord. It will be interesting to see whether the community action movement can provide an effective voice for the people who live in working-class areas of Northern Ireland. No one has managed it in the past.

Evaluation

People in Northern Ireland are born into communities which are often physically and structurally divided, and the divisions are ratified and reinforced by different social patterns. In such circumstances it is not suprising that many of the voluntary organisations which people support are segregated—indeed anything else would be abnormal and unnatural. Still, any claim

160

that such segregation is general must be heavily qualified. The points of contact between Catholic and Protestant are just as remarkable as the points of separation. The counter pull of class divisions, for example, has created a middle-class identity which may be as cohesive as that based on religion, particularly among the professional classes. Furthermore, apart from Belfast, Derry and some other towns which have recognisable segregated housing, communities in most other parts of the province are essentially integrated in their social activities, group membership, housing and employment. Too often generalities which apply to Belfast are inaccurately attributed to the entire province.

The major difficulty in discussing the real extent of voluntary segregation is the apparent lack of interest about the matter among researchers, which is all the more surprising in light of constant public interest. In particular, the prevalence of discrimination in private employment and the influence of the media in Northern Ireland are virtually uncharted territories. With the important exceptions of some research studies, one is likely to gain as much insight into the nature of social segregation from a study of Ulster's literature than from her researchers.[39]

So assessment of the evidence is difficult. Nevertheless some points are clear, and one of these is the influence of sectarianism on the social, leisure and economic activities of many Ulster people. Relationships are rarely reached in ignorance of the religion of each party—they are frequently made, but the information is important because it will determine or delineate the boundaries of acceptable conversation. Catholics will often avoid areas of .discussion with Protestants which they would happily join with other Catholics, and vice versa. The necessity of having this sort of conversational taboo certainly demonstrates the extent of social segregation in the province; but it also shows a willingness to overcome its effects.

CHAPTER VII

Theories about the conflict

If men define situations as real, they are real in their consequences.
Georges Soroe, 1961

Then we have people genuinely trying to be helpful who advocate a kind of reciprocal emasculation. No national anthem or loyal toast to offend one side; no outward signs or symbols of Nationalism to offend the other. This approach, too, I believe to be misconceived; it is rather like trying to solve the colour problem by spraying everyone a pale shade of brown.
Terence O'Neill, 1968

What we need is an active fraternity of pessimists. They will not aim at immediate radical solutions, because they know that these cannot be achieved in the hollow of the historical wave; they will not brandish the surgeon's knife at the social body, because they know that their own instruments are polluted. They will watch with open eyes and without sectarian blinkers for the first sign of the new horizontal movement; when it comes they will assist its birth; but if it does not come in their lifetime, they will not despair. And meantime their chief aim will be to create oases in the interregnum desert.
Arthur Koestler, 1969

The Goldfish Bowl

There is nothing new in the recent interest shown by outsiders in Irish tensions, and it is clear that Ireland's attraction has been the starkness of her contrasts and the uncompromising bitterness of her conflicts. De Beaumont's observation in 1839 holds the key to Ireland's particular fascination for Victorian politicians and political theorists: 'In Ireland the traveller sees magnificent castles and wretched cabins : but no house which stands midway between the palaces of the great and the hovels of the indigent, for in this country there are only rich and poor.'[1]

Various British radicals endorsed de Beaumont's analysis of the Irish problem and most of them were in agreement about both the causes and symptoms of the disease. The land question, in one form or another, was believed to lie at the root of Ireland's difficulties. Some felt that the system of land management was sound, but that it was being unfairly or inefficiently worked; Ricardo, for example, believed that there was nothing wrong with landlordism as such, but that Irish landlords were notoriously corrupt; and Trower thought that the average land holding in Ireland was too small. 'It appears to me that no permanent or substantial good can be done till all small farms and small tenancies are got rid of. These are the curse of Ireland.'[2] Others took more radical stands. John Stuart Mill, for example, attacked the introduction of capitalist farming into Ireland, and brought the argument down to earth with the reminder, 'the people are there, and the problem is not how to improve the country, but how it can be improved by and for its present inhabitants'.[3] Cobden and Bright too were concerned with the Irish question, the former soon becoming convinced that the only way to remove the 'landlord spirit' was the giving of 'Ireland to the Irish' both in church and state.[4]

Many of these early analyses of the Irish problem were based, to a greater or lesser degree, upon economic considerations, and especially on the nature of the relationship between landlord and tenant. It is interesting to note that it was the agrarian reformer, Arthur Young, who added the extra dimension of legal and social discrimination. 'To discover what the liberty of people is, we must live among them, and not look for it in the statutes of the realm; the language of written law may be that of liberty, but the situation of the poor may speak no other language than that of slavery. There is too much of this contradiction in Ireland : and where manners are in conspiracy against law, to whom are the oppressed to have recourse?'[5]

Marx and Engels were also among those nineteenth-century political thinkers who became interested in Ireland. They were fascinated by the land question, its connection with the growing demand for Irish independence and the possibility that Ireland, with its obvious social discrepancies, might spark off a general social revolution; but, quite apart from these, Professor Mansergh has shown how both Marx and Engels used Irish developments to refine, change or confirm their theories about social revolution.

Much of the revival of interest by theoreticians in Ireland which took place in the 1960s was based on a similar realisation by researchers that Ireland's qualities as a goldfish bowl, into which they might gaze and test their theories against the behaviour of the specimens, were as great as ever. The effects of the rediscovery of this rich source of material was the greater from following many decades of neglect, decades in which some of the conflicts which had been observed in the nineteenth century had become institutionalised by partition and by growing segregation inside Northern Ireland. The influx of researchers into Northern Ireland from the late 1960s represented many interests and many philosophies, but some were only interested in the conflict insofar as it might support more generally held views about communal discord. Such an approach removed from the researcher any obligations to those actually caught up in the struggle, and the resulting studies were frequently superficial and unashamedly selective, ignoring data which might force a modification of their original viewpoint. The broadcasting of such studies on every continent, and the rapidity with which academic and journalistic reputations were made abroad, sometimes by people with only a passing acquaintance with Ireland, has vastly oversimplified the problem. One of the results of this process is that the Northern Ireland problem is often regarded in analogical terms, and very naïve ones at that. So the Russian press has regarded the problem as a typical post-colonialist situation, and Americans are encouraged to regard it as similar to their racial problem without the colour differences; similarly the IRA is seen, depending on the reception area, as freedom fighters or terrorists or proletarian revolutionaries. It is perhaps superfluous to add that such oversimplifications, far from throwing light on the problems, often divert discussions about Ireland along paths which, to Irishmen, are most incredibly erroneous.

Fortunately these exercises in opportunism have been countered by a far greater number of useful and illuminating studies which have been produced since Barritt and Carter's *The Northern Ireland Problem* was first published in 1962—the first serious sociological analysis of the situation since the previous century.[6] Some of these argue that the Ulster problem is best understood in terms of some general universal theory about human behaviour; others that it is essentially an Irish phenomenon, only properly understandable in Irish terms. While there is naturally considerable borrowing of data and ideas between these theorists, this chapter is designed to discuss their different views about why there is community disharmony in Northern Ireland.

Universal Aspects
Economic Theories
It is quite impossible to summarise the views of all those observers who see economic factors as both the cause and the means of solution of the Northern Ireland problem. Their approaches are almost as varied as the depth of their analyses. Nevertheless there is general agreement about some of the areas of discussion, including the colonial relationship between Britain and Ireland since (at least) the seventeenth century, class differences within the province, the economic connections between both parts of Ireland and Great Britain after the Second World War, and the nature of the sectarian conflict between Catholic and Protestant working classes.

The common starting point is the means by which Britain exploited her Irish colony since the Plantation of Ulster. This dominance was maintained both by the control of Irish resources, especially exploitation through the landlord system, and by commercial exploitation through legislation. An example of the latter was the body of laws passed during the seventeenth century to restrict Irish trade, which systematically destroyed those Irish commercial enterprises—commercial shipping, cattle exports, production of wool, cotton, glass—which offered competition to British commerce or industry; only those trades which benefited Britain, or at least did not compete with her interests, like linen and the provisions trade, were allowed to be practised. The act of Union of 1800 between the British and Irish parliaments was, according to this view of conflict, necessitated by the success of the independent Irish parliament from 1782 to 1800 in stimulating successful commercial competition with Britain. To maintain efficient exploitation, it was necessary for Britain to destroy the Irish parliament and restore a situation in which Britain's economic interests could be efficiently safeguarded.

Such a viewpoint maintains that the British control of Ireland before and during the nineteenth century was economic rather than political. Thus the 1921 settlement which partitioned Ireland had little real consequence since British control continued through ownership of property and by commercial dominance—a situation which applied in the south as well as the north of the island. Indeed the settlement was necessary to maintain this control, because without it popular feeling in Ireland might have gone on to threaten Britain's economic interests. Control of Northern Ireland was left to the local bourgeoisie, which employed sectarianism to stabilise the area.

The years following the Second World War are critical ones to Marxist analysts of the Northern Ireland situation. The important development in this period was the decline of the traditional industries—especially ship-building and textiles—which were largely controlled by Northern Ireland industrialists. This had two important effects. The first was the weakening of the economic base of Unionism, and the second was its replacement by new industries which were mostly controlled from Britain. The new factories which came into Ulster during the 1950s and 1960s, and the increased subsidisation of the Belfast shipyards, largely from British funds, increased the dependency of Northern Ireland on Great Britain. It also served to accentuate the economic disparity between Northern Ireland and the Republic of Ireland. The principal result, as Greaves put it, was 'the subordination of the Irish bourgeoisie to English monopoly capitalism.'[7] Boserup claimed in 1970 that the increasing trade contacts between Britain and both parts of Ireland represented a reintegration of the Republic into the British economy : 'In economic terms the Union is rapidly being restored.'[8] The entry of both the United Kingdom and the Republic of Ireland into the European Economic Community in 1973 is seen as merely the latest manoeuvre to maintain and strengthen bourgeois and capitalist control.

One of the greatest problems to Marxist analysts has been

the absence of overt inter-class conflict in Northern Ireland and the persistence of an internecine conflict within the working classes. Jenkins attempts to deal with this apparent contradiction by claiming that in Northern Ireland the bourgeois elite has successfully diverted the 'real' class differences into the 'unreal' field of religious differences.[9] The answer then, is to demonstrate this subterfuge by all means necessary and to encourage the working classes to abandon the false conflict and demand satisfaction of their real needs.

His proposition is that ethnic or sectarian differences cannot exist in isolation but are in fact class conflicts in disguise. Other theorists find his explanation unsatisfactory. Boserup in particular points to the fact that the dominant group in Northern Ireland is not clearly characterised by its ownership of the means of production.[10] Instead it includes adherents who, in most other societies, would be members of the oppressed minority. The class concept which appears more satisfactory to Boserup is that proposed by Dahrendorf, which defines classes by their relation to the exercise of power rather than by their control of the means of production. By this definition the key to understanding the Ulster problem is the way in which divergent class interacts were successfully united under the Protestant loyalist banner. Boserup describes this as the Orange System, defining it as 'a system in which Orange lodges, local business, the Unionist party machine, local government and administration and the hierarchies of the Protestant sects and denominations are all knit together tightly into a stable bloc which maintains its ascendancy through discrimination, patronage, and the fear of real or imagined bogeymen such as the spectres of Home Rule and Popery'.[11] The failure of the Nationalists to construct a similar edifice does not arise from unwillingness, but from the fact that their support is confined within a minority of the population, and perhaps a minority of that minority. Gibbon called them 'the miserable Catholic obverse of the Unionist Party—miniature and mirror of it'.[12] Both parties depended on polarised sectarian divisions, and upon each other's existence.

According to Boserup's analysis it is unrealistic to expect solutions to Ulster's problems from liberal reforms by a Unionist administration; any reforms sufficiently radical to restore equality of opportunity to Catholics would destroy the very basis of Unionism, thus removing the means of carrying them through. Such reforms could only be implemented by an outside agency.

Although Boserup's analysis is significantly different to that of Jenkins and Greaves, they both find agreement in the unreality of the conflict. However, Jenkins sees the unreality in the fact that sectarianism diverted the struggle away from 'real' class issues, and Boserup sees it in institutional terms: 'The religious conflict in Ulster is an artificial conflict in the sense that the relationship between the two communities is no longer a necessarily antagonistic one, but only the social institutions make it remain so'.[13] The extension of this argument is, of course, that any workable solution will ultimately depend on altering these institutions.

Not all those who believe that the Northern Ireland conflict is based on economic considerations would accept a Marxist analysis. A less dramatic but more easily quantified explanation is that of relative deprivation. The basis of this theory is that frustration and possible conflict tends to arise when a group in society perceives a gap between their situation and that of its reference group—the wider the gap, the more the discontent. Runciman has identified three areas of such inequality[14]—economic disparity, social inequalities and political inequalities—and Birrell applied these tests to the situation of Catholics in Northern Ireland. He found that Catholics certainly felt that they were deprived and that there is 'some evidence of a factual basis for Catholics' perception of their deprivation in relation to Protestants'.[15] The Civil Rights Campaign of the late 1960s, he argued, was a conventional attempt to alter the *status quo* and, when it failed, the increase in frustration led to violence. 'Relative deprivation,' he concluded, 'provides a persistent, underlying cause of civil disturbance in Northern Ireland. The only effective solution seems to be to remove its causes.'[16] What it does not satisfactorily explain is why civil disturbances at the post-1969 level were delayed for forty years.

As has been previously indicated, there is considerable variation in the depth of the analyses employed by students of the Irish conflict. Some of the more superficial and selective studies sometimes ignore the obvious in favour of obscure trivia; not surprisingly, the result resembles a building constructed of twigs when the massive logs which litter the Ulster scene lie unused beside it. One example is the zeal with which instances of Catholic-Protestant working class solidarity—like the 'hunger riots' of 1932, or the (almost invariably rejected) overtures of the Official IRA to Protestant working-class bodies—are seized upon hopefully as evidence that the workers have at last seen the futility of sectarian differences. Conveniently overlooked is the mass of evidence which points in the opposite direction.

On the other hand the category of economic theorists also includes some of the most comprehensive and painstaking examinations of all. Jenkins and Macrae were in advance of the entire field in basing their study of polarisation in 1966 on a survey which they conducted themselves; and Boserup's historical analysis is among the most stimulating and illuminating which have been written. No student of the Northern Ireland conflict can hope to understand what has happened without a close study of them.

Racial/Ethnic Theories

Liam de Paor's book, *Divided Ulster*, begins uncompromisingly : 'In Northern Ireland Catholics are Blacks who happen to have white skins. This is not a truth. It is an oversimplification and too facile an analogy. But it is a better oversimplification than that which sees the struggle and conflict in Northern Ireland in terms of religion . . . Racial distinction between the colonists and the natives is expressed in terms of religion.'[17] A number of observers believe that a racial analysis, with all its inconsistencies, nevertheless offers the most fruitful means of understanding what is happening in Ulster.

It is probable that the growing tendency to regard the conflict in these terms arises from the comparative abundance of literature and scholarship into the problems of racial and ethnic minorities both in the United States and in Great Britain. In some cases administrators have found this comparison too easy to resist. Thus the first legislation introduced in Northern Ireland to tackle its community problems was very closely based on British legislation concerning its coloured minorities; the act establishing the Northern Ireland Community Relations Commission is identical in parts to that which established the Com-

169

mission in Britain; and the Prevention of Incitement to Hatred act (NI) of 1970 closely follows parts of the British Race Relations act.[18] But while the growth of interest in racial interpretations of the Irish problem is undoubtedly partly due to the existence of convenient racial models elsewhere, it is by no means a new concept. In fact it revives an attitude which had considerable support during the eighteenth and nineteenth centuries, and which was well presented by a parish minister in 1814:

> The inhabitants of the parish are divided into two races of men as totally distinct as if they belonged to different countries and religions. These may be distinguished by the usual names of Scotch and Irish; the former including all the descendants of the Scotch and English colonists who emigrated hither since the time of James I, and the latter comprehending the native and original inhabitants of the country. Than those no two classes of men can be more distinct: The Scotch are remarkable for their comfortable houses and appearance, regular conduct and perseverance in business, and their being almost entirely manufacturers; the Irish, on the other hand, are more negligent in their habitation, less regular and guarded in their conduct, and have a total indisposition to manufacture; both are industrious, but the industry of the Scotch is steady and patient and directed with foresight, while that of the Irish is rash, adventurous, and variable.[19]

A similarly racial attitude was often reflected in the blatantly anti-Irish pages of *Punch* during the nineteenth century:

> A gulf, certainly, does appear to yawn between the Gorilla and the Negro. The woods and wilds of Africa do not exhibit an example of an intermediate animal . . . Philosophers go vainly searching abroad for what they would readily find if they sought for it . . . in some of the lowest districts of London and Liverpool. It comes from Ireland . . . it belongs in fact to a tribe of savages, the lowest species of the Irish Yahoo. When conversing with its kind it talks a sort of gibberish. . . . The Irish Yahoo generally confines itself within the limits of its own colony, except when it goes

170

out of them to get its living. Sometimes, however, it sallies forth in states of excitement, and attacks civilised human beings that have provoked its fury.[20]

More recently the theories about minority groups developed by Wagley and Harris have been applied to the Ulster situation because they are mainly concerned with groups which emerged as a result of historical developments.[21] They argued that there are three situations from which racial minorities emerge: slavery in the past; large-scale immigration of poor people; and situations in which the minority emerged from a defeated enemy. The third has obvious relevance in Northern Ireland and researchers like Robert Moore begin their analysis with the Plantations and the emergence of a colonial relationship between conqueror and conquered. This relationship is characterised by the fact that colonists are interested in exploitation rather than development, and Moore quotes the decline of western Ulster as evidence that this exploitation continues despite various attempts to encourage its challenge by class rivalries.

When arguing that the Northern Ireland situation is essentially racial, Moore accepts as the best yardstick the tests suggested by Rex.[22] Rex had argued that three criteria distinguish structures of those social relations which are racial, and Moore claims that all three conditions apply to Northern Ireland. They are:

1. *The existence of two or more groups with distinct identities, forced to live together in a society.* In Northern Ireland, the main groups are identifiable by their economic status, by where they live and where they are educated, and by social behaviour.

2. *The presence of a high degree of inter-group conflict, in which members of the rival group are recognisable.* Moore argues that the conflict is evident, and that religious adherence is the means of identifying group members, which is why there are so many restraints on mixed-religious marriages in Ulster.

3. *The use of some kind of deterministic theory which justifies the allocation of roles and rights.* This theory, ac-

171

cording to Moore, is that '99% of Catholics are traitors or potential traitors, that they reject the Northern Ireland constitution, that they will always use their might and power to overthrow the Protestant order'.[23]

While there is some debate as to whether or not Rex's criteria apply to the Northern Ireland situation, there is a strange willingness to accept almost without question that they are the proper criteria for defining a racial situation. Some other writers, however, believe that it is a waste of time to argue whether any general objective criteria apply to Northern Ireland. What is important, especially to Barth[24] and to Wagley and Harris, is whether or not people perceive themselves to be participants in a racial or ethnic struggle. Such a situation, described by Wagley and Harris as 'ethnocentricity', applies when a minority group protects its cultural values (by opposing intermarriage, for example), perceives itself in conflict with the majority group, and believes itself to be the object of discriminatory practices or policies. Whether or not such discrimination takes place is relatively unimportant; the authors point to French Canada where, they claim, there was little or no discrimination but all the characteristics of a racial situation.

There is a strong implication in racial and ethnic theory that one group is dominant over the other. To those who emphasise this aspect, the question of how the dominant group maintained its ascendancy offers the most fruitful way of testing whether a situation is racial. Simpson and Yinger, for example, list six possible policies by which the stronger ethnic group may deal with its opponents.[25]

1. Assimilation; (a) forced or (b) permitted
2. Pluralism
3. Legal protection for minorities
4. Population transfer; (a) peaceful or (b) forced migration
5. Continued subjugation
6. Extermination

Various exponents of racial analyses of the Northern Ireland problem argue that one or more of the first five solutions have been or are still being implemented in the province. The increased external pressures since 1969, in the forms of the international press and greater direct involvement by Westminster in Northern Ireland, make the last three possibilities improbable, and it could be argued that Westminster has been mainly responsible for the application of assimilative policies, accompanied by legislative protection for the minority.

There are undoubtedly many aspects of inter-group relations in Northern Ireland which resemble symptoms of a racial struggle—the presence of discrimination; the claim to be able to recognise Catholics or Protestants by alleged physical characteristics; the attribution of generic characteristics by one group to the other—Catholics being described as lazy, dirty, glib, untrustworthy, and Protestants as bigoted, stiff, unimaginative and uncultured. Most of all, the apparent permanence and immutability of the conflict could be cited as a perfect example of Wagley and Harris' ethnocentric theory, with both groups staunchly defending their cultural and social values, and resisting any attempts towards assimilation.

Given these circumstances, some observers have cautiously suggested that a pluralist approach offers the best avenue out of an apparently insoluble situation—cautiously, because pluralist 'solutions' are often misread as apartheid. The argument runs like this : It is clear to all but the most optimistic onlooker that the community's divisions are, for all practical purposes, permanent. Hopes that some of these divisions were starting to dissolve in the 1960s were dashed by the inter-communal strife of the early 1970s. Assimilative policies therefore are misdirected and doomed to failure. Those advocating a united Ireland are also misguided, since this would amount to the transfer of the same racial problem into another geographical unit; the ethnic conflicts in the north would continue, and probably intensify. Policy therefore should instead be directed towards the construction of plural institutions, which would ensure the equal distribution of economic, social, political and human rights but allow the continuation of voluntary cultural separation in areas like education, marriage, religion etc. At least, the argument goes on, this solution would be based on the realities of the situation. The suggestion is by no means unique; the Dutch developed a system similar to this, and it appears to have solved their main problem. Furthermore, pluralism is the only strategy from those suggested by Simpson and

173

Yinger which has not been attempted and failed—except for that of minority extermination.

Caste Theories

The existence of Catholics at all levels of Northern society causes problems for advocates of both economic and racial interpretations of the problem. The former find difficulty explaining the presence of working-class Protestants in positions of relative control; the latter find equal difficulty explaining the presence of Catholics at almost every economic level of Northern Ireland society, a finding verified by many observers, notably Barritt and Carter, Richard Rose and the Cameron Commission. Patrick McNabb attempted to get around this difficulty by postulating that the social structures in Northern Ireland most resemble a caste system—a sort of amalgam of the class and racial theories.

McNabb describes the system which, he claims, was introduced with the conquest: 'the society was divided into two castes; Protestant and Catholic. Each caste had its own class structure; that is, its own middle class, which includes a wide range of occupations, wealth and social statuses, and its own working class. In addition, the Protestant caste had a class of gentry which had considerable political influence'.[26] This was not the first occasion that a suggestion of caste was made. Lecky, the famous historian, wrote, 'The most worthless Protestant, even if he had nothing else to boast of, at least found it pleasing to think that he was a member of the dominant race.'[27]

This theory is used to explain why discrimination is not applied in any absolute or overall sense. It is quite acceptable, and McNabb supplies illustrations, for Protestants to employ Catholics, but only if there are no qualified Protestants available. Consequently, Catholics have the opportunity of upward class mobility and are to be found at all class levels. They also discriminate, although their opportunities for doing so are fewer. But the Catholic has no opportunity to reach the top positions for which his abilities might qualify him. This applies to all classes. Able working-class Catholics will find it as difficult to become a factory floor foreman as his middle-class co-religionist to become Chairman of the Board.

174

The difficulties which faced the Northern Ireland Labour Party and the trade union movement may be used as illustrations of the caste nature of Ulster's society. Class issues have never seriously looked like replacing sectarian ones as the main social divisions in the province, because the caste system has ensured that the class war has been channelled along divided sectarian lines. It is not unusual to find Protestant working-class movements like the Loyalist Association of Workers, the Ulster Workers Council, or the abortive working-class unionist political parties which have been formed; Catholics have always supported to some degree parties like the Republican Labour party and the Republican Clubs as well as men like Jim Larkin and James Connolly. It was proven very difficult to create genuine cross-religious working-class groups, unless such groups carefully avoided basic issues which might threaten their unity.

McNabb, in common with many other observers of the Northern Ireland scene, is particularly interested in the social role of the Orange Order. Rosemary Harris emphasised the practice of complete equality of opportunity for members of Orange lodges to express opinions, and McNabb sees it as a vital institution for it provided the social cement which held together the diverse class interests of Ulster Protestants. It was the collapse of this unity, as the result of both external and internal factors, which precipitated the events of the late 1960s. The cement was no longer able to hold the structure together.

Psychiatric Theories

Morris Fraser, a Belfast child psychologist, borrows freely from American studies of their racial problems in developing a basically psychiatric analysis of the Irish situation. Consequently there is much emphasis on theories of race and caste, and a central tendency to see the conflict as between in- and out-groups, suspicious and hostile towards each other.

The first stage in the development of prejudice and discrimination, according to Fraser, is the definition in stereotyped terms of an out-group. It is important for the elite group to find a 'pariah' group so that it can maintain its status. Berkowitz claims that there are four requirements necessary for the identification of such scapegoats—visibility, strangeness, prior dislike and proximity.[28] Fraser believes that all four characteristics are present in Northern Ireland—even visibility, since it is possible to recognise members of the out-group by their education, addresses, names and even, some claim, features. When the 'pariah' group has been defined, and attributed with such racial defects as unreliability, dirtiness, over-breeding and superstition, such defects are then used to justify discrimination against them. As Fraser put it, 'exclusion of the minority group from employment is rationalised by attributing to its members undesirable qualities. Frustrated by this discrimination, the out-group finally takes to open demonstration against the majority, who then point to this behaviour as illustrative of the out-group's essential unworthiness.'[29] This is sometimes supplemented by the contentment myth, which argues that the minority actually enjoy living in overcrowded, dirty surroundings. 'They're like that'.

The whole process is accelerated and heightened by the advent of economic prosperity. At such times the threat of upward social mobility disturbs the middle-class elite, and causes frustration to those who demand admission to the elite. This frustration also increases among the workers, who become more aware of relative deprivation and of competition for increased resources. In the Northern Ireland context competition tends to become sectarian, and leads to increased polarisation and a strengthening of the ghettos. The increase in ghettoisation during times of prosperity, when one might expect increased mobility, arises from the minority's frustrated ambitions : this results in the minority group turning inwards, becoming more conscious of itself and acquiring an aggressive pride; in the United States this is symbolised in the slogan, 'Black is beautiful'.

The frustration-aggression hypothesis which, in its most simple form, proposes that the existence of frustration always leads to some form of aggression, is rejected by Fraser as inadequate in explaining the complexities and the longevity of the Northern problems.[30] Instead he concentrates on the educative processes by which fears and prejudices are transmitted from generation to generation. While accepting the importance of the family in the transmission of these feelings he maintains that schools have an unusual pertinence in Ulster. The segregation of Catholic and Protestant children, while perhaps acceptable elsewhere, has particularly dangerous effects in a situation where children have very limited opportunities to meet each other naturally outside school hours because of social and residential segregation. In addition to the fact of segregation, which is bad enough in itself, Fraser argues that the schools transmit, partly unintentionally, different myths and values. Consequently, since it will be necessary to break into the circle of reinforcing conflict at some point, he suggests that the integration of schools is the most obvious stage to begin the re-education of society.

Some reviewers have criticised what they consider an over-emphasis by Fraser on the integrated education question. It is certainly true that he gives very little emphasis to the overwhelming corpus of evidence that most attitudes and prejudices have already been implanted before children reach the age of school attendance; in comparison with the home, schools have relatively little influence on the acquisition of attitudes. But the argument is not quite so clear-cut. As well as the transmission of knowledge, school involves contact with peer groups, teachers and other influences. Although these may or may not create prejudices, the evidence suggests that they reinforce and strengthen them unless corrective measures are taken. Segregated schools may not create prejudices. But by not doing anything to remedy or modify them it is legitimate to claim that schools play a part in the perpetuation of discord.

Comparative Studies

The tendency of Northern Ireland people to see their conflict as unique has often been remarked. As Elliot and Hickie put it, 'the situation in Ulster is rarely, if ever, compared with similar conflicts in Cyprus, Belgium and Fiji'.[31] Certainly some general authors have looked towards other situations to supply analogies and insights—Rose, for example, sees similarities between Northern Ireland and the southern United States, and Fraser not only compares the positions in society of the American negroes (this time mainly in the northern cities) and Ulster Catholics but also draws heavily on American medical evidence of the effects of riot situations on children. But these are concerned with particular surface similarities and are not in-depth analyses of the social characteristics which produced the underlying tensions. There has been a shortage of researchers who are sufficiently familiar with the Ulster conflict and with another conflict situation to write with authority about both, and to draw useful conclusions from their similarities or differences. Apart from Rose and Fraser, very little has been published. John Bayley has compared the Ulster and Cyprus situations[32] indicating how rapidly hostility between communities can change in short periods of time; but most of all he stresses the failure of palliative measures in both places—mediation attempts, community relations exercises, etc.—and the need for more radical approaches which would change the whole politico-economic structure which contains the conflict.

G.B. Newe has discussed the relevance to Northern Ireland of the Dutch phenomenon of *verzuiling* or pillarisation, which is based on the view that the national structure is supported by separate pillars (*zuilea*), which are the various blocs in the population.[33] The consequence of this view is that the main denominational and a number of secular groups have established 'an array of organisations encompassing practically every sphere of social and political life, including separate schools and universities, political parties, trade unions, employer associations, newspapers, and radio and television stations'.

There have been other brief studies. The similarities between Northern Ireland and Rhodesia have been described, and there have been comparisons between Switzerland and Ulster, based on some familiarity with the former, but little with the latter.[34] Indeed it is clear that attempts to demonstrate points or ideas from analogous situations are at best difficult and at worst misleading. In a place where social debate really disguises political or cultural gulfs there is an unfortunate tendency to select analogies which confirm prejudices rather than suggest new approaches. An example is in the area of the debate on integrated schools. Extensive use is made by defenders of Catholic schools of Greeley and Rossi's comparisons between American Catholics who were educated in mixed-religious schools and those who were educated in Catholic schools.[35] The comparison is spurious because the term 'Catholic' has completely different implications in America than it has in Ulster, where it has much wider cultural implications. Many would argue that segregation between American blacks and whites would be a more accurate comparative study, since they comprise the two main cultural groups in conflict there.

Treated carefully, however, there can be no doubt that studies of comparative conflicts are not only useful but essential. They can supply international experience for the solution of precise problems, like Fraser's and Lyons' use of American studies on the psychiatric effects of riot situations. They can suggest, and have suggested, institutional and legislative approaches—indeed, some would argue that the failure of some reformist legislation has been caused by insufficient or inaccurate analyses of the situations from which they were borrowed, specifically the transfer of anti-racialist legislation from Great Britain. The publication in 1975 by the Northern Ireland Office of a discussion paper on the government of Northern Ireland, which included an Annex on the experience of other countries with community problems, may be the first indication of a greater willingness to adopt techniques developed by other countries.[36]

Irish Aspects
The Nationalist View

The nationalist view of the Irish problem, which has attracted a considerable number of polemicists, has perhaps been best summarised in the *Handbook of the Ulster Question* published by the Southern Government in 1923 :

Ireland is by natural design a complete geographical entity. This natural design enforced on the political life of Ireland at a very early date the ideal of national unity, and it is doing violence, not only to nature, but to the whole trend of the political life of the island to divorce politically at this late date in her national existence a considerable section of the northern part of the country from the motherland.[37]

In historical terms, it is argued, this natural unity was threatened and finally destroyed as a result of conquest and colonisation. This attempt to subordinate the Irish people to the interests of Britain has been resisted, often by force, since the sixteenth century and before, until the struggle for independence which followed the 1916 rising secured a measure of independence for the greater part of the island. The road to 1916 is paved with the martyrology of Nationalism—O'Neill,

179

Sarsfield, Tone, Pearse—demonstrating that the ideal of national unity was always present, despite hardships and oppression.

The ideal and the struggle still remain. The 1921 settlement was, to nationalists, a betrayal in that it secured the independence of twenty-six of Ireland's thirty-two counties at too high a cost—the abandonment of the other six. Partition was in fact the ultimate gerrymander, the exclusion of an area from national unity, not for geographical, historical, social or even religious reasons, but because it was the largest unit which could be safely controlled by unionists—an infuriating concept, not least because unionists made little or no attempt to pretend otherwise.

Apart from their fundamental antipathy to the existence of Northern Ireland as a contradiction to national unity, nationalists also claim that the Northern government has discriminated against the nationalist minority, both in the institutions created by the new state and by depriving it of social, civil, political and economic rights. But although nationalists campaigned for the removal of these restrictions, supporting civil rights campaigns, many of them did so rather sceptically, believing that as long as the unnatural Northern Ireland unit remained, it would be necessary for the majority to repress the minority. The only solution to the Northern Ireland problem, therefore, would be to dissolve the state of Northern Ireland and unite the two parts of the island.

A number of writers, not all of them unsympathetic to the nationalist cause, have strongly attacked its historical roots. One was Michael Tierney, who wrote :

A very popular way of looking at our history is to conceive of it as having been guided in all its phases by one true doctrine, the doctrine of Nationality, all other explanations being dismissed as abhorrent. This one true doctrine is often believed to be of immortal native origin and is invoked with equal rigour to explain the course of events in the twelfth, seventeenth, or the nineteenth century. Thus construed and invoked, it makes nonsense of a great part of our history; for in this rigid form it is a product of the late eighteenth century and was first popularly preached only a little more than a hundred years ago.[38]

Jack Magee went on to describe how this nationalist view of the past was propagated both inside and outside schools by politicians, many of whom used the medium of history books. 'Nationalist politicians used the past, and the patterns they wove of events which occurred then, as material for speeches, propaganda and political journalism. The result was that Irish history in the popular mind had a single theme—the struggle for independence.'[39] The problem here is that the message which was transmitted was essentially divisive. There were at least two important qualities in this sort of nationalism which effectively excluded the northern Protestant from embracing it. The first was the emphasis on an exclusively Gaelic culture and heritage, best demonstrated by Padraig Pearse's aspiration towards an 'Ireland, not free only but Gaelic as well, not Gaelic only but free as well'—an aspiration which leaves no room for other traditions; the other important component in Irish nationalism has been its close association with the Catholic church. This is not to say that there have not been prominent Protestant nationalists; but, not only has nationalism never been able to boast wide Protestant support, it has never made serious attempts to secure it. In fact, Irish nationalism has been a static creed which leaves little room for serious development. Nationalists have certainly used many arguments, like the commercial and developmental advantages which would follow in a United Ireland, to support their beliefs, but these are really irrelevant to their real motives. The fact is that, if it could be proven that there were no commercial or developmental advantages to be gained by removing the border, nationalists would still remain nationalists. Nationalism is fundamentally an act of faith.

The difficulty with such a stand, of course, is that it limits the means by which one's opponents may be converted. Padraig O Snodaigh attempted to do this by arguing from linguistic evidence that there has always been a Protestant Gaelic culture, but such an approach, whether valid or not, is not likely to win many converts from unionism.[40] The contradiction of nationalism might be compared to a zealous religious sect which has made little or no attempt to convert the infidels. Unionists have tended to be consigned to whatever fate their heresy deserves.

The Unionist View

Unionism as the term is generally recognised today emerged in the late nineteenth century as the organised resistance to the threat of home rule for Ireland. It was firmly based on the intrinsic unity of the British Isles. The New Ulster Movement pointed out in 1972, 'Southerners must face the fact that, to a large majority in Northern Ireland, British nationality seems as natural as the air they breathe'.[41] The introduction of partition was therefore opposed to basic unionist beliefs, and was regarded as secession by the twenty-six counties of southern Ireland. One unionist supporter put it like this: 'The true partitionists are those who would (in a political sense) remove Ulster from what anyone who glances at a map of Europe will recognise as a natural, geographical, social and economic unit, namely the British Isles.'[42]

Just as the new state of Northern Ireland was not of their choosing, but accepted as the lesser of two evils, the alleged repressions in Northern Ireland were nothing more than necessary means of defending it, forced upon unionists by a recalcitrant minority. The nationalist minority in Northern Ireland, unionists argue, refused to accept normal democratic standards like majority rule, and have at times resisted them by force. Given the opportunity, they would overthrow the state. Indeed, Northern Ireland is the only state which permits as the main opposition grouping politicians who are openly traitors. It is in circumstances like these that the majority has attempted to administer and legislate, and it has-been necessary, for government to operate at all, to introduce extraordinary measures. Every government in the world would do the same in similar circumstances. The treasonable views of the opposition justify whatever means are necessary—special legislation, predominantly unionist security organisations and even manipulation of electoral boundaries. Faced with constant intransigence, what were the alternative strategies open to government?

There is no doubt that unionists are much less well served by their apologists than nationalists. Jack Magee attributed this to the superior skill of the nationalist propagandists, but it probably is more closely related to the essentially defensive nature of the unionist case. Unionists are better known for the policies they oppose than for those they advocate. They opposed

182

Home Rule; they opposed the influence of the Catholic church; after partition they opposed unification. These negative qualities imbue their slogans: 'No Popery', 'Not an inch', 'No Surrender'. The reactionary nature of unionism springs from its role in defending the *status quo*—first the Union, then the Northern Ireland state and its institutions. It is noticeable that unionists have been moving towards a more positive viewpoint since partition. The key to this change is contained in one of Lord Brookeborough's statements about the border: 'The border between Northern Ireland and Eire exists because of the ideological gulf which divides the two peoples.'[43] The case on which modern unionism rests is that the Northern Ireland unit —which was opposed in the years preceding the Government of Ireland act, but is now defended with absolute devotion— represents particular values and a culture quite different than those accepted south of the border. Its history, culture, economic structure and general standards of morality mark it out as different from the rest of the island and an intrinsic part of the United Kingdom.

This emphasis on the British connection and on 'British standards' has caused considerable difficulties for some unionists. The growth of local pride—a form of Ulster nationalism —has sometimes become so powerful as to challenge the British nationalism from which it emerged. The difficulty of pinning one's hopes on membership of a nation which might reject them was already evident when the Liberal government introduced a Home Rule Bill in 1910—thus forcing unionists into the prospect of militarily resisting Great Britain in order to remain British. It appeared again after 1969 when the British government threatened such fundamental unionist tenets as Northern Ireland's control of her own security, the independence of her parliament and (so some unionists feared) partition itself. In the face of such threats some unionists— known generally and without apparent irony as Loyalists*— began to consider the possibility of an independent Ulster

* *Punch* magazine expressed some nineteenth-century cynicism about the term:
'Loyal to whom, to what?
to power, to pelf
to place, to privilege, in a word to self.
Those who assume, absorb, control, enjoy all
must find it vastly pleasant to be loyal.'

183

divorced from Britain. Loyalists argue that this is not incompatible with their support of British values, since they conceive such standards to have absolute rather than transitory values. These values, which are undefined but vaguely colonial and strongly Protestant, would be retained in Northern Ireland even if Britain abandons them.

The betrayal of British and traditional unionist values, as seen by Loyalists, has been described by Louis Gardner, at the time a leading member of Vanguard, one of the new loyalist groups: The trouble, he claimed, began with the conciliatory policies introduced by Terence O'Neill in the 1960s, and which were contrary to unionist precepts. He argues that 'Craig and the others were penalised for professing principles which until a few months before were taken for granted by everyone calling himself a Unionist; however moderate, and which are held by most Unionists today.'[44] There can be no doubt that his judgement was correct. O'Neill's proposed changes challenged the basic Unionist deterministic theory that most Catholics were potential or actual traitors and would never rest until the Northern state was overthrown.

The Two Nations Theory

As has been seen, the two major political groupings in Northern Ireland are in basic disagreement about whether they should be part of an all-Ireland unit or an integral part of the United Kingdom. These are political differences, but represent a more fundamental debate about the perceptions which the Irish people have about themselves. Do they have more in common with each other—north and south—than they have points of difference? Or are the differences so great that the two parts could be regarded as in all major characteristics, quite distinct? Are there living in Ireland two separate nations?

The term was first popularised by W.F. Moneypenny, more famed as the biographer of Disraeli, in his book *The Two Irish Nations*, published in 1912. He wrote: 'The Home Rule struggle is a struggle between two nations, the Protestant and the Roman Catholic, or as, to avoid the semblance of ministering to religious bigotry, they had better perhaps be called, the Unionist and the Nationalist.'[45] Having made the point, Moneypenny did not labour it. In fact he went on to stress the common characteristics between his two nations, observing that, despite the differences, 'there is at the bottom a common ground of sympathy and intelligence . . . in the very depths of their antagonism there is something essentially Irish'. The obvious differences between Ulster and the rest of Ireland had been remarked by many earlier commentators like Nassau Senior in 1868, who had found the northern part of Ireland like a different country, 'not merely dissimilar but opposed' to the rest of the island.[46]

Many current advocates of the Two Nations theory argue that these fundamental differences have been reinforced and strengthened by the new institutions and policies developed north and south of the border after partition. Northerners in particular point to the Gaelicisation campaign in the south which attempted to exalt the Irish language by making it compulsory both in schools and for admission into the Irish civil service, and to the prominence of the Catholic church in legislation and the social affairs of the nation. In the latter respect they agree with Father John O'Brien, who said, 'Ireland is a Catholic nation : the activities of the Church and her priests are intertwined with the daily life of the Irish people.'[47] These differences and the fact of fifty years' separate development, they argue, have reduced Moneypenny's 'essential Irishness' to purely superficial dimensions. Estyn Evans summed it up when he wrote that most Northerners, 'while proud to call themselves Irish on St Patrick's day or at Twickenham on the rugby football field, think of themselves first and foremost as British'.[48]

M.W. Heslinga brought a wealth of scholarship to his consideration of the problem and examined the geographical, historical, religious and political settings to determine whether or not the land border in Ireland represents a cultural divide. He found strong arguments in favour of the overall unity of the British Isles, and that the differences between the northern and southern parts of the British Isles are at least as great as those between the land blocs on either side of the Irish sea. Within Ireland the people of the north, despite their obvious conflicts, share 'a sense of regional fellowship, a sense of difference from southerners, that mixture of contempt and defensiveness that is typical of the strongly-marked provincial character'.[49] Heslinga's central point is that, although it is possible to quibble about the precise position of the border, it nevertheless does divide two separate cultures. He concludes that 'the two parts of the Irish border . . . demonstrate that a so-called artificial frontier (line) can be a greater cultural divide than a so-called natural frontier (zone)'.[50]

Institutions and Discord

Surprisingly few of the writers who concerned themselves with the causes of Ulster's conflict have seriously considered the effects of institutions in a polarised community. It is true that a number of authors have discussed the province's public bodies, but mainly as manifestations of a more fundamental and less easily definable conflict. While this is the proper context in which the issue should be considered, one result has been a failure to examine the effect of institutions on the very nature of the Ulster conflict.

Institutions are the grammar of the state. They are the formal arrangement of human conduct, which is essentially informal. Thus the evolution of any police force and of a formal judiciary has its origin in the individual's need for protection, a need which, in less institutionalised circumstances, is satisfied by the strength of his arm. As with language and grammar, the formal arrangements came later, and attempted to impose a pattern on procedures which were spontaneous. The result of this search for formality was not only the rejection of non-conformist values and procedures, but the creation of a new system of norms and values which were rigidly defended. Deviance from these values became unacceptable, and loyalty became directed towards the institutions themselves rather than the principles and rights which they were created to defend. It is for this reason that statutes are so difficult to repeal, no matter how obviously obsolete they may be. The instinct to abandon or change institutions only when their inefficiency or corruption becomes intolerable is based on the fear that the devil one knows is preferable to the devil one does not know—that the removal or radical change of an institution almost invariably means its replacement by another institution.

This law of administrative inertia may have persuaded some people to underestimate the importance of institutions in producing changes. Every institution has been introduced to deal with a particular problem. If the problem is a specific adminis-

186

trative one, like the provision of 2,000 houses or 5,000 school places, the innovation may succeed or be adapted; its success or failure soon becomes evident. But the greater social agencies, like those responsible for education or housing or public welfare, have not such precise objectives. As well as performing administrative functions, their activities may also have important social consequences, some intended and some accidental. It is not easy to control these social effects, and the law of inertia ensures that dysfunctional institutions often are allowed to continue in existence and become an obstacle to the attainment of the objectives which they were introduced to attain. Far from helping the situation, they obscure the problem by coming between it and its solution, thus creating a secondary administrative obstacle which must be removed before the basic issue can be tackled. The trouble is that it is not possible to return to the basic issue simply by abolishing the institution, because its very existence has changed the problem. The League of Nations supplies an analogy : when it collapsed in the 1930s it had already failed in its prime objective of improving international relations. If it had been abolished at that time, no other body could have successfully replaced it without taking into account the League's effect on international relations—both its successes and its failures—because its enterprises had altered both international power balances and the public perception of international agencies. The world problem in 1938 was different, in essence as well as in degree, from that in 1918, and the League itself had contributed to the process. As with the League, so with other institutions; all of them, negatively or positively, alter the problems they were designed to remedy. The greater the change from past practice, and the longer the institution lasts, the more it will redefine and alter the problem.

Northern Ireland's recent experiences amplify the point. It would be foolish and misleading to claim that the community divisions in the province were created by its institutions. In the first place there is ample evidence that these divisions existed before partition was introduced, and that a substantial proportion of the polarisation in the community is voluntary; this is demonstrated by such matters as where people choose to live and where they send their children for schooling. But the development of institutions which were viewed differently by the two communities certainly accelerated and sharpened divisions within Northern Ireland. Before 1921, the Northern problem was generally regarded as part of a wider Irish problem and the conflict between the nationalist and unionist supporters in the province as the greater issue in miniscule—in rather the same way as the troubles in Derry city today are regarded merely as one manifestation of the Ulster problem. After 1921 the problem changed both in its manifestations and in essence. Instead of revolving around such great matters as the ideal of a united Ireland or the British connection, it came to concern such mundane and real issues as attitudes towards the state or the local authority or the 'other sort' within one's own immediate area. Correspondingly it became more bitter. Whether one regarded this development as focusing at last on the 'real' issue of community relations, or as an attempt to avoid the 'real' issue of the Irish problem, there is general acceptance of one point : the new state and its institutions have themselves had important effects on the very nature of the problem.

The most obvious of these effects has been to intensify and institutionalise Northern Ireland's community divisions. The methods of allocating local authority houses in a number of parts of the province have encouraged the tendency towards demographic polarisation; the failure of the two main political groupings to search for common ground has created a tradition of separateness and intransigence which hinders all attempts to create normal political relationships; the separation of primary school children into Catholic and state schools has expanded in the passage of time to include teacher training and secondary education. The continuation and growth of the cultural differences between the two religious communities in Northern Ireland has created a situation where a Protestant's socialisation makes it very difficult for him to even consider voting for an anti-partitionist political party, or for a Catholic to send his children to a non-Catholic school. To make such a break would not only mean defying the instincts which one's cultural community had considered normal; it would also mean, in a more concrete sense, inviting the censure and suspicion of one's own community. While it is easy to point to particular institutions and show how they may have encouraged social divisiveness, the most marked and far-reaching effect of the half century since the Government of Ireland act has certainly been in the way in which its citizens have come to accept the institution of the state itself. Before 1920 there was little enthusiasm anywhere for the proposed new state. To Unionists it was a patched-up settlement which was reluctantly accepted as the best guarantee for the maintenance of the British connection, and their prime loyalty was towards a Great Britain which had threatened to abandon them on a number of occasions during the previous decade. Fifty years have changed this position completely. There is still deep suspicion of the motives of all parties at Westminster; but Protestant nationalism—and this does not refer only to right-wing Unionists—is now primarily attached to the state of Northern Ireland. And while it is true that Northern Ireland has never attracted such support from a substantial minority of its citizens, the fifty years have produced a wide acceptance of the six-county unit, if only because any alternative area would raise even greater conflict. Almost every poll and survey which allows such analysis shows that a considerable number of Catholics have accepted the Northern Ireland state, at least in the short term; Rose's 1968 survey found that 33% of Catholics approved of the constitutional position of Northern Ireland, on balance, and a further 32% did not express an opinion. The *Fortnight* magazine poll of July 1972 revealed that 41% of Catholics would vote against the unification of Ireland, and a further 26% would abstain. None of this is particularly surprising. Any constitutional arrangement which has lasted for half a century is bound to have acquired a degree of *de facto* recognition, even from its most bitter opponents.

If one accepts that institutions have contributed towards the polarisation of Northern Ireland, it is not unreasonable to look towards institutional innovations to erode community divisions and distrust. Few did, however, until the 1960s. Despite Terence O'Neill's frequently expressed concern with the problem of community relations, it was not until 1969 that the first institutional changes were introduced in an attempt to deal with some of the grievances highlighted during the civil rights campaign. Some of these changes—notably the replacement of the corrupt Derry Council by an appointed Development Commission—were intended as temporary measures. Others, however, introduced new institutions which were intended to be permanent. These new institutions were designed either to tackle the problem of community relations or to meet grievances about the fair allocation of public resources. They included a ministry of Community Relations, a Community Relations Commission, a Commissioner for Complaints, a Parliamentary Commissioner for Administration and a Housing Executive which assumed responsibility for the allocation of all public housing including that previously controlled by the local authorities: all these decisions, as well as the replacement of the Special Constabulary by a newly-formed Ulster Defence Regiment, were carried out between 1969 and 1971. The reform of local government was accelerated and the new system came into force in 1973 and, between 1970 and 1975, no fewer than five different governments attempted to establish acceptable constitutional arrangements, without success.

All these changes were inspired by the desire to right inequalities. But the very inequalities which supplied the motivation for change had been in part produced by normal democratic procedures administered in a sectarian manner. Consequently, some of the reforms reflected a distrust of democracy itself. The allocation of public housing, for example, was placed under the control of an appointed central body, the Northern Ireland Housing Executive, which was in turn responsible to the Northern Ireland Ministry of Development; the possibility of local bias was thus removed, but housing allocation passed to the control of bodies which were only indirectly under public scrutiny. When local government was reorganised in 1973 the same trend towards centralisation was marked. Many of the powers which had resided with the local authorities—including education, planning and even control over the raising and collection of rates—were removed or partly removed from them and passed to various ministries. As a result of these developments, some of the sectarian abuses which had caused concern were removed, but they were replaced by a whole series of new procedures which have caused perhaps even greater public concern. The problem of local government discrimination was successfully tackled, but this was only achieved at the price of greatly reduced public control.

190

Whether or not this concern was justified, it is clear that a new problem was created, and that it may amount to an artificial secondary abuse which will make even more difficult the successful solution of basic community divisions. It may have been wiser to retain the old powers of local authorities and to seek means of remedying their defects. At least in that way any solution reached would be based on principles of self-determination and democracy. It is not beyond the realms of possibility that it will yet come to this.

The introduction of the British army in 1969 provides another and more pointed example of an administrative innovation altering the nature of the problem it was designed to remedy. The army was ordered on to the streets to deal with a serious and immediate problem, and with the approval of the Catholic community. The immediate problem was solved, but it is clear that the army presence created new problems which had not existed before. The growth of the Provisional IRA was greatly encouraged by the physical presence of the traditional enemy in the streets. Certainly many of the people who had initially welcomed the soldiers came to regard them with hatred and suspicion, and to see their removal as a prerequisite for any solution. Bernadette Devlin's dry comment in August 1969, 'You're giving them tea now. What will you be giving them in six months?', was to prove ominously true. This is not to argue that the decision to send in the army was, in retrospect, a wrong one; it could be argued that it was the least unattractive alternative open to government at the time. But it suggests that the decision was taken without sufficient consideration being given to the long-term effects of the move, and consequently that insufficient thought was applied to finding means of countering these effects. The general point, of course, is that institutions and procedures hurriedly introduced to deal with some manifestation of a problem may have the real effect of broadening and deepening the problem itself.

Northern Ireland's first institutions directly aimed at improving community relations were introduced in 1969 and soon ran into difficulties. In that year a ministry of Community Relations was created, and later a Community Relations Commission. Since the ministry became exclusively involved in the provision of grants—mainly for the administration of the Social

191

Needs act and the construction of community centres, which were certainly seriously lacking in the province—it was not seen to perform any unique function which could not be easily carried out by another ministry. As the smallest ministry in Northern Ireland it appears to have carried little weight in cabinet; consequently the government's commitment to the problem of community relations was queried by many of its critics. The reaction of the Northern Ireland Executive to such criticism was to discover other tasks for the ministry, or department, as it came to be called. The provision of sport and recreational facilities was transferred from the department of Education for no very obvious reason. These new responsibilities were undoubtedly very important ones, but hardly provided the sort of radical innovative policy which many had hoped for.

In addition to the ministry, an independent Community Relations Commission was established to advise government and to seek more radical approaches to the community problems which were peculiar to Northern Ireland; in the event, the Commission was never consulted for advice on any legislative proposal by the Stormont government and all its recommendations were rejected or ignored. The independence too was soon seen to be illusory. Although the Commission was allowed to determine its own strategies, it had no control over the resources required to implement them. Expenditures exceeding £500 required the approval of the ministry of Community Relations, a situation which provided the ministry with both the power of rejection and the more subtle, and perhaps more pervasive, power of deterrent—that is, the failure by the Commission to propose schemes because they were likely to be rejected by the ministry. As a result, after five years of operation, the Commission's field staff amounted to only sixteen people, its first chairman and director had both resigned in frustration and relations between Commission and department had steadily deteriorated.[51] In October 1974 it was abolished, to be followed within months by the department of Community Relations whose functions returned to the other government departments from whence they had come.

Events subsequent to the 1969–72 reforms clearly demonstrate their failure to reduce the level of violence in Northern Ireland, far less to provide a springboard for healing the

192

deeper community discord. Apart from observing that institutional reforms introduced at the time of escalating violence are unlikely to have any effect on public attitudes, there appear to have been two main reasons for their failure. The first was their refusal to accept that the Ulster problem was a comprehensive one and could not be approached by random tinkering with a few institutions; and the second was that they were implemented without real public participation and support.

The very longevity of the Irish problem suggests that no interim and unco-ordinated initiatives are likely to dent its fundamental conflicts, but the initiatives so far introduced have been short-term and unco-ordinated. Whatever the achievements of the ministry of Community Relations, its establishment supported the view that the problem of community relations could be compartmentalised within one department. Instead of recognising that it was a central problem of government, which ought to be a consideration in almost every decision taken by every department, it allowed other ministries to avoid tackling the issue on the grounds that there was a specific ministry to deal with it. The Incitement to Hatred act and the office of Commissioner for Complaints were also peripheral changes, directed at penalising malpractices rather than tackling their more fundamental causes. Indeed, the Northern Ireland Community Relations Commission was the only institution with sufficiently broad terms of reference to examine basic community conflicts. Its unfortunate history and rapid demise should not disguise the need for an independent institution which would have both the authority and the resources to approach community relations problems on a wide front.

The other reason for the failure of institutional reform in Northern Ireland has been the failure of the decision-makers to involve the community in their decisions. The reforms carried out since 1969 may have been well-intentioned but, far from establishing greater democratic control, some of them have considerably reduced the popular voice in decision-making. This is particularly the case in the introduction of a central Housing Executive and in the greatly increased central control of local government. Most important of all, the failure of Northern Ireland's politicians to agree on even the framework of their government led in 1972 to the prorogation of Northern

Ireland's legislature and executive, and to the introduction of direct rule from Westminster. Each of these developments further removed the decision-making processes from the people in the communities and inevitably produced a paternalistic style of administration. Increasingly the criteria for innovations became liberal values rather than democratic agreements. Consequently, many of the reforms were rejected. The Hunt proposals, for example, suggested changes in the Royal Ulster Constabulary which were regarded as eminently fair in Britain, but came nowhere near to satisfying Nationalist suspicions nor to securing the return of the police to minority areas. The fall of the power-sharing Executive in 1974 as a result of a political strike remains perhaps the prime example of how dependent are successful political initiatives in Northern Ireland on grassroots loyalist approval. If nothing else, the events of the early 1970s have demonstrated that the main determinants of change in Northern Ireland have been the local communities, not politicians or planners.

Evaluation

The importance of considering analyses and theories about the Northern problem is that they determine, whether or not the legislator or administrator is conscious of it, what policies are introduced to deal with it. Even in a conflict situation as dynamic as Northern Ireland's where policy appears at times to be mere reaction to external phenomena, the way in which the administrator or legislator looks upon the conflict will determine whether he will advocate the introduction of more soldiers or more factories or a charter of human rights.

There has been a plethora of analyses and policies directed towards the solution of the Northern Problem since 1969. A number of voluntary organisations, notably Protestant and Catholic Encounter (PACE), have adopted a basically ethnic interpretation and have offered themselves as centres for Catholics and Protestants to meet and work towards reconciliation between the two communities;[52] some of these organisations have experienced great difficulty in securing the interest and participation of working class people. A broadly ethnic/racial approach has also guided much of the legislative innovation which has taken place since 1969 and British anti-racial legis-

194

lation has on occasions been adopted in Northern Ireland with virtually no alterations, notably in the cases of the Incitement to Hatred act and the Community Relations act. On the other hand, the new institutions of the Ministry of Community Relations and the Commissioner for Complaints appear to have been based on the belief that the overt conflict since 1968 arose from maladministration of a system which was basically sound, but required the removal of some discrepancies such as discrimination by local authorities; the corollary of this liberal analysis is that the conflict, and perhaps even the problem, will disappear when these abuses are removed.

Perhaps the most pervasive influence of all on the formation of policy has been the hope that the proven correlation between deprivation and discontent is the essential key to the Ulster solution and that the injection of massive resources will be sufficient to improve community relations in the province. This rather vague liberal analysis is often simplified into the phrase, 'there's nothing wrong in Northern Ireland that 20,000 jobs wouldn't put right'. The evidence quoted in support of this approach was the stability of Northern Ireland during the relatively prosperous war and post-war years, but this argument received a severe knock when the events following 1969 revealed that the old divides had been lurking close to the surface and re-emerged in all too familiar forms. However, as long as it is recognised that there are aspects of the Northern problem which cannot be explained in economic terms—these aspects have been called the 'unreal' problems—such an approach has much to commend it. If it is accepted that the formation of a united working class is a desirable objective, then efforts could be directed towards the creation of a social structure similar to that in most western countries, where the main conflicts are between social classes. At least, if this strategy succeeded, the conflict would have been diverted into areas which were familiar and which most democracies could contain with relative ease—rather like injecting a smallpox victim with cowpox because physicians knew how to treat the lesser complaint.

All of these approaches assume that community integration is a desirable objective. It has been argued, however, that this assumption flies in the face of the evidence, that the polarisation of the communities is comprehensive and that this

195

should be recognised by the creation of separate institutions for Catholics and Protestants. Certainly this would offer a number of answers to apparently insoluble difficulties. The problem of policing for example, might be more easily resolved, and the allocation of public resources, always a key issue in the dispute, would be removed at a stroke from the field of community disharmony and dispute. Indeed to carry this analysis to its logical conclusion is to argue that the search for an integrated society is a barrier to any settlement and should be immediately abandoned. To adapt a Cypriot analogy, the two communities are like two scorpions in a bottle. If you cannot persuade them to mate, it is better to recognise the fact and look around for a second bottle.

The difficulty lies in determining at what point the mating attempts should be abandoned. It cannot be argued that integrative policies have failed in Northern Ireland, because they have never been systematically introduced. To opt for a segregationist policy before all others have been attempted is virtually to rule out the possibility of integration in the future. Not only would the separate institutions formalise existing community divisions and create new ones, they would be virtually impossible to remove. It is for these reasons that acceptance of community polarisation and the introduction of appropriate institutions is a final option, only to be attempted when all others have failed. Nevertheless, it is foolish to ignore the possibility that the desire for an integrated community and the need for popular support for it may be mutually exclusive aspirations.

Whatever the values of the various theories about the conflict the one factor which emerges with greatest force is its Ulster character. Clearly it is also an Irish problem and a British problem, but its roots lie in the social, economic, cultural and geographical structure of Northern Ireland. Whatever political formulae are introduced to reduce its violent manifestations—whether a united Ireland, or union with Great Britain, or an independent Ulster—a peculiarly local conflict will still continue. Consequently, any theory which is not based on a painstaking analysis of the Ulster background—and this includes an historical analysis—cannot hope to understand either the nuances or the essence of the problem. This applies to decision-makers as well as to researchers. Comparative studies and general theories of conflict are useful for providing insights. But it is noticeable that those researchers who approached the Northern problem from the basis of a more general theoretical background and who also took the trouble to examine the background to the problem in detail invariably were forced to make major readjustments to their original premises. Northern Ireland is at least as remarkable for its peculiarities as for its general characteristics.

Bibliography:
Conflict in Ireland

THIS bibliography contains two main parts. The list of sources towards its end is an attempt to record, without comment, the fast growing mass of literature relating to the Irish problem; it includes books, articles, as well as both published and unpublished papers. Where it appeared appropriate some undergraduate dissertations have been included, and these are clearly indicated in the list of sources. Because more than 500 sources are listed, the earlier part of the bibliography attempts to select a representative variety of publications which are most likely to lead to an understanding of the Northern Ireland problem. This selection is, of course, a subjective one, and has been arranged to correspond with the appropriate chapters.

There is also a list of publications which regularly deal with Irish affairs, and a selection of relevant government publications.

Background
A number of bibliographies of the Irish problem have been printed recently, and provide a useful starting point for serious researchers. The most comprehensive is by Richard Rose in *Political Studies* (1972) although T. Moody's summary of *Irish Historiography* (1971) also covers the period 1936–70. For earlier periods J. Carty's two *Bibliographies of Irish history* (1936 and 1940) cover the period 1870 to 1921, and E. Johnston's select *Bibliography of Irish History* (1969) is an essential reference work for historians. More recent publications are discussed in R. Scott's *Revolution in Northern Ireland* (1971) and in the July 1972 issue of the *Campaign Newsletter* of the Campaign for Social Justice in Northern Ireland. Useful bibliographical information is also contained in an article in *Political Quarterly*

by Cornelius O'Leary (1971) and in Martin Wallace's *Northern Ireland* (1971). The Institute of Irish Studies at Queen's University Belfast has published a list of *Theses relating to Ireland* (1968) and the Northern Ireland Community Relations Commission a *Register of completed and on-going research into the Irish conflict* (1972).

All students of Northern Ireland affairs must lean heavily on the three daily newspapers which are published in the province. The *Belfast Newsletter* presents the news from a basically Unionist standpoint, while the *Irish News* caters for the anti-partitionist minority; if the number of attacks from both sides is anything to go by, the *Belfast Telegraph* treads a middle path and is the only evening paper. The *Irish Times* although printed in Dublin, carries a great deal of Ulster news, and is highly recommended for reliable information and perhaps more astute comment than any of the other three. Of the British papers, the *Guardian, Times* and *Sunday Times* cover Irish news most diligently. *Fortnight*, a liberal magazine which has a useful chronological summary in each issue, is also highly recommended. All these publications are easily obtainable. The problem for the modern researcher is the mass of political literature which has sprung up, especially since 1968, much of it ephemeral. Publications are produced by, among others, the Unionist and Alliance parties, Republican Clubs, the People's Democracy, the Northern Ireland Civil Rights Association and some of its branches, the Ulster Defence Association, Ulster Vanguard and the Free Presbyterians. G. Smith has discussed some documentary sources in the *Journal of Librarianship* (1971), and J. Gracey and P. Howard in the first issue of *Irish Booklore* (1971) which always contains interesting bibliographical information.

History

Since Irish historiography is experiencing a renaissance which appears to be totally unrelated to the present troubles, it is becoming more difficult to shortlist for the general reader. Two books are, however, particularly highly recommended—J.C. Beckett's *The Making of Modern Ireland* (1966) and F.S.L. Lyons' *Ireland Since the Famine* (1971). R. Dudley Edwards has recently written *A New History of Ireland* (1972) which is sound but rather short. An extremely bright and readable publication, aimed primarily at schools, is the three volume *History of Ireland* (1969) edited by Margaret MacCurtain, and the two booklets entitled *Ulster since 1800*, edited by T.W. Moody and J.C. Beckett in 1954 and 1957 are still admirable, if increasingly difficult to find; the eleven-volume *Gill History of Ireland* (1972–75) is also first rate. From the numerous other historical works published, three are particularly recommended for stimulation and interest. They are: A.T.Q. Stewart's *The Ulster Crisis* (1967), Robert Kee's *The Green Flag* (1972), which has an admirable bibliography, and E. Strauss's *Irish Nationalism and British democracy* (1951).

Three collections of essays also provide useful background reading. T. Moody and F. Martin's *Course of Irish History* (1967) and K. Nowlan and T. Williams's *Ireland in the war years and after* (1969) are rather mixed in quality, but the *Irish Parliamentary Tradition* (1973) edited by B. Farrell, maintains a very high standard. *The Ulster debate*, published by the Institute for the study of Conflict in 1972, is unlikely to be of lasting use, although some essays in it are interesting.

There are a number of books which help to explain the background to and course of the present troubles in the province. D. Barritt and C. Carter's *Northern Ireland problem* (1962) was the first and is still one of the best. Martin Wallace's *Northern Ireland* (1971) is very reliable and balanced, as is R. Lawrence's *Government of Northern Ireland* (1965) which considers London-Belfast relations. The largest survey conducted in Northern Ireland is described in *Governing without Consensus* (1971) by Richard Rose, while Basil Chubb's *Government and Politics of Ireland* (1970) is a useful introduction to affairs south of the border. Nevertheless it is likely that *Divided Ulster* (1970) by Liam de Paor will turn out to be the most original of all the recent publications on the background to the troubles. De Paor apportions a lot of the blame for the Northern Ireland problem to the Unionist party, as do a number of recent contributors, such as Desmond Greaves (1972), T.P. Coogan (1966) and, less emotionally but with greater insight, Nicholas Mansergh (1936). But the Unionists have had their apologists too, particularly Sir Douglas Savory (1958) and Hugh Shearman (1971). T. Wilson's *Ulster under Home Rule*

(1955) is also sympathetic to the regime. However both extreme wings are not well served by their apologists, although Louis Gardner's *Resurgence of the majority* (1971) is a good expression of right-wing unionism, and the Provisional IRA has produced its version of recent history in *Freedom struggle* (1973), a polemical and scrappy publication.

It is hardly surprising that the troubles of the last few years have encouraged a remarkable upsurge in the number of books published about them. It will be some years before a measured assessment of these books is possible, but some have clearly added to an understanding of the situation. The *Sunday Times* Insight team's *Ulster* (1972) throws new light on the formation of the Provisional IRA, and Elliot and Hickie's *Ulster* (1971) approaches the problem from a conflict theory angle. The publications by O. Dudley Edwards (*The sins of our fathers*), A. Boyd (*Holy war in Belfast*), M. Wallace (*Guns and Drums*) and M. Hastings (*Ulster 1969*) all have considerable interest despite their publication so close to the actual events. R. Riddell's *Fire over Ulster* (1970) is idiosyncratic and B. Devlin's *The Price of my Soul* (1969) subjective. B. Egan and V. McCormack's *Burntollet* (1969) and Sean O Fearghall's *Law(?) and Orders* (1970) are interesting narratives of particular episodes.

Very little has been published from sources close to the government, but the reports published from the Northern Ireland Stationery Office are very useful, especially the *Cameron Report* (1969) which attempted an analysis of the roots of the problem. The views of Terence O'Neill are the subject of two books (1969 and 1972) but it is clear from James Callaghan's *A House Divided* (1973) that the British Home Secretary was much more aware of what was happening than the Northern Ireland Prime Minister.

Finally, two pamphlets are particularly recommended for anyone who has only rudimentary knowledge of the situation in Northern Ireland and requires a brief but accurate introduction. These are H. Jackson's *The Two Irelands* (1971) and the Northern Friends' Peace Board's *Orange and Green* (1969).

Demography
The most stimulating and far-reaching research into the

201

Northern Ireland problem in recent years has been concerned with demographic and population problems. There is no doubt that this situation is partly due to the energy and enterprise of the Geography department at Queen's University, Belfast. Academics like Emrys Jones, Estyn Evans, and Fred Boal have provided the impetus. Evans has written a number of books related to the interaction of geography and the people of Ireland, and Jones's *Social Geography of Belfast* (1960) establishes a base on which many others have built. Two other recent books on Belfast deserve mention: Budge and O'Leary's *Belfast—approach to Crisis* (1973) describes an interesting period in the city's evolution, and the collection of essays entitled *Belfast* (1967) edited by J.C. Beckett and Robin Glasscock, is the most up-to-date description of its birth and growth. Fred Boal's various publications provide the best insights into its urban problems.

The demographic pattern outside Belfast has been less fully described. Tom Hadden's article on *Interlocking Ulstermen* (1972) is an interesting short introduction, and John Macrae's *Polarisation* (1966) was one of the earliest studies of small towns in the province. Rosemary Harris's *Prejudice and tolerance in Ulster* (1972) looks in detail at a small village community, and theses by T. Kirk (1967), A. Robinson (1967), W. Rooney (1965) throw considerable light on population patterns and interaction respectively in Lurgan, Derry, Newcastle and Cullybackey. It is important to add that the published material is strongly underpinned by detailed studies like Carleton's *The growth of south Belfast* (1964) and by a large number of local studies in the form of dissertations (see for example, E. Crilly (1959), F. Mercer (1971), M. Neill (1971) and A. Williamson (1970). In this respect the Geography department has succeeded in marrying the work of its students and the research interests of its staff.

The question of religion and demographic behaviour in Ireland is intelligently discussed by Brenda Walsh in two publications for the Economic and Social Research Institute (1968 and 1970). Emigration and immigration, two vital factors in determining the population structure in Ireland, are naturally considered in these papers. Three other publications are more directly concerned with migration; they are *Internal migration in Ireland* (1970) by R. Geary and J. Hughes, *Emigration and demographic change in Ireland* (1961–62) by S. Cousins and *Irish seasonal migration* (1942) by B. Kerr.

The periodic outbursts of violence and intimidation since the eighteenth century have been a major factor in determining where people have chosen to live. Andy Boyd's *Holy War in Belfast* (1969) documents some of these outbreaks but, apart from official reports like that into the 1854 riots, none of them have been closely examined until 1969. M. Poole and E. Stewart conducted separate enquiries into the enforced movement of families during that year, and a research unit of the Northern Ireland Community Relations Commission carried out a similar investigation into the movements, following the introduction of internment in 1971. The problem was researched in more detail by John Darby and Geoffrey Morris in 1973, and a report published entitled *Intimidation in housing* (1974). Clearly, the consequences of these movements will be the subject of further research studies in the future.

The State and State Institutions

It is certain that no aspect of the debate on the Northern Ireland situation has produced more writing and controversy than that dealing with the machinery and offices of the state. The trouble is that much of it is uninformed, some of it polemical and little of it contains acceptable data. There are very few government publications to help clarify the situation, although some of the reports commissioned since 1969 and the *Annual Reports* of the Commissioner for Complaints, both published by the Stationery Office in Belfast, do provide useful information. This can be supplemented by recent general publications—for example, those of Martin Wallace (1971), D. Barritt and C. Carter (1962), Liam de Paor (1970) and Richard Rose (1971) —since most of them consider the allegations levelled at the government, local authorities, police, the law courts and, since 1969, the security forces.

The events of the last few years in Northern Ireland, with considerable increases in both the extent of violence and the number of arrests and detentions related to terrorist activities, have focused a lot more attention on the prosecution and administration of law and order. No authoritative book has yet been written on the Royal Ulster Constabulary, but a number of papers and articles have been published on the subject. Kevin Boyle, who is compiling a history of policing in Ireland, has written articles on the history of the force, and on the possibilities for its future (1970). J. Tobias also adopts a historical approach (1970) as does G. Dobbie, whose paper highlights the dual role of the force, *Protectors and Partisans* (1971). An investigation by B. White into the state of the police was printed in the *Belfast Telegraph* in September 1973. A. Peacock, former Inspector General of the force has written a defence of the force's record entitled *The Royal Ulster Constabulary* (1970). The *Black paper* (1973), published by the Central Citizen's Defence Committee, is an attack on the force's record both before and after the Hunt reforms. It perhaps goes without saying that the *Hunt report* (1969) on the police and the *Cameron report* (1969) on civil disturbances are essential reading for an understanding of the bitterness aroused in the province when policing is discussed. James Callaghan's narrative of his role as Home Secretary, *A House Divided* (1973), sketches the background to the commissioning and publication of these reports. Callaghan's book is also important for its references to a report carried out for him by D. Osmond and R. Mark into the RUC which has not been published elsewhere. Finally, Catholics attitudes towards policing are described in a survey conducted for the *Andersonstown News* in July 1973, and G. Boehringer has a number of interesting observations on the future of the force in *The future of policing in Northern Ireland* (1973).

Two publications which eulogise the 'B' Specials are A. Hazlett's *The Fermanagh B Specials* (1972) and M. Dane's paper with the same title (1970). Neither deals seriously with the allegations levelled against the force.

The role of the army has aroused considerable controversy since its arrival in 1969, and publications are beginning to appear. D. Kennally and E. Preston's *Belfast August 1969* (1971) and a thesis by P. Pistoi (1972) are critical of the army's actions following the introduction of internment, and Rona Fields chronicles a number of case studies in her scrappy and declamatory *A Society on the run* (1973). D. Barzilay's *The British Army in Ulster* (1973) is generally sympathetic towards the army, as is *Four months in Winter* (1972) by the same author. The strategic problems posed by the campaign are the subject of books by F. Kitson (1971) and R. Clutterbuck (1973). A number of publications consider the Special Powers act and the general question of extra-ordinary legislation. These include Harry Calvert's *Constitutional Law in Northern Ireland* (1968) and F. Newark's *Devolution in Government* (1953) both written by academic lawyers. The National Council for Civil Liberties published an important attack on the Special Powers act in 1936. Cedric Thornberry has written a valuable article on *International Law and emergency situations* (1973), and *Emergency powers: a fresh start* (1972), compiled by an informal and anonymous group based in Queen's University Belfast, identifies the local difficulties and suggests some remedies. Regarding the actual operation of justice in the province, allegations of bias against Catholics in the courts have been made by Kevin Boyle and Denis Faul, and discussed in two newspaper articles by E. Curran (1971) and S. Riley (1972). The most up to date publications on the administration of justice are Tom Hadden and Paddy Hillyard's *Justice in Northern Ireland* (1973) and *Law and State: the Case of Northern Ireland* by the same authors and Kevin Boyle (1975). A substantial amount of evidence confirming discrimination by local authorities was accepted by the Cameron commission and some of it appears in the *Cameron Report* (1969). Further data has been printed elsewhere. *Fermanagh facts* (1969) compiled by the Fermanagh Civil Rights Association, is a particularly comprehensive collection of evidence, but A. Corrigan's *Eyewitness in Northern Ireland* (1969), the other main collection of material, is less convincingly researched and presented. *Housing in Northern Ireland* (1972) written by Derek Birrell et al., also cites instances of discrimination by local authorities. Here more than anywhere else it is essential for the serious researcher to study *Hansard*, since many of the allegations of discrimination by local authorities were made and answered there. Finally allegations have also been made of discrimination in the employment of Catholics in the Northern Ireland civil service. Barritt and Carter discuss this charge, and their findings should be supplemented by reading *The Northern Ireland Civil Service* (1973) by David Donnison, *The Press notice* (1973) from the

Northern Ireland Office in response to it, and Michael Mc-Keown's *Civil Service discrimination* (1973).

Politics

There is a serious dearth of literature and reliable research relating to politics in Northern Ireland which is perhaps related to the lack of basic data. For example, there was no reliable information on election results for the Northern Ireland parliament until Sidney Elliott's very useful *Northern Ireland election results 1921–1972* in 1973. Similarly with local government elections : until Knight and Baxter-Moore's *Elections of the twenties* (1971) no serious work had been carried out in this field. The authors of both these works have also had analyses published of the 1973 Assembly and local government elections respectively, and there are a few studies of particular elections, like F. Boal and R. Buchanan's article on *The 1969 Stormont election* (1969). To these sources should be added P. McGill's thesis on the Northern Ireland Senate (1965) and A.G. Donaldson's article on the same subject (1958).

Some surveys could be used to supplement these meagre offerings. R. Jenkins and J. Macrae's *Polarisation* study in 1966 has considerable political content, as does the *Belfast Telegraph* poll of 1968. Both Richard Rose's *Governing without consensus* (1971) and R. Elliot and J. Hickie's *Ulster—A Case Study in Conflict Theory* (1971) are based on surveys, although they differ in extent and depth. It is interesting to compare the survey of voters conducted by *Fortnight* magazine in July 1972 with the results of the 1973 Assembly elections, even if it only serves to throw doubts on the validity of everything which has been written in this paragraph and on the value of polls as indicators of electoral intentions.

The Unionist, Alliance and Northern Ireland Labour parties all issue their own publications with some regularity. The Unionists have been the most dependable in producing publications, issuing a regular *Unionist Review* and occasionally papers from their research department, papers which have so far not been remarkable for depth or originality. The Alliance party also publishes a regular publication *Alliance Bulletin*, which is well presented and informative. The Northern Ireland Labour party publishes less frequently and more irregularly, and the Social and Democratic Labour party have so far produced very little. Apart from occasional papers from Vanguard, which appear to have dried up since 1971, and privately published political pamphlets, like those of C. Smyth, the other local parties are inactive. It is difficult to know whether to categorise Ian Paisley's *Protestant Telegraph* as a political or a religious paper; it contains material in each sphere, and quite a lot in both. All the parties, at least all those who boast permanent addresses, will supply policy manifestos on request.

Regarding the parties themselves, the books by Martin Wallace (1971) and D. Barritt and C. Carter (1962) provide short introductions. J. Sayers has written a valuable article on the *Political parties and the social background* (1955). The Unionist party is best served by detailed studies: D. Savage (1961) and J. Boyle (1962) have both written admirable studies of the early years of Unionism, and St John Ervine's *Craigavon, Ulsterman* (1949) deals effectively with the party's middle years. The publication in 1973 of *The Ulster Unionist party* by John Harbinson has at last provided a standard reference book. Two theses for the Political Science Department at Queen's University, Belfast deal with the *Northern Ireland Labour Party* from 1884 to 1967; John Harbinson (1966) covers the period up to 1949 and J. Graham (1973) the period following that date, publishing a shortened version of his work in *The Irish Press* (1971). The problems of the centre parties were discussed in 1972 by Erskine Holmes in *A Centre Party Coalition Government*, problems which increased considerably after their poor showing in the elections of that year. Not surprisingly very little has been written about the new parties—Alliance, the Social Democratic and Labour party and the right-wing unionist groupings; they have not been in existence for long enough. But the real surprise is the dearth of material on the Nationalist and Republican parties. The reason may well be related to the absence of formal organisation for which both parties were renowned. Whatever the reason, researchers will be forced either to rely on newspaper articles and the publications of pressure groups close to the nationalists and republicans, or to produce themselves the underpinning research on which more general studies might be based. Books like Tim Pat Coogan's *The I.R.A.* (1970), Bowyer Bell's *The Secret Army* (1970) and the *Sunday Times* Insight team's *Ulster* (1973) provide a fairly comprehensive history of the IRA; the publications of People's Democracy, the Northern Ireland Civil Rights Association and the Central Citizens' Defence Committee express various Catholic viewpoints, but the virtual absence of reliable information about constitutional anti-partitionist activities remains the most serious research gap in this field.

The Churches

Considering the frequency with which religion and the churches have been charged with contributing towards community divisions in Northern Ireland, surprisingly little research has been conducted into their role and influence. John Whyte's *Church and State in Modern Ireland* (1971) is primarily concerned with the relations between the Catholic church and the government of Southern Ireland, but is by far the outstanding work in the field. *Irish Anglicanism* (1970) edited by M. Hurley, is the most substantial book on a Protestant church which has appeared recently, and *The development of Methodism in Ireland* was described in an unpublished thesis in 1964. Another relevant thesis by A. Megahey looks at the part played by *The Irish Protestant churches in social and political issues between 1870 and 1914* (1969).

As usual, however, it is difficult to find reliable data on which intelligent discussion might be based. *The Irish Ecclesiastical Record* is the best guide to thinking by the Catholic hierarchy, but only appears annually; many of the Catholic dioceses also publish annual directories. The Church of Ireland has two annual publications—*The Journal of its General Synod* and the *Annual Report* laid before the General Synod. The Presbyterian Church annually publishes the *Reports to the General Assembly* and the *Minutes of the General Assembly*. Apart from these, the Anglicans publish the weekly *Church of Ireland Gazette*, and the Presbyterians the *Presbyterian Herald*; there is no equivalent locally published Catholic newspaper. An interesting and unrestrained insight into evangelical Protestantism can be gained from the *Ulster Protestant* and Dr Ian Paisley's weekly *Protestant Telegraph*. These publications can be supplemented by four independent studies: the title of Brendan Walsh's *Religion and demography in Ireland* (1970) is self-explanatory; John Greer's *A Questioning Generation* (1972) is a report on the attitudes of pupils to Religious teaching; the two surveys conducted by the *Independent Television Authority* (1970) and *Opinion Research Centre* (1970) are examinations into religious attitudes in the province, and the former compares these with British attitudes. A number of theses and dissertations—for example, those by E. Turner .(1970), E. O'Neill (1967) and V. McCormack (1970)—have also investigated the relationship between religious attitudes and prejudice. Considering that some of these found a positive connection between strength of religious feeling and prejudice, it is surprising that the churches themselves have not encouraged research into the problem. Some understanding of the strong reactions which greet any attack on the part played by the churches in Northern Ireland's sectarian conflict can be gathered by reading the New Ulster Movement's pamphlet *Tribalism or Christianity in Ireland* (1973) and the public controversy which preceded and followed it in the local newspapers. Clifford Longley's article in *The Times* (1972) is an astute discussion of the problem, and some more general books devote considerable attention to the Northern Ireland churches. These include Martin Wallace's *Northern Ireland* (1971), Richard Rose's *Governing without consensus* (1971), D. Barritt and C. Carter's *Northern Ireland problem* (1962) and Owen Dudley Edwards' *The sins of our fathers* (1970). In 1973 there was considerable concern expressed at the annual meeting of the World Council of Churches about the failure of the churches to come to terms with the peculiar problems in Ireland, and it is likely that the Irish churches will soon initiate research into such matters as the problem of mixed marriages.

The Schools
More serious research activity has been evident in the field of Irish education than in almost any other area, but many of the products of this research have been detailed and specialised. Don Akenson's *Enmity and Education* (1973), with its excellent bibliographical chapter, is certainly the main work on the subject, although his other book and those of T. McElligott (1966) and N. Atkinson (1969) are also useful. A number of more general books—notably R. Lawrence's *The Government of*

Northern Ireland (1965), M. Wallace's *Northern Ireland* (1971) and the Open University's *Education in Great Britain and Ireland* (1973) have sound sections on the subject for anyone requiring a shorter introduction on the subject. *The Education Times* and, to a lesser degree, the *Times Education Supplement* contain articles of interest to Irish educationalists, and the Northern Ireland Council for Educational Research publishes papers on the subject, including two registers of research in education. The two main teachers' unions, the Irish National Teachers' Organisation (INTO), the Ulster Teachers' Union (UTU) and the National Association of Schoolmasters (NAS) all produce magazines. *Northern Teacher* jointly produced by the INTO and UTU is by far the best. The Marquess of Londonderry describes the thinking behind the 1921 Education act in *Public Education in Northern Ireland* (1924), but many of the other descriptions of the new system are frankly partisan. W. Corkey's *Episode in the history of Protestant Ulster* (undated) presents the Protestant view, as do the relevant sections of *Orangeism* (1967) by M. Dewar *et al.* *Aspects of Catholic Education* (1971) is an intelligent defence of Catholic schools, and Cardinal Conway has also written a pamphlet on *Catholic schools* (1971). J. Campbell's *Catholic Schools* (1964) describes a survey on the same problem. Queen's University Belfast has produced a number of theses and dissertations which concentrate on more detailed aspects of education in the province; among these are unpublished works by E. Holmes (1968), V. McCormack (1970), E. Knox (undated), J. Graham (undated), N. Ross (1969), J. Salters 1970), W. Spense (1959), E. Turner (1970) and A. Webb (undated), and to these should be added D. Miller's *Paper to the American Historical Association* (1969), P.J. McCormack's *Youth in Derry* (1972) and G. Dent's thesis at the University of London (1965). Some of these papers deserve a much wider publication.

The publications of the Northern Ireland Ministry of Education are printed by the Stationery Office in Belfast. Apart from papers on particular subjects, like *The Burgess Report on Secondary Education* (1973), the ministry publishes an *Annual Report* and *Education Statistics* twice a year. Unfortunately many of the ministry's early publications are out of print, and the *Education Statistics*, though useful, do not contain much data which would be an aid to the current public debates on integrated and comprehensive education.

The concentration among educational researchers on curricular influences within schools may be partly caused by the difficulty of investigating more subtle influences, such as those of school systems and teachers' backgrounds. Whatever the reason, a number of empirical and discoursive studies, which are summarised by the author in *Divisiveness in Education* (1973), have been published. John Magee's paper on *The teaching of Irish History* (1969) is highly recommended, and other articles by Lorna Hadkins (1971) and Alan Robinson (1971) are also concerned with the effects of history teaching in Ireland. James Russell's paper on *Civic Education* (1972) contains useful data, as does John Greer's booklet on sixth-form religion (1972). *Practice 73* from Queen's University Education department, is an interesting description of a project in Anglo-Irish literature in a Protestant grammar school. The teaching materials produced by John Malone's *School Project in Community relations* (1971) were the first attempt to remedy the defects which were revealed in some of these other studies, and J. McCormick's *Ulster in your hands* (1971) is another attempt to encourage a broader approach to educational problems.

The debate on integrated education has so far benefited little from the energies of researchers. M. Dallat and W. Moles debate the issue in *Community Forum* (1972) and E. McEldowney's description of *The Vere Foster Affair* (1971) demonstrates some of the problems involved. Apart from these, there are only descriptions of personal experiences, like those of Edward Curran (1971), Bernadette Devlin (1969) and Robert Harbinson (1960). While these help to transmit personal reactions to segregated schooling it is impossible not to agree with the first annual report of the Community Relations Commission that one of the few undisputed facts about integrated education was the need for more research on the problem.

Voluntary Segregation

However much one demonstrates the pressures which force the two cultural communities in Northern Ireland apart, there is evidence that voluntary choice also plays a part. The evidence is by no means overwhelming, but is certainly sufficient to invoke more comprehensive investigation. Fred Boal's research in the Falls-Shankill area of Belfast (1969) reveals that the segregation in housing in the area also extends to such mundane matters as visiting patterns, shopping habits, choice of newspaper and selection of marriage partners; it is interesting to point out that he found segregation of a comparable level, this time on a class level rather than a religious basis, in two Protestant parts of the city. A dissertation by Susan Starling on *The Sociology of Voluntary Organisations in Belfast* (1971) found extensive segregation between and within such organisations, even ones which had no obvious relationship to the sectarian problems in the province.

Rosemary Harris's *Prejudice and tolerance in Ulster* (1972) is the most significant in-depth examination of social patterns in a small Northern Ireland village. It demonstrates the degree to which segregation is enforced by such matters as the quality of land owned by the two communities, but it also clearly shows that social relationships between the communities by their own choice were only possible within mutually acceptable limits and that they rarely exceeded these limits. Drinking and shopping habits, as well as membership of and support for organisations, were manifestations of this voluntary separation. Tom Kirk found the same phenomenon in his thesis on *The religious distribution of Lurgan* (1967), a larger town, where segregation has produced a high degree of duplication in the field of voluntary activities.

D. Bleakley's book *Peace in Ulster* (1972) attempts to balance the picture by describing some of the organisations in which the two communities work together.

Conflict Theory

Most of the recent writers who have attempted to analyse the Irish situation from a theoretical viewpoint have leant heavily on research conducted abroad. This applies in particular to those who see the problem as a racial one. Robert Moore (1973) and Rosemary Harris (1972), in the section of her book where she searches for a theoretical framework, both refer to the presence of two distinct and hostile cultures in Ireland and define the Ulster problem as basically racial. Leading racial theorists are examined for definitions and strategies which are then applied

212

to Ireland. Liam de Paor (1970) also describes a racial situation, but from a historian's viewpoint. The trouble is that these, as well as P. McNabb's caste theory (1971), while providing interesting insights, stop short at the point where analysis normally moves into recommendations.

Robin Jenkins and John Macrae were among the first of the new school of researchers to examine the Northern problem; Jenkins suggests that real class differences have been diverted in 'unreal' religious disputes by the elite. Their study, *Polarisation* (1966) like R. Elliot and J. Hickie's *Case study in Conflict Theory* (1971) has the benefit of being based on a survey conducted by the authors. Anders Boserup (1969 and 1971) argues that the communal differences are related more closely to power than class, and are maintained by the 'Orange system'. Other authors who adopt an interpretation which is class-based are P. Gibbon (1969) and C. Greaves (1972) but neither of them with the cogency or insight of Boserup.

Morris Fraser in *Children in Conflict* (1973) sees the problem in terms of in- and out-groups, and approaches the problem from a psychiatric angle. He too applies approaches pioneered by Americans, especially that of L. Berkowitz (1962).

Not everyone, of course, sees the struggle in Northern Ireland fitting into more general theories of conflict. Many, even before M. Moneypenny's book *The Two Irish Nations* (1912), saw it as a peculiarly Irish phenomenon. The best consideration of the literature on this matter is unquestionably M. Heslinga's *The Irish border as a cultural divide* (1962). Not surprisingly, much of the other literature on the subject is highly partisan. L. Gardiner (1971) and W. Carson (1957) present the partitionist argument, and many books, including the North-Eastern Boundary Bureau's *Handbook of the Ulster Question* (1921), the nationalist one. P. O Snodaigh attempts to demonstrate the continued existence of a Gaelic Protestant tradition in Ulster, and his pamphlet *Hidden Ulster* (1973) was strongly countered by the Marxist Workers' Association. M. Sheehy (1955) argued the existence of two cultures from a southern Irish viewpoint, and the question was discussed from a variety of angles in a special issue of *Community Forum* (1973). The New Ulster Movement also devoted a special publication to *Two Irelands or One?* (1972) and all the works of Estyn

Evans are both enlightening and readable on the subject. Since the whole question of national identity is the one which divides the two communities, or at least is widely seen in this light, it is unlikely that the debate will end there.

SOURCES

BOOKS

Akenson, Donald, *The Irish Education experiment: The National system of Education in the Nineteenth Century*, Routledge and Kegan Paul, 1970.

Akenson, Donald, *Education and Enmity*, David and Charles, 1973.

Ancient Order of Hibernians, *Its Order and Record*, AOH Dublin 1967.

Arthurs, Paul, *The Peoples Democracy*, Blackstaff, Belfast 1973.

Atkinson, Norman, *Irish Education: A History of Educational Institutions*, Allen Figgis, 1969.

Ayearst, M., *The Republic of Ireland—Its Government and its Politics*, University of London Press, 1971.

Baker, S., 'Conflict Groups in Belfast', *Studies in Urban History*, Arnold, 1972.

Barritt, Denis, and Carter, Charles, *The Northern Ireland Problem*, Oxford 1962.

Barrow, J., *Tour round Ireland*, John Murray, 1836.

Barth, F., *Ethnic Groups and Boundaries: The Social Organisation of Cultural Differences*, London 1969.

Barzilay, David, *Four Months in Winter*, Belfast 1972.

Barzilay, David, *The British Army in Ulster*, Century Services, Belfast 1973.

Beckett, J.C., *A Short History of Ireland*, London 1952.

Beckett, J.C., *The Making of Modern Ireland*, Faber, 1966.

Beckett, J.C., *et al., The Ulster Debate*, Bodley Head, 1972.

Beckett, J.C., and Glasscock, Robin (eds.), *Belfast: The Origin and Growth of an Industrial City*, BBC, London 1967.

Bell, J. Bowyer, *The Secret Army*, Blond, London 1970.

Bell, R., (ed.), *Education in Great Britain and Ireland*, Routledge and Kegan Paul, 1973.

Berkowitz, L., *Aggression: A Social Psychological Analysis*, Mc-Graw-Hill, New York 1962.

Biggs-Davidson, John, *The Hand is Red*, Johnson, London 1974.

Birrell, Derek, *et al., Housing in Northern Ireland*, Centre for Environmental Studies, London 1972.

Bleakley, David, *Peace in Ulster*, Mowbrays, London 1972.
Boland, Kevin, *We Won't Stand Idly By*, Dublin 1972.
Boulton, David, *The UVF*, Torc Books, Dublin 1973.
Boyd, Andrew, *Holy War in Belfast*, Anvil, Tralee 1969.
Boyd, Andrew, *The Rise of the Irish Trade Unions*, Anvil, Tralee 1972.
Boyd, Andrew, *Brian Faulkner and the crisis of Ulster Unionism*, Anvil, Tralee 1973.
Boyle, J., *Leaders and Workers*, Mercier, Cork 1965.
Boyle, Kevin, Hadden, Tom, and Hillyard, Paddy, *Law and State: The Case of Northern Ireland*, Martin Robertson, 1975.
Buckland, P., *The Anglo-Irish and the New Ireland 1885–1922*, Gill and Macmillan, 1972.
Buckland, P., *Irish Unionism: Select Documents*, HMSO, Belfast 1972.
Buckland, P., *The Origins of Northern Ireland: Ulster Unionism 1885–1923*, Gill and Macmillan, 1973.
Budge, Ian, and O'Leary, Cornelius, *Belfast: Approach to Crisis*, Macmillan, 1973.
Bustead, M.A., *Northern Ireland*, Oxford University Press, 1974.
Callaghan, James, *A House Divided*, Collins, 1973.
Calvert, Harry, *Constitutional Law in Northern Ireland*, Stevens and Son, 1968.
Camblin, G., *The Town in Ulster*, Mullan, Belfast 1951.
Campbell, J.J., *Catholic Schools: A Survey of a Northern Ireland Problem*, Fallons, c.1964.
Campbell, T.J., *Fifty Years of Ulster 1890–1940*, Irish News, 1941.
Carasso, Jean-Pierre, *La Rumeur Irlandaise*, Paris 1970.
Carson, W., *Ulster and the Irish Republic*, Belfast 1957.
Carty, J., *Bibliography of Irish History 1911–1921*, Dublin 1936.
Carty, J., *Bibliography of Irish History 1870–1911*, Dublin 1940.
Chubb, Basil (ed.), *A Source Book of Irish Government*, Institute of Public Administration, Dublin 1964.
Chubb, Basil, *The Government and Politics of Ireland*, Oxford University Press, 1970.
Churchill, Winston, *Lord Randolph Churchill*, Odhams edition, 1951.
Clark, W., *Guns in Ulster*, Northern Whig, Belfast 1967.
Clutterbuck, R., *Protest and the Urban Guerrilla*, Cassell, 1973.
Colvin, I., *The Life of Lord Carson*, Gollancz, 1934.
Connell, K., *The Population of Ireland*, Oxford 1950.
Conlon, L., *Cumann na mBan and the Women of Ireland*, Kilkenny People Ltd, 1969.

215

Connery, Donald S., *The Irish*, Eyre and Spottiswoode, 1968.
Connolly, James, *Labour in Irish History*, 1910, Reprinted New Books, Dublin 1956.
Connolly, James, *The Reconquest of Ireland*, 1915; Reprinted New Books, Dublin 1968.
Connolly, James, *The New Evangeline*, 1910, Reprinted New Books, Dublin 1972.
Coogan, T.P., *Ireland Since the Rising*, Pall Mall, 1966.
Coogan, T.P., *The IRA*, Pall Mall, 1970.
Corkery, Daniel, *The Hidden Ireland*, Dublin 1925.
Corkey, William, *Episode in the History of Protestant Ulster 1923–47*, Belfast, privately printed, n.d.
Cronin, Sean, *Ireland Since the Treaty*, Dublin 1971.
Crotty, R., *Irish Agriculture: Its Volume and Structure*, Mercier, Cork 1966.
Cullen, L., *An Economic History of Ireland Since 1660*, Batsford, 1972.
Curtis, E., *A History of Ireland*, London 1936.
Curtis, L., *Apes and Angels: The Irishman in Victorian Caricature*, David and Charles, 1971.
Curtis, R., *The History of the Royal Irish Constabulary*, Dublin 1869.
Dane, Mervyn, *The Fermanagh 'B' Specials*, The Impartial Reporter, Enniskillen, 1970.
de Beaumont, G., *L'Irlande Sociale, Politique et Religieuse*, Paris 1839.
de Paor, Liam, *Divided Ulster*, Penguin, 1970.
Deeny, James, *The Irish Worker*, Institute of Public Administration, Dublin 1971.
Deutsch, Richard, and Magowan, Vivien, *Northern Ireland: Chronology of Events*, Blackstaff, Belfast, *Volume 1, 1968–71*, 1973; *Volume 2 1971–73*, 1974.
de Tocqueville, Alexis, *Journeys to England and Ireland*, J. Mayer, (ed.), Faber, 1958.
Devlin, Bernadette, *The Price of my Soul*, Pan, 1969.
Dewar, M.W., Brown, J., and Long, S.E., *Orangeism, a new Historical Perspective*, Belfast 1967.
Dillon, Martin, and Lehane, Denis, *Political Murder in Northern Ireland*, Penguin, 1973.
Dowling, P.J., *A History of Irish Education*, Mercier, Cork 1971.
Edmunds, S., *The Gun, the Law and the Irish People*, Anvil, Tralee 1971.

Edwards, Owen Dudley, *The Sins of our Fathers*, Gill and Macmillan, 1970.

Edwards, R. Dudley, *A New History of Ireland*, Gill and Macmillan, 1972.

Edwards, Ruth Dudley, *An Atlas of Irish History*, Methuen, 1973.

Elliot, R.S.P., and Hickie, John, *Ulster: A Case Study in Conflict Theory*, Longman, 1971.

Elliott, Sidney, *Northern Ireland parliamentary election results 1921–1972*, Political Reference Publications, 1973.

Ellis, B., *History of the Irish Working Class*, Gollancz, 1972.

Ervine, St John, *Craigavon, Ulsterman*, Allen and Unwin, 1949.

Evans, E. Estyn, *Irish Heritage: The Landscape, the People and Their Work*, Dundalk 1942.

Evans, E. Estyn, *Portrait of Northern Ireland*, Collins, 1951.

Evans, E. Estyn, (ed.), *Belfast in its Regional Setting*, Belfast 1952.

Evans, E. Estyn, *Irish Folk Ways*, Routledge and Kegan Paul, 1957.

Evans, E. Estyn, *The Irishness of the Irish*, Irish Association, 1967.

Farrell, Brian, (ed.), *The Irish Parliamentary Tradition*, Gill and Macmillan, 1973.

Faul, Denis, *Testimony to the Sub-Committee of the House of Representatives of the USA*, Feb/March 1972.

Fiacc, Patrick, (ed.), *The Wearing of the Black*, Blackstaff, 1974.

Fields, R., *A Society on the Run: A Psychology of Northern Ireland*, Penguin, 1973.

Fitzgerald, Garret, *Towards a New Ireland*, Charles Knight, 1972.

Fitzgibbon, C., *Red Hand: The Ulster Colony*, Michael Joseph, 1972.

Fraser, Morris, *Children in Conflict*, Secker and Warburg, 1973.

Gallagher, F., *The Indivisible Island*, Gollancz, 1957.

Gray, T., *The Orange Order*, The Bodley Head, 1972.

Greaves, C.D., *The Irish Crisis*, Lawrence and Wishart, 1972.

Greeley, A., and Rossi, P., *The Education of Catholic Americans*, Aldine, Chicago 1966.

Green, E.R.R. (ed.), *Essays in Scotch-Irish History*, Routledge and Kegan Paul, 1969.

Gwyn, D., *The History of Partition 1912–1925*, London 1950.

Hand, Geoffrey J., *Report of the Irish Boundary Commission, 1925*, Irish University Press, 1969.

Harbinson, John F., *The Ulster Unionist Party*, Blackstaff, Belfast 1973.

Harbinson, Robert, *Song of Erne*, Faber and Faber, 1960.
Harris, H., *The Royal Irish Fusiliers*, Belfast 1972.
Harris, Rosemary, *Prejudice and Tolerance in Ulster*, Manchester University Press, 1972.
Harrison, J., *The Scot in Ulster*, Blackwood, 1888.
Hastings, Max, *Ulster 1969: The Fight for Civil Rights in Northern Ireland*, Gollancz, 1970.
Hawthorne, J., *Two Centuries of Irish History*, BBC, 1966.
Hazlett, A., *The Fermanagh 'B' Specials*, Tom Stacey, 1972.
Heslinga, M.W., *The Irish Border as a Cultural Divide*, Van Gorcum and Company, Assen 1962.
Hewitt, J., and Montague, J., *The Planter and the Gael*, Arts Council of Northern Ireland, Belfast 1970.
Hurley, Michael, (ed.), *Irish Anglicanism, 1869–1969*, Dublin 1970.
Ireland, Denis, *From the Jungle of Belfast*, Blackstaff, 1973.
Irish Republican Army (Provisional), *Freedom Struggle*, Dundalk, 1973.
Isles, K.S., and Cuthbert, Norman, *An Economic Survey of Northern Ireland*, HMSO, Belfast 1957.
Joannon, P., *Histoire de l'Irlande*, Plon, Paris 1973.
Johnston, E., *Ireland in the Eighteenth Century*, Gill and Macmillan, 1972.
Jones, Emrys, *A Social Geography of Belfast*, Oxford University Press, 1960.
Jones, Emrys (ed.), *Belfast in its Regional setting: A Scientific Survey*, Belfast 1952.
Jones, T., *Whitehall Diary*, London 1971.
Kee, Robert, *The Green Flag: A History of Irish Nationalism*, Weidenfeld and Nicolson, 1972.
Kelly, James, *Orders for the Captain?*, Privately Published, 1971.
Kelly, Henry, *How Stormont Fell*, Gill and Macmillan, 1972.
Kennedy, R., *The Irish: Emigration, Marriage and Fertility*, University of California Press, 1972.
King, Cecil, *On Ireland*, Jonathan Cape, 1973.
Kitson, Frank, *Low-intensity Operations*, Faber, 1971.
Lawrence, R.J., *The Government of Northern Ireland: Public Finance and Public Services 1921–1964*, Oxford 1965.
Lecky, W., *History of Ireland in the Eighteenth Century*, London 1892.
Leyburn, James, *The Scots-Irish: A Social History*, University of North Carolina Press, 1962.
Limpkin, C., *The Battle of Bogside*, Penguin, 1972.

218

Livingstone, Peadar, *The Fermanagh Story*, Cumann Seanchias Chlochair, Fermanagh 1969.
Lydon, James, and MacCurtain, Margaret, (eds.), *The Gill History of Ireland*, (Eleven volumes), Gill and Macmillan, 1972–1975.
Lyons, F.S.L., *Ireland Since the Famine*, Weidenfeld and Nicolson, 1971.
McCann, Eamonn, *War in an Irish Town*, Penguin, 1974.
Macardle, D., *The Irish Republic*, Corgi, London 1968.
McCormick, J., *Ulster in Your Hands*, York 1971.
McCreary, Alf, *Corrymeela*, Christian Journals Ltd, Belfast 1975.
MacCurtain, Margaret, *A History of Ireland*, (three volumes), Gill and Macmillan, 1969.
McElligott, T., *Education in Ireland*, Dublin 1966.
McGuffin, John, *Internment*, Anvil, 1973.
McGuffin, John, *The Guineapigs*, Penguin, 1974.
MacIntyre, T., *To the Bridewell Gate*, Faber and Faber, 1971.
McManus, Francis, *The Years of the Great Test*, Mercier, Cork 1967.
Magee, John, *Northern Ireland, Crisis and Conflict*, Routledge and Kegan Paul, 1974.
Maguire, Maria, *To Take Arms*, Macmillan, 1973.
Maltby, Arthur, *The Government of Northern Ireland*, Irish University Press, 1974.
Manhatton, Avro, *Religious Terror in Ireland*, Paravision Books, London 1970.
Mansergh, Nicholas, *The Government of Northern Ireland*, Allen and Unwin, 1936.
Mansergh, Nicholas, *The Irish Question 1840–1921*, Allen and Unwin, 1965.
Marrinan, Patrick, *Paisley—Man of Wrath*, Anvil, Tralee 1973.
Meenan, James, *The Irish Economy Since 1922*, Liverpool University Press, 1970.
Mewitt, J. (ed.), *Eyewitness of Ireland in Revolt*, Osprey, Reading 1947.
Milne, K., *The Church of Ireland*, Dublin 1966.
Mogey, John M., *Rural Life in Northern Ireland*, Oxford University Press, 1947.
Moneypenny, M., *The Two Irish Nations*, London 1912.
Moody, T.W. (ed.), *Irish Historiography 1936–70*, Irish Committee of Historical Sciences, Dublin 1971.
Moody, T.W., and Beckett, J.C. (ed.), *Ulster since 1800*, Two volumes, BBC, 1954 and 1957.
Moody, T.W., *The Ulster Question, 1603–1973*, Mercier, 1974.

Moody, T.W., and Martin, F.X., *The Course of Irish History*, Mercier, 1967.

Moss, Robert, *Urban Guerrillas*, Maurice Temple Smith, 1972.

Murphy, M., *Education in Ireland: Now and the Future*, Mercier, 1970.

Narain, B.J., *Public Law in Northern Ireland*, Printed by Appletree Press for the author, Belfast 1973.

Nassau, Senior, *Journals, Conversations and Essays Relating to Ireland*, London 1868.

Nelson, Sarah, 'Protestant Ideology Considered', in Ivor Crewe (ed.) *British Political Sociology Yearbook*, II, 1975.

Newark, F., *The Constitution of Northern Ireland*, Belfast 1950.

Newark, F., (ed.), *Devolution in Government*, London 1953.

North-Eastern Boundary Bureau, *Handbook of the Ulster Question*, Stationery Office, Dublin 1923.

Nowlan, K.P., and Williams, T.D. (ed.), *Ireland in the War Years and After*, Dublin 1969.

Cruise O'Brien, Conor, (ed.), *The Shaping of Modern Ireland*, London 1960, Gill and Macmillan, 1969.

O'Byrne, Cathal, *As I Roved Out*, Belfast 1946.

O'Farrell, Patrick, *Ireland's English Question*, Batsford, 1971.

O'Mahony, D., *The Irish Economy*, Mercier, Cork 1967.

O'Neill, Terence, *Ulster at the Crossroads*, Faber, 1969.

O'Neill, Terence, *Autobiography*, Hart-Davis, 1972.

O'Sullivan, Michael, *Patriot Graves*, Chicago 1973.

Pomfret, J., *The Struggle for Land in Ireland*, Princeton 1930.

Poole, Michael, and Boal, F.W., 'Religious Residential Segregation in Belfast in mid-1969', in Clark, B., and Cleave, M., (ed.), *Social Patterns in Cities*, London 1973.

Queckett, A., *The Constitution of Northern Ireland*, HMSO, Belfast 1928.

Rafferty, J. (ed.), *The Celts*, Mercier, Cork 1964.

Rex, John, *Race Relations in Sociological Theory*, London 1970.

Ricardo, David, *The Works of David Ricardo*, edited by P. Sraffa, Cambridge 1970.

Riddell, Patrick, *Fire over Ulster*, Hamish Hamilton, 1970.

Rose, Richard, *Governing Without Consensus*, Faber, 1971.

Royal Belfast Academical Institution, *The History of the Royal Belfast Academical Institution, 1910–1960*, RBAI, Belfast 1959.

St Joseph's College of Education, *Aspects of Catholic Education*, Belfast 1971.

Sayers, John E., 'The Political Parties and the Social Background' in Tom Wilson (ed.), *Ulster Under Home Rule*, Oxford University Press, 1955.

Senior, Hereward, *Orangeism in Ireland and Britain 1795–1836*, Routledge and Kegan Paul, 1966.

Sheehy, M., *Divided We Stand*, Faber and Faber, 1955.

Shearman, Hugh, *Northern Ireland 1921–1971*, HMSO, Belfast 1971.

Simpson, G., and Yinger, J., *Racial and Cultural Minorities*, Harper and Row, 1965.

Spencer, A.E.C.W., *Ballymurphy*, Social Studies Department, Queen's University Belfast, 1973.

Stetler, Russell, *The Battle of Bogside*, Sheed and Ward, 1970.

Stewart, A.T.Q., *The Ulster Crisis*, Faber, 1967.

Strauss, E., *Irish Nationalism and British Democracy*, Methuen, 1951.

Sunday Times Insight Team, *Ulster*, Penguin, 1972.

Sutherland, Margaret, 'Education in Northern Ireland', in Bell, R., (ed.), *Education in Great Britain and Ireland*, Routledge and Kegan Paul, 1973.

Sweetman, Rosita, *On our Knees*, Pan, 1972.

Symons, L., and Hanna, L., *Northern Ireland: A Geographical Introduction*, University of London Press, 1967.

Targett, G., *Unholy Smoke*, Hodder and Stoughton, 1969.

Targett, G., *Bernadette, the Story of Bernadette Devlin*, Hodder and Stoughton, 1975.

Tierney, M. (ed.), *Daniel O'Connell: Centenary Essays*, Dublin 1949.

Utley, T.E., *Lessons of Ulster*, Dent, 1975.

Wagley, C., and Harris, M., *Minorities in the New World*, New York 1958.

Wallace, Martin, *Guns and Drums: Revolution in Ulster*, Geoffrey Chapman, 1970.

Wallace, Martin, *Northern Ireland: 50 Years of Self-Government*, David and Charles, 1971.

Whale, John, *The Half-shut Eye*, London 1971.

Whyte, J.H., *Church and State in Modern Ireland 1923–1970*, Gill and Macmillan, 1971.

Wilson, Thomas (ed.), *Ulster Under Home Rule*, Oxford University Press, 1955.

Winchester, Simon, *In Holy Terror*, Faber and Faber, 1974.

Young, A., *Travels in Ireland*, London 1780.

Younger, C., *A State of Division*, Fontana, 1972.

PERIODICALS : ARTICLES
Administration, Institute of Public Administration, Dublin, quarterly.
Alliance Bulletin, Alliance Party, Belfast, monthly.
Aquarius, Servite Priory, Benburb, annual.
Community Forum, Northern Ireland Community Relations Commission, Belfast, quarterly (last issue 1974).
Fortnight, Belfast, fortnightly.
Furrow, Maynooth, twice yearly.
Irish Booklore, Belfast, twice yearly.
Irish Ecclesiastical Record, Dublin, six times yearly (last issue, 1966).
Irish Geography, Dublin, annual.
Irish Historical Studies, Dublin, twice yearly.
Irish Journal of Education, Dublin, twice yearly.
Irish Theological Quarterly, Maynooth, quarterly.
Journal, Church of Ireland, Dublin, annual.
Journal of Irish Medical Association, Dublin, monthly.
Newman Review, Belfast, annual.
Northern Ireland Legal Quarterly, Belfast, quarterly.
Northern Teacher, Irish National Teachers' Organisation and Ulster Teachers' Union, Belfast, quarterly.
PACE, Belfast, quarterly.
Profile, Dublin, fortnightly (1972–1973).
Social Studies, Dublin, quarterly.
This Week, Dublin, fortnightly (last issue 1972).
Ulster Commentary, Belfast, monthly.
Unionist Review, Ulster Unionist Party, Belfast, monthly.
Akenson, Donald, 'National Education and the Realities of Irish Life 1831–1900', *Eire-Ireland*, IV/4, 1969.
Arnold, Sam, and Clark, Mike, 'Integration : What About the Teachers?', *Fortnight*, 16 April 1971.
Barritt, Denis, '1961–1971 : Progress or Retrogression', *Community Forum*, 1/2, 1971.
Bayley, John, 'The Failure of Palliatives', *Community Forum*, 2/3, 1972.
Bayley, John, and Loizos, Peter, 'Bogside off its Knees', *New Society*, 1969.
B.E., 'The Church and Society', *This Week*, 15 June 1972.
Bell, C., 'Ireland: The Dynamics of Insurgency', *New Society*, 25 November 1971.
Bell, J. Bowyer, 'The Escalation of Insurgency: The Provisional IRA's Experience', *Review of Politics*, 35/3, 1973.

222

Birrell, Derek, 'Relative Deprivation as a Factor in Conflict in Northern Ireland', *The Sociological Review*, 20/3, 1972.
Birrell, Derek, et al., 'Housing Policy in Northern Ireland', *Community Forum*, 2/2, 1972.
Black, Richard, 'Flight in Belfast', *Community Forum*, 2/1, 1972.
Blumer, Jay C., 'Ulster on the Small Screen', *New Society*, 23 December 1971.
Boal, F.W., 'Territoriality on the Shankill/Falls Divide in Belfast', *Irish Geography*, 6/18, 1969.
Boal, F.W., 'Territoriality and Class: A Study of two Residential Areas in Belfast', *Irish Geography*, VI/3, 1971.
Boal, F.W., 'The Urban Residential Sub-community—a Conflict Interpretation', *Area*, Institute of British Geographers, 4/3, 1972.
Boal, F. W., 'Close Together and Far Apart: Religion and Class Division in Northern Ireland', *Community Forum*, 2/3, 1972.
Boal, F.W., and Buchanan, Ronnie, 'The 1969 Northern Ireland Election', *Irish Geography*, VI/1, 1969.
Boehringer, Kathleen, 'Discrimination: Jobs', *Fortnight*, 14 May 1971.
Boehringer, Gill, 'The Future of Policing in Northern Ireland', *Community Forum*, 3/2, 1973.
Boserup, Anders, 'Power in a Post-Colonial Setting', *Peace Research Society Papers XIII*, 1969.
Boserup, Anders, 'Revolution and Counter-Revolution in Northern Ireland', *Varldspolitikens Dagsfragor*, 1971.
Boserup, Anders, 'Contradictions and Struggles in Northern Ireland', *Socialist Register*, 1972.
Boyle, J., 'The Belfast Protestant Association and the Independent Orange Order', *Irish Historical Studies*, XIII, 1962–63.
Boyle, Kevin, 'The Minimum Sentences Act', *Northern Ireland Legal Quarterly*, Belfast, XXI, 4, 1970.
Brett, C.E.B., 'The Lessons of Devolution in Northern Ireland', *Political Quarterly*, 14, 1970.
Burke, V., and Murphy, S., 'Springfield Riot Report', *Newman Review*, III/1, Belfast 1971.
Burrows, P., 'Schools Community Relations Project', *Community Forum*, 1/1, 1971.
Bustead, M.A., and Mason, Hugh (ed.), 'Local Government Reform in Northern Ireland', *Irish Geography*, VI/3, 1971.
Caldwell, J., 'Ballymena, an Urban Ulster', *Fortnight*, 26 January 1972.

223

Calvert, Harry, 'Special Powers Extraordinary', *Northern Ireland Legal Review*, XX/1, Belfast 1968.

Calvert, Harry, 'Human Rights in Northern Ireland', *The Review of the International Commission of Jurists*, 2 June 1969.

Calvert, J., 'Housing Problems in Northern Ireland: A Critique', *Community Forum*, 2/2, 1972.

Canavan, J., 'The Future of Protestantism in Ireland', *Studies*, XXIV, 12.

Carroll, Don, 'The Search for Justice in Northern Ireland', *New York Journal of International Law and Politics*, 1973.

Carter, A., 'The Use and Abuse of History in Northern Schools', *The World and the School*, 1970.

Cathcart, Rex, 'BBC Northern Ireland: 50 Years Old', *The Listener*, 12 September 1974.

Chapman, P., 'Housing Reform in Northern Ireland', *Journal for the Built Environment*, 35/3, 1972.

Chinoy, Michael, 'How Not to Resolve a Conflict', *New Society*, 4 September 1975.

Clark, H., 'Why an Ulster Defence Regiment', *Solon*, 1/2, 1970.

Common, R., 'Some Concerns of Regional Geography, with Illustrations from Northern Ireland', *Scottish Geographical Magazine*, 87, 1971.

Cooper, R., and O'Shea, T., 'Northern Ireland: A *New Society* survey of the social trends', *New Society*, 7 June 1973.

Cousins, S., 'Emigration and Demographic Change in Ireland 1951–1961', *Economic History Review*, XIV, 1961–62.

Craig, J., 'Ulster is British', *The Spectator*, 23 February 1924.

Cranston, Des, 'Endlessly Marching Men: The Ulster Protestant, Confused', *Cambridge Review*, 18 May 1973.

Daly, M., 'The Special Powers Act', *Newman Review*, III/1, Belfast 1971.

Dallat, Michael, 'Integrated Education', *Community Forum*, 2/1, 1972.

Darby, John P., 'Divisiveness in Education: Its Extent and Effects in Northern Ireland', *Northern Teacher*, Winter 1973.

Darby, John P., 'History in the School: A Review Article', *Community Forum*, 4/2, 1974.

Darby, John P., and Morris, Geoffrey, 'Community groups and Research in Northern Ireland', *Community Development Journal*, 10/2, 1975.

Davey, Ray, 'Corrymeela is Not an Island', *Community Forum*, 1/2, 1971.

224

Davies, R., and McGurnaghan, M.A., 'Northern Ireland: The Economics of Adversity', *National Westminster Bank Quarterly Review*, May 1975.

de Bhaldraithe, E., 'Joint Pastoral Care of Mixed Marriages', *The Furrow*, Dublin 1971.

Dickie, Anthony, 'Anti-Incitement Legislation in Northern Ireland', *New Community*, 1/2, 1972.

Donaldson, A.G., 'The Constitution of Northern Ireland: Its Origins and Development', *University of Toronto Law Journal*, XI/1, 1955.

Donaldson, A.G., 'The Senate of Northern Ireland', *Public Law*, 1958.

Donaldson, A.G., 'Fundamental Rights in the Constitution of Northern Ireland', *Canadian Bar Review*, XXXVII, 1959.

Donnison, David, 'The Northern Ireland Civil Service', *New Society*, 5 July 1973.

Duff, Niall, 'Community Self-surveys', *Community Forum*, 3/1, 1973.

Dunham, Arthur, 'Community Organisations in Times of Change', *Community Forum*, 2/1, 1972.

Edwards, J., 'Special Powers in Northern Ireland', *Criminal Law Review*, 1956.

Fahy, Patrick A., 'Some Political Behaviour Patterns and Attitudes of Roman Catholic Priests in a Rural Part of Northern Ireland', *Economic and Social Review*, 1971.

Farrell, Michael, 'People's Democracy: A Discussion on Strategy', *New Left Review*, 55, 1969.

Ferguson, J., 'Community Relations in schools in Northern Ireland', *Trends in Education*, HMSO, London 1973.

Fields, R., 'Ulster a Psychological Experiment', *New Humanist*, London, March 1973.

Firth, Gay, 'Polar Press', *Fortnight*, 14 May 1971.

Fortnight Publications Ltd, *Survey into Political Attitudes*, July 1972.

Fortnight, 'Guide to Ulster demography', *Fortnight*, 9 February 1972.

Fortnight, 'Unionism—The State of the Party', *Fortnight*, 18 January 1973.

Fortnight, 'Integrated education', *Fortnight*, 1 February 1973.

Fortnight, 'The RUC: A Troubled Force', *Fortnight*, 16 February 1973.

Fraser, Morris, 'The Cost of Commotion', *British Journal of Psychiatry*, March 1971.

Fraser, Morris, *et al.*, 'Children and Conflict', *Community Forum*, 2/2, 1972.
Fry, Anne, 'Struggle for Power in Newry', *Community Care*, 27/2, October 1974.
Fulton, J., 'Some Reflections on Catholic Schools in Northern Ireland', *Studies*, LVIII, Winter 1969.
Gibbon, Peter, 'Ulster: Religion and Class', *New Left Review*, 55, 1969.
Gibbon, Peter, 'Orange and Green Myths', *Fortnight*, August 1972.
Gibbon, T., 'The Origins of the Orange Order and the United Irishmen', *Economy and Society*, 1/2, 1972.
Gibson, Norman, 'The Northern Problem', *Community Forum*, 1/1, 1971.
Gibson, Norman, 'Economic Conditions and Poverty in Northern Ireland', *Economic and Social Review*, 4/3, 1973.
Goodchild, Norman, 'The Bogside Community Association', *Community Forum*, 4/2, 1974.
Gracey, Jim, and Howard, Paula, 'Northern Ireland Political Literature 1968–1970', *Irish Booklore*, 1/1, 1971.
Gray, T., 'The Religious Dimension', *New Humanist*, London, March 1973.
Gretton, J., 'Belfast: The Social and Economic Reality', *New Society*, 31 December 1970.
Griffiths, J.H., 'Community Development and Community Relations', *Community Forum*, 1/2, 1971.
Griffiths, J. H., 'The Northern Ireland Community Relations Commission', *New Community*, 1/2, 1972.
Griffiths, J.H., 'Why I Resigned', *Fortnight*, 11 May 1972.
Hadden, Tom, 'Interlocking Ulstermen', *New Society*, 1972.
Hadden, Tom, and Boyle, K., 'The Hunt Report—Convincing Justice', *New Law Journal*, London, 18 December 1969.
Hadkins, Lorna, 'Textbooks', *Community Forum*, 1/1, 1971.
Hamilton, I., 'The Irish Tangle', *Conflict Studies*, 6, 1971.
Hamilton, I., and Moss, R., 'The Spreading Irish conflict', *Conflict Studies*, 17, 1971.
Hayes, Maurice, 'Some Aspects of Local Government in Northern Ireland', *Public Administration*, 1967.
Heatley, Fred, 'Northern Ireland Civil Rights Association', (five articles) *Fortnight*, 23 March, 5 April, 26 April, 10 May, and 7 June 1974.
Hill, Ian J., 'Pamphlets Galore', *Fortnight*, 20 November 1970.
Hoggart, Simon, 'The Army PR men of Northern Ireland', *New Society*, 11 October 1973.

Holmes, Erskine, 'A Centre Party Coalition Government', *Community Forum*, 2/2, 1972.

Howard, Paula, *et al.*, 'What the Other Papers Say', *Community Forum*, 2/2, 1972.

Howard, Paula, 'The Paper War', *Fortnight*, (three articles) 11 January, 25 January, and 8 February 1974.

Institute for the Study of Conflict, 'Ulster: Politics and Terrorism', *Conflict Studies*, London 1973.

Irish Association for Cultural, Economic and Social Relations, *Attitudes of school leavers: A Survey*, unpublished, but extracts in *Community Forum*, 3/3, 1973.

Irish Marketing Survey, *A Survey of Public Opinion* for *This Week*, May 1970.

Jamieson, David, 'Local Government in Belfast', *Local Government Review*, 13 May 1972.

Jenvey, Sue, 'Sons and Haters: Ulster Youth in Conflict', *New Society*, 20 July 1972.

Johnson, James, J., 'Reorganisation of Local Government in Northern Ireland', *Area*, 4, 1970.

Johnston, R., 'The Composition of British Capital Investment in Northern Ireland', *Irish Democrat*, December 1959 and January 1960.

Jones, Emrys, 'The Distribution and Segregation of Roman Catholics in Belfast', *Sociological Review*, 4, 1956.

Jordan, John, 'Northern Poets and Northern Politics', *Hibernia*, 1974.

Kane, J.J., 'Civil Rights in Northern Ireland', *Review of Politics*, 33, 1970.

Kaye, J., 'The Irish Prisoners', *New Society*, 6 September 1973.

Kerr, B., 'Irish Seasonal Migration', *Irish Historical Studies*, III, 1942–43.

Kinehan, Robin, 'Economic Development: Large-scale Investment or Self-help Projects', *Community Forum*, 2/3, 1972.

Lahinch, C., 'Rhodesia and the North: A Parallel', *This Week*, 15 June 1972.

Lakeman, Enid, 'Proportional Representation in Northern Ireland', *Community Forum*, 1/2, 1971.

Lawrence, R.J., 'Devolution Reconsidered', *Political Studies*, IV/1, 1956.

Lee, G., 'The Constitution and State of Emergency', *Irish Law Times*, 103, 1969.

Lee, T., 'Immigrants in London: Trends in Distribution and Concentration 1961–1971', *New Community*, II/2, 1973.

227

Leon, G., 'The Politics of Civil Rights in Northern Ireland', *Cithera*, X/1, 1970.

Leyton, Elliott, 'Opposition to Integration in Ulster', *Man*, 9, 1974.

Lijphart, Arend, 'The Northern Ireland Problem: Cases, Theories, and Solutions', *British Journal of Political Science*, 5, 1975.

Londonderry, Lord, 'Public Education in Northern Ireland: The New System', *19th Century and After*, XCV, 1924.

Loughran, Gemma, 'The Moral Education Project in Northern Ireland', *Community Forum*, 1/2, 1971.

Lyons, H.A., 'The Psychiatric Sequelae of the Belfast Riots', *British Journal of Psychiatry*, 118/544, March 1971.

Lyons, H.A., 'The Effects of Civil Disturbances on Mental Health', *Proceedings of the Medical Association for Prevention of War*, 2/3, 1971.

Lyons, H.A., 'Depressive Illness and Aggression in Belfast', *British Medical Journal*, February 1972.

Lyons, H.A., 'Riots and Rioters in Belfast', *Community Forum*, 3/2, 1973.

McCarthy, Charles, 'Civil Strife and the Growth of Trade Union Unity: The Case of Ireland', *Government and Opposition*, 8/4, 1973.

Macauley, A., 'Catholics in the North 1870–1970', *Newman Review*, 2/1, 1970.

McClung Lee, Alfred, 'Insurgent and "Peace-Keeping" Violence in Northern Ireland', *Social Policy*, 20/4, 1973.

McCormack, P., 'Times Past', *Community Forum*, 2/2, 1972.

McCormick, J., 'Political Games', *Fortnight*, 12 November 1971.

McInerney, Michael, 'Noel Browne: Church and State', *University Review*, V, 1968.

Mackel, Sean, *et al.*, 'Co-operative and Industrial Self-help in Northern Ireland', *Community Forum*, 3/1, 1973.

McKeown, Michael, 'Civil Service Discrimination', *Hibernia*, 5 October 1973.

Mansfield, Frank, 'Focus on Northern Ireland', *Municipal and Public Services Journal*, 5 March 1972.

Moles, W., 'Integrated Education', *Community Forum*, 2/1, 1972.

Moore, Robert, 'Race Relations in the Six Counties', *Race*, 1973.

Moore, Robert, 'Plural Societies', *Race*, XIV/1, 1972.

Neill, Desmond G., 'Some Consequences of Government by Devolution in Northern Ireland', in F. Newark, *Devolution in Government*, Allen and Unwin, 1953.

Neill, D., *et al.*, 'The Role of Educational Institutions in Northern Ireland', *Community Forum*, 2/1, 1972.

Newark, F., 'Legislation in Northern Ireland', *Northern Ireland Legal Quarterly*, 23/1, 1972.

Newe, G.B., 'Living Together', *Community Forum*, 2/3, 1972.

O'Brien, Conor Cruise, 'What Rights Should Minorities Have?', *New Community*, II/2, London 1973.

O'Leary, Cornelius, 'Northern Ireland: The Politics of Illusion', *Political Quarterly*, XL/3, 1969.

O'Leary, Cornelius, 'The Northern Ireland Crisis and its Observers', *Political Quarterly*, XLII/3, 1971.

O'Malley, P., 'Attempted Suicide Before and After the Communal Violence in Belfast, August 1969', *Journal of the Irish Medical Association*, 65/5, 1972.

Orr, Lawrence, 'The Orange Order', *Solon*, 1/2, 1970.

Paisley, Ian K., 'Ecumenism', *Community Forum*, 1/1, 1971.

Park, A.T., 'An Analysis of Human Fertility in Northern Ireland', *Journal of the Statistical and Sociological Society of Ireland*, 21, 1962–63.

Patten, Pat, 'Local Government Reform: Health and Social Services', *Community Forum*, 3/1, 1973.

Peacock, A., 'The Royal Ulster Constabulary', *Solon*, 1/2, 1970.

Pearce, David (ed.), 'Northern Ireland', *Built Environment* (Special issue), 3/2, 1974.

Poole, K.P., 'The Northern Ireland Commissioner for Complaints', *Public Law*, Summer 1972.

Poole, Michael, 'Religious Displacement in the Summer of 1969', *Fortnight*, August 1971.

Rankin, H., 'On the Psychostasis of Ulster', *Psychotherapy and Psychosomatics*, 19, 1971.

Riley, S., 'Some Lawyers ask: Is the Law Past Reproach?', *Sunday News*, 28 May 1972.

Robb, J.D.A., and Matthews, J.G.W., 'The Injuries and Management of Riot Casualties', *British Journal of Surgery*, 58/6, June 1971.

Roberts, Alan, 'Passive Resistance in Ulster', *New Society*, 6 June 1974.

Robinson, Alan, 'Education and Sectarian Conflict in Northern Ireland', *New Era*, January 1971.

Robinson, Alan, 'Londonderry, Northern Ireland: A Border Study', *Scottish Geographical Magazine*, 86, 1970.

Roche, D.J.D., et al., 'Housing Requirements for Northern Ireland', *Economic and Social Review*, 3/3, 1972.

Roche, D.J.D., et al., 'Some Determinants of Labour Mobility in Northern Ireland', *Economic and Social Review*, 5/1, 1973.

Rose, Richard, 'Ulster, the Problem of Direct Rule', *New Society*, 10 June 1971.
Rose, Richard, 'Discord in Ulster', *New Community*, 2/2, 1972.
Rose, Richard, 'Ulster Politics: A Select Bibliography of Political Discord', *Political Studies*, XX, June 1972.
Rose, Richard, and McAllister, Ian, 'Repartition not the Solution to Northern Ireland's Problems', *Irish Times*, 16 September 1975.
Rose, Richard, and Simpson, Harry, 'Where Can People Live?' *Community Forum*, 3/1, 1973.
Russell, James, 'Violence and the Ulster Schoolboy', *New Society*, 26 July 1973.
Russell, James, 'The Sources of Conflict', *Northern Teacher*, Winter 1974/75.
Rutan, J.F., 'The Labour Party in Ulster: Opposition by Cartel', *Review of Politics*, 1967.
Savage, D.C., 'The Origins of the Ulster Unionist Party 1885–86', *Irish Historical Studies*, XII/47, 1961.
Schutz, Barry, and Scott, Douglas, 'Northern Ireland and Rhodesia', in Crewe, Ivor, (ed.), *British Political Sociology Yearbook*, II, 1975.
Scott, Roger, 'The 1970 British General Election in Ulster', *Parliamentary Affairs*, 1971.
Scott, R.D., 'Ulster in Perspective', *Australian Outlook*, December 1969.
Scott, R.D., 'Revolution in Northern Ireland: An Historiography', *Lakehead University Review*, IX/2, 1971.
Shallice, T., 'The Ulster Depth Interrogation Techniques and Their Relation to Sensory Deprivation Research', *Cognition*, 1/4, 1973.
Shearman, Hugh, 'Conflict in Northern Ireland', *The Year book of World Affairs*, 24, 1970.
Simpson, H., 'The Northern Ireland Housing Executive', *Housing Review*, 22/3, June 1973.
Sloan, Harold, 'Ecumenism', *Community Forum*, 1/1, 1971.
Smith, A., 'Bias in Broadcasting', *This Week*, Dublin, 21 September, 1972.
Smith, G., 'Recent Disturbances in Northern Ireland: Some Documentary Sources', *Journal of Librarianship*, II/3, 1971.
Taylor, Robert, 'Shopfloor Ulster', *New Society*, 23 May 1974.
Taylor, Robert, 'Images of the Irish', *New Society*, 28 November 1974.

Thornberry, Cedric, 'International Law and Emergency Situations', *Community Forum*, 3/2, 1973.
Tobias, J., 'The Policing of Ireland', *Criminologist*, 5, 1970.
Trevor, Michael, 'Why segregation?', *Fortnight*, 5 February 1971.
Tweed, Bill, 'Community Work Comment in Northern Ireland', *Social Work Today*, 2/15, 1971.
Wallace, Martin, 'Home Rule in Northern Ireland—Anomalies of Devolution', *Northern Ireland Legal Quarterly*, 18/1, 1967.
Walsh, D., 'From Battle Front to Peace Line', *New Humanist*, March 1973.
Watson, Alex, 'Liberal Watershed', *Community Forum*, 3/1, 1973.
Whale, John, 'Modern Guerrilla Movements', *Community Forum*, 3/2, 1973.
White, Barry, 'The Alliance Party', *Fortnight*, 23 October 1970.
White, Barry, 'Faulkner', *Fortnight*, 2 April 1971.
White, J., 'Partition', *The Month*, XVII, 1957.
Whyte, J.H., 'Intra-Unionist Disputes in the Northern Ireland House of Commons, 1921–72', *Economic and Social Review*, 1974.
Wilson, Derick, 'An Approach to some Early School Leavers', *Community Forum*, 1/1, 1971.
Wilson, Desmond, 'Economic Development: Large-scale Investment or Self-help Projects?', *Community Forum*, 2/3, 1972.
Wright, Frank, 'Protestant Ideology and Politics in Ulster', *European Journal of Sociology*, XIV, 1973.

PAMPHLETS
Belfast Urban Study Group, *The A to Z of Belfast Housing*, Belfast 1974.
Biggs-Davidson, John, *Catholics and the Union*, Unionist Research Department, Belfast 1972.
Birrell, Derek, *et al.*, *Housing in Northern Ireland*, Northern Ireland Community Relations Commission Research Paper, 1972.
Blake, John, *Northern Ireland in the Second World War*, HMSO, Belfast 1956.
Boal, F.W., Doherty, P. and Pringle, D., *The Spatial Distribution of some Social Problems in the Belfast Urban Area*, Northern Ireland Community Relations Commission, Belfast 1974.
Boyd, Andrew, *The Two Irelands*, Fabian Research Series No. 269, 1968.

Boyd, Andrew and Ireland, John, *The New Partition of Ireland*, Private, n.d.

Calvert, Harry, *The Northern Ireland problem*, United Nations Association, 1972.

Campaign for Social Justice in Northern Ireland, *The Plain Truth*, Dungannon 1969.

Campaign for Social Justice in Northern Ireland, *Northern Ireland —The Mailed Fist*, Dungannon 1971.

Catholic Chaplaincy, Queen's University Belfast, *Annual Reports*.

Central Citizens' Defence Committee, *The Black Paper: The Story of the Police*, CCDC, Belfast 1973.

Chichester-Clark, James, *Spotlight on Northern Ireland*, Royal Commonwealth Society, 1971.

Child Poverty Action Group, *Downpatrick Survey*, CPAG, 1972.

Community Groups' Conference, *Community Action: The Way Forward*, Derry 1974.

Community Relations Commission Research Unit, *Flight*, Northern Ireland Community Relations Commission, Belfast 1971.

Community Development Forum, *Social Need and Social Need Legislation in Northern Ireland*, CDF, Belfast 1972.

Conway, A., *There are no Evil Men—A Fresh Look at the Irish question and a Suggested Way Forward*, Dublin 1971.

Conway, William, *Catholic Schools*, Catholic Communication Institute of Ireland, 1971.

Corrigan, Aidan, *Eyewitnesses in Northern Ireland*, Voice of Ulster Publications, 1969.

Corrigan, P.J. and Crone, R., 'A Sixth-Form Experiment', *Practice '73*, Queen's University Belfast, 1973.

Coughlan, Anthony, *Trade Unionism in Ireland Today*, Connolly Publications, London 1965.

Coughlan, Anthony, *The Northern Crisis*, Solidarity Publications, Dublin 1969.

Crozier, Brian (ed.), *Ulster: Politics and Terrorism*, Institute for the Study of Conflict, London 1973.

Darby, John P., *Register of Research into the Irish Conflict*, Northern Ireland Community Relations Commission Research Paper, Belfast 1972.

Darby, John P., and Morris, Geoffrey, *Intimidation in Housing*, Northern Ireland Community Relations Commission, 1974.

Dash, S., *Justice Denied: A Challenge to Lord Widgery's Report on Bloody Sunday*, National Council for Civil Liberties, London 1972.

Dowling, J.D.H., *Nothing to Hide: The Boehringer Case and*

Academic Freedom in Northern Ireland, Council for Academic Freedom and Democracy, 1974.

Economic and Social Research Institute, *Register of Research Projects in the Social Sciences*, ESRI, Dublin, annual.

Egan, Bowes, and McCormack, V., *Burntollet*, ERS Publishers, London 1969.

Electoral Reform Society, *The Electoral System of Northern Ireland*, ERS, London 1970.

Farrell, Michael, *Struggle in the North*, People's Democracy, Belfast 1969.

Faul, Denis, and Murray, Raymond, *Brutalities*, Association for Legal Justice, Belfast 1972.

Fermanagh Civil Rights Association, *Fermanagh Facts*, 1969.

Gardner, Louis, *The Resurgence of the Majority*, Vanguard Publications, 1971.

Geary, R., and Hughes, J., *Internal Migration in Ireland*, Economic and Social Research Institute, Dublin, 1970.

Gibson, Norman, *Partition Today*, Tuairim Extern Lectures, Dublin 1958.

Gibson, Norman (ed.), *Economic and Social Implications of the Political Alternatives that may be open to Northern Ireland*, New University of Ulster, Coleraine 1974.

Greer, John, *A Questioning Generation*, Church of Ireland Board of Education, Coleraine 1972.

Griffiths, J.H., and Black, Richard, *The Future of Local Government*, Northern Ireland Community Relations Commission, 1971.

Griffiths, J.H., *A Case Study in Agency Conflict: The Northern Ireland Community Relations Commission*, Occasional Paper, New University of Ulster, Coleraine 1974.

Hadden, Tom, and Hillyard, Paddy, *Justice in Northern Ireland: A Study in Social Confidence*, Cobden Trust, London 1973.

Hauser, Richard, *A Social Option*, published by the author, 1975.

Hayes, Maurice, *Community Relations and the Role of the Community Relations Commission in Northern Ireland*, Runnymede Trust, 1972.

Independent Television Authority, *Religion in Great Britain and Northern Ireland*, ITA, 1970.

An Informal Group, *Emergency Powers: A Fresh Start*, Fabian Tract 416, The Fabian Society, London 1972.

Institute of Irish Studies, *Theses on Subjects Relating to Ireland Presented for Higher Degrees*, Queen's University Belfast, 1968.

Intergroup Project, *Working paper No. 4*, Grubb Institute, 1972.
Irish Congress of Trade Unions, *Industrial Relations in Northern Ireland*, Belfast 1971.
Jackson, Harold, *The Two Irelands: A Dual Study of Inter-Group Tensions*, Minority Rights Group Report No. 2, 1971.
Jenkins, Robin, *Conflict and Polarisation*, Peace Research Centre, London 1968.
Jenkins, Robin, and Smoker, Paul, *Northern Ireland: A Case Study in Polarisation*, Peace Research Centre, London 1971.
Johnston, E., *Irish History: A Select Bibliography: Historical Association Pamphlet No. 73*, 1969.
Johnston, J., *Why Ireland needs the Common Market*, London 1962.
Kennally, D., and Preston, E., *Belfast, August 1971: A Case to be Answered*, National Labour Press, London 1971.
Knight, J., and Baxter-Moore, N., *The Northern Ireland Elections of the 1920's*, Electoral Reform Society, London 1971.
Lee, G., and Taylor, R., *Ulster*, Reprinted from *The Economist*, 1971.
McCafferty, Niall, *'If We Were Given a Chance . . .'*, Northern Ireland Community Relations Commission, 1974.
McCann, Eamonn, *The British Press and Northern Ireland*, Northern Ireland Socialist Research Centre, London 1971.
McCann, Eamonn, *What Happened in Derry*, London 1972.
McCormack, P., and Rhodes, E., *Youth in Derry*, Magee University College, Derry 1972.
McInerney, Michael, *Trade Unions Bid for Peace in North*, Irish Times Publications, n.d.
McKeown, Michael, *The First 500*, Irish News Ltd, Belfast 1972.
Macrae, John, *Polarisation in Northern Ireland: A Preliminary Report*, Peace Research Centre, Lancaster, 1966.
Magee, John, *The Teaching of Irish History in Irish Schools*, Irish National Teachers' Organisation, 1969, and NI Community Relations Commission, 1971.
Malone, John, *Schools Project in Community Relations*, Northern Ireland Community Relations Commission, 1972.
New Society, *Northern Ireland, A New Society Social Studies Reader*, New Society Publications, London 1973.
New Ulster Movement, *The Reform of Stormont*, NUM, Belfast 1971.
New Ulster Movement, *A Commentary on the Programme of Reforms for Northern Ireland*, NUM, Belfast 1971.
New Ulster Movement, *The Legal Basis of Partition in Ireland*, NUM, Belfast 1971.

New Ulster Movement, *The Way Forward*, 1971
New Ulster Movement, *Northern Ireland and the Common Market*, 1972.
New Ulster Movement, *Two Irelands or one?* 1972.
New Ulster Movement, *Violence and Northern Ireland*, 1972.
New Ulster Movement, *A New Constitution for Northern Ireland*, 1972.
New Ulster Movement, *Towards the Return of the Rule of Law*, 1972.
New Ulster Movement, *Tribalism or Christianity in Ireland*, 1973.
Northern Friends' Peace Board, *Orange and Green: A Quaker Study of Community Relations in Northern Ireland*, Yorkshire 1969.
Northern Ireland Council for Educational Research, *Register of Research in Education*, Two volumes, 1972.
O Fearghall, Sean, *Law(?) and Orders: The Belfast Curfew of 3–5 July 1970*, Central Citizens' Defence Committee, 1970.
O'Mahony, D., *Industrial Relations in Ireland: The Background*, Economic Research Institute, Paper 19, 1964.
O'Mahony, D., *Economic Aspects of Industrial Relations*, Economic Research Institute, Paper 24, 1965.
Opinion Research Centre, *Religion in Northern Ireland*, ORC, London 1970.
O Snodaigh, P., *Hidden Ulster*, Abbey Printers, Cavan 1973.
Patterson, Monica, *The Hungry Sheep of Ulster*, Platform Publications, 1974.
Police Authority of Northern Ireland, *The First Three Years*, Police Authority, Belfast 1973.
Pyne, P., *The Irish Bureaucracy*, New University of Ulster: Institute of Continuing Education, Derry 1973.
Queen's University Belfast, Education Department, *Project 1973*, Belfast 1973.
Queen's University Belfast, Geography Department, *List of Theses*, Belfast 1973.
Research Services Limited, *Readership Survey of Northern Ireland*, RSL, 1970.
Robb, J.D.A., *New Ireland—Sell Out or Opportunity?*, published by author, 1972.
Russell, James, *Some Aspects of the Civic Education of Secondary Schoolboys in Northern Ireland*, Northern Ireland Community Relations Commission, 1972.
Sandy Row Redevelopment Association, *Sandy Row at the Public Enquiry*, Belfast 1972.

Savory, D., *Contemporary History of Ireland*, Unionist Headquarters, Belfast 1958.
Smyth, Clifford, *Ulster Assailed*, Belfast 1970.
Smyth, Clifford, *Politics of Deception*, Puritan Printing Company, Belfast 1971.
Smyth, Martin, *The Battle for Northern Ireland*, County Grand Orange Lodge of Belfast, 1972.
Ulster Defence Association, *The Shankill Disturbances*, Belfast 1972.
Ulster Workers' Council, *Ulster General Strike*, Belfast 1974.
Unionist Research Department, *The Case for Internment*, Belfast 1971.
Vogt, H., *Nordirland*, Evang, Missionsverlag, Stuttgart 1972.
Walsh, B.M., *Some Irish Population. Questions Reconsidered*, Economic and Social Research Institute, Dublin 1968.
Walsh, B.M., *Religion and Demographic Behaviour in Ireland*, Economic and Social Research Institute, Dublin 1970.
Walsh, B.M., *Ireland's Demographic Transformation*, Economic and Social Research Institute, (Internal draft), Dublin 1972.
Walsh, D., *Crisis in Ireland*, Dublin 1971.
West Ulster Unionist Council, *It Matters to You*, Enniskillen, 1970.
Whyte, J.H., *The Reform of Stormont*, New Ulster Movement, 1971.
Whyte, J.H., *Governing Without Consensus: A Critique*, Northern Ireland Community Relations Commission, 1972.
Wilson, J., *Environment and Primary Education in Northern Ireland*, Northern Ireland Council for Education Research, 1972.

NEWSPAPERS: ARTICLES
Andersonstown News, Belfast, weekly.
Belfast Newsletter, Belfast, daily.
Belfast Telegraph, Belfast, daily.
Church of Ireland Gazette, Dublin, weekly.
Education Times, Dublin, weekly.
Hibernia, Dublin, fortnightly.
Irish Independent, Dublin, daily.
Irish News, Belfast, daily.
Irish Press, Dublin, daily.
Irish Times, Dublin, daily.
Presbyterian Herald, Belfast, weekly.
Protestant Telegraph, Belfast, weekly.
Republican News, Belfast, weekly.

Sunday Independent, Dublin, weekly.
Sunday Press, Dublin, weekly.
Sunday News, Belfast, weekly.
Sunday World, Dublin, weekly.
Ulster Protestant, Belfast, weekly.
United Irishman, Dublin, weekly.
Acheson, Alan, 'The Media and the Crisis', *Church of Ireland Gazette* (two articles), 21 and 28 June 1972.
Belfast Telegraph, *Survey Conducted by National Opinion Polls*, December 1967.
Bell, Brian, 'The Making of a Party', *Belfast Telegraph*, 28 April 1970.
Boehringer, Gill, 'Andersonstown Policing Survey', *Andersonstown News*, 11 July 1973.
Chartres, J., and Macbeth, I., 'Ian Paisley', *The Times*, 29 January 1969.
Clark, Ric, 'Sixteen Days in May', *Sunday News* (four articles), 16 March, 23 March, 30 March and 6 April 1975.
Cummins, M., 'The Alliance Party', *The Irish Times*, 26 February 1972.
Curran, E., 'Why Cardinal Conway is Wrong About the Schools', *Belfast Telegraph*, 17 February 1971.
Curran, E., 'Is Justice Being Done in Northern Ireland?', *Belfast Telegraph*, 2 June 1971.
Dowling, J., 'Trade Unionism in Ireland', *Irish Press*, 8–10 March 1971.
Downey, J., 'Anglo-Irish Relations', *Irish Times*, 10–14 January 1972.
Feeney, J., 'The Provisional IRA in the south', *The Irish Press*, 22–22 January 1972.
Graham, John, 'The Nature and Development of the NILP', *Irish Press*, Dublin, 26–27 March 1971.
Hanson, Richard, 'Politics and the Pulpit', *The Guardian*, 14 September 1973.
Kelly, John, 'Towards a Northern Policy', *Irish Times*, 31 August and 8 September 1970.
Kemp, D., 'Ian Paisley', *Glasgow Herald*, 5 February 1969.
Longley, Clifford, 'Odd Men out in all Christiandom', *The Times*, 21 February 1972.
McEldowney, Eugene, 'The Vere Foster Affair', *Irish Times*, 17 and 18 June, 1971.
McInerney, Michael, 'Whitehall Looks at Westminster', *Irish Times*, 17 and 18 June, 1971.

McKeown, C., 'Inside Orangeism', *The Irish Press,* 21 July 1971.
Oliver, Ted, 'Violence and Our Children', *Belfast Telegraph*, 15 and 16 January 1975.
O'Mahony, T., 'Segregated Education in the North', *Irish Press,* 27 February–1 March 1972.
Taylor, D., 'The Welfare Gap Between North and South', *The Times*, 8 March 1972.
Viney, M., 'The Protestant million', *Irish Times*, 6–9 December 1971.
Watson, P., 'The Long-term Costs of Fear', *Sunday Times*, 24 September 1972.
White, Barry, 'John Hume', *Belfast Telegraph*, 14 September 1971.
White, Barry, 'The State of the Police', *Belfast Telegraph*, 21 September 1973.
Winchester, Simon, 'Along the Ulster Terror Trail', *The Guardian*, 23 June 1972.

THESES

Carleton, S.T., *The Growth of South Belfast*, M.A., Queen's University Belfast, 1967.
Cooke, J.H., *Development and Distribution of Methodism in Ireland*, M.A., Queen's University Belfast, 1964.
Crilly, E., *Newtownabbey, Rathcoole and Belfast: A study in Urban Relationships*, Dissertation, Geography department, Queen's University Belfast, 1959.
Davies, Mary, *The Role of the Press in the Recent Northern Ireland Crisis*, Dissertation, London School of Economics, 1970.
Dent, George I., *The Law of Education in Northern Ireland and the Influence of English Law*, Ph.D., University of London, 1965.
Elliott, Sidney, *The Electoral System in Northern Ireland since 1920*, Ph.D, Queen's University Belfast, 1972.
Foy, M., *The Ancient Order of Hibernians*, M.A., Political Science Department, Queen's University Belfast, 1972.
Gillespie, A., *Spatial Variation of Unemployment in Northern Ireland*, Geography Tripos, Clare College, Cambridge 1970.
Graham, J., *Divergent Thinking*, dissertation, Psychology department, Queen's University Belfast, n.d.
Graham, John, *The Northern Ireland Labour Party 1949–c.1967*, M.A., Queen's University Belfast, 1973.
Harbinson, John F., *History of the N.I. Labour Party 1884–1949*, M.Sc., Queen's University Belfast, 1966.

Holmes, Erskine, *Public Opinion and Educational Reform in Ireland*, M.A., Queen's University Belfast, 1968.

Huczynski, A.A., *A Contents Analysis of English, Eire and Ulster Newspapers*, Dissertation, London School of Economics, 1970.

Johnston, D., *A Study in local education planning and development 1965–1971*, Education Department, Queen's University Belfast 1971.

Kirk, Thomas, *The Religious Distribution in Lurgan*, M.A., Queen's University Belfast, 1967.

Knox, E., *The Effects on Moral Judgement of Social Pressure*, Dissertation, Psychology Department, Queen's University Belfast, n.d.

McCormack, V., *Authoritarianism, Guilt and Political Attitudes in Two Groups of Different Denominations of Northern Irish School Children*, Dissertation, Psychology Department, Queen's University Belfast, 1970.

McElligott, T., *Intermediate Education and the Work of the Commissioners 1870–1922*, M.Litt, Trinity College Dublin, 1969.

McGill, Patrick F., *The Senate in Northern Ireland 1921–1962*, Ph.D., Queen's University Belfast, 1965.

Macourt, M., *Bigger and Better: An Explorative Comparative Study of Catholic and Protestant Farmers in the Republic of Ireland*, Economics Department, University of Dundee, 1973.

Megahey, A., *The Irish Protestant Churches and Social and Political Issues 1870–1914*, Ph.D., Queen's University Belfast, 1969.

Mercer, F., *Sandy Row: A Study Before Redevelopment*, Dissertation, Social Studies Department, Queen's University Belfast, 1971.

National Council for Civil Liberties, *The Special Powers Act of Northern Ireland*, NCCL, London 1936.

Neill, M., *Rathcoole: A Study in Social Relationships*, Dissertation, Geography Department, Queen's University Belfast, 1971.

O'Neill, E., *Stereotypes and Prejudice of Protestant and Catholic boys*, Dissertation, Psychology Department, Queen's University Belfast, 1967.

Pistoi, P., *Operation Motorman in Ballymurphy*, M.A., Essex University, 1972.

Robinson, Alan, *A Social Geography of Londonderry*, M.A. Queen's University Belfast, 1967.

Rooney, W., *Newcastle and Castlewellan: A Comparative Study in Local Geography*, M.A., Queen's University Belfast, 1945.

239

Ross, N., *Identification from Faces of Religious Affiliations,* Dissertation, Psychology Department, Queen's University Belfast, 1969.
Rutan, G.F., *Northern Ireland under Unionist Rule,* Ph.D., University of North Carolina, 1964.
Salters, John, *Attitudes Towards Society in Protestant and Roman Catholic Schoolchildren in Belfast,* M.A., Queen's University Belfast, 1970.
Spense, W., *The Growth and Development of the Secondary Intermediate School in Northern Ireland since the Education Act of 1947,* M.A., Queen's University Belfast, 1959.
Starling, Susan, *The Sociology of Voluntary Organisations in Belfast,* Dissertation, Geography Department, Queen's University Belfast, 1971.
Toman, E., *Adult Education in Northern Ireland,* Dissertation, New University of Ulster, Coleraine, 1970.
Turner, E., *Religious Understanding and Religious Attitudes in Male Urban Adolescents,* Ph.D., Queen's University Belfast, 1970.
Webb, A., *Religion and Prejudice,* Dissertation, Psychology Department, Queen's University Belfast, n.d.
Williamson, A., *Community Integration in a West Belfast Housing Estate,* Dissertation, Geography Department, Queen's University Belfast, 1970.

UNPUBLISHED DOCUMENTS
Appeals of Conscience Foundation, *Tensions in Northern Ireland,* ACF, New York, 1970.
Boyle, Kevin, *Police and Police Reforms in Northern Ireland,* Paper read to National Conference on Research and Training in Criminology, Cambridge, July 1970.
Boyle, Louis, *Statement on Resignation from the Unionist Party,* 1969.
Cohan, A., *Religious values and an end to Partition,* Paper read at Lancaster Conference on Northern Ireland, 1971.
Dobbie, G., *The Police in Northern Ireland,* Paper read at Lancaster Conference on Northern Ireland, 1971.
Hillyard, Paddy, *The Army in Northern Ireland,* Paper read at Lancaster Conference on Northern Ireland, 1971.
Hughes, E., *Has Swiss Experience Lessons for Ulster?,* Paper read at Lancaster Conference on Northern Ireland, 1971.
McNabb, Patrick, *A People Under Pressure,* Paper read at Lancaster Conference, 1971.

Miller, D., *Education and Sectarian Conflict in Northern Ireland,* Paper presented to American Historical Association, 30 December 1969.

Obershall, A., *Conflict and Conflict Regulation in Northern Ireland,* Paper read to American Sociological Association, New York, 1973.

Osmond, D., and Mark, R., *Report into the Royal Ulster Constabulary,* Unpublished but described in James Callaghan, *A House Divided,* Collins, 1973.

Overy, Bob, *A Pacifist Perspective on Civil Rights,* Paper read at Lancaster Conference on Northern Ireland, 1971.

Scott, Olive, *The Cultural Divide,* Paper read at Lancaster Conference on Northern Ireland, 1971.

Spencer, A.E.C.W., *Urbanisation and the Problem of Ireland,* Paper read to Social Studies Conference, Donegal, 1972.

Stewart, E., *Housing Movements in 1969,* unpublished survey by ad-hoc group, Belfast 1969.

White, C., *Collective Behaviour in Northern Ireland: A Sociological Perspective,* Paper read at Lancaster Conference on Northern Ireland, 1971.

Wilson, Thomas, *The Ulster Crisis,* Paper read at Lancaster Conference on Northern Ireland, 1971.

GOVERNMENT PUBLICATIONS

The Benson Report: Northern Ireland Railways, HMSO, Belfast, Cmd 458 1963.

Adult Education in Northern Ireland, HMSO, Belfast, Cmd 473 1964.

The Lockwood Report: Higher Education in Northern Ireland, HMSO, Belfast, Cmd 475 1965.

The Wilson Plan: Economic Development in Northern Ireland, HMSO, Belfast, Cmd 479 1965.

The Reshaping of Local Government, HMSO, Belfast, Cmd 517 1967.

Reshaping of Local Government—Further Proposals, HMSO, Belfast, Cmd 530 1969.

The Cameron Report: Disturbances in Northern Ireland, HMSO, Belfast, Cmd 532 1969.

A Commentary by the Government of Northern Ireland to accompany the Cameron Report, HMSO, Belfast, Cmd 534 1969.

The Hunt Report: Report of the Advisory Committee on Police in Northern Ireland, HMSO, Belfast, Cmd 535 1969.

Public Education in Northern Ireland, HMSO, Belfast 1970.

241

Law Reform in Northern Ireland, HMSO, Belfast, Cmd 543 1970.
The MacRory Report: Local Government in Northern Ireland, HMSO, Belfast, Cmd 546 1970.
A Record of Constructive Change, HMSO, Belfast, Cmd 558 1971.
The Future Development of the Parliament and Government of Northern Ireland, HMSO, Belfast, Cmd 560 1971.
Northern Ireland and the European Community, HMSO, Belfast, Cmd 563 1971.
The Compton Report: Allegations against the Security Forces of Physical Brutality in Northern Ireland, HMSO, London, Cmnd 4823 1971.
The Future of Northern Ireland, Northern Ireland Office, Belfast 1972.
The Scarman Report: Violence and Civil Disturbances in Northern Ireland in 1969, HMSO, Belfast, Cmd 566 1972.
Political Settlement, HMSO, Belfast, Cmd 568 1972.
The Parker Report: Authorised Procedures for the Interrogation of Persons Suspected of Terrorism, HMSO, London, Cmnd 4901 1972.
Report of the Widgery Tribunal, HMSO, London, H.C.220 1972.
The Diplock Report: Legal Procedure to deal with Terrorist Activities in NI, HMSO, London, Cmnd 5185 1972.
The Burgess Report: The Reorganisation of Secondary Education in Northern Ireland, HMSO, Belfast, Cmd 574 1973.
Northern Ireland Constitutional Proposals, HMSO, London, Cmnd 5259 1973.
The Gardiner Report: Measures to Deal with Terrorism in Northern Ireland, HMSO, London, Cmnd 5847.
Government of Northern Ireland, Northern Ireland Office, Belfast 1975.

Notes

CHAPTER I: HISTORICAL BACKGROUND (pp. 1–24)

1. There has been a flourishing of Irish historiography over the last few decades, so there is no shortage of excellent material. Two books are particularly recommended for the historical background to community tensions in Ireland: J.C. Beckett, *The Making of Modern Ireland 1603–1923*, Faber, 1966, and F.S.L. Lyons, *Ireland since the Famine*, Weidenfeld and Nicolson, 1972. Rather shorter accounts are contained in Liam de Paor, *Divided Ulster*, Penguin, 1970, and D. Barritt and C. Carter, *The Northern Ireland Problem*, Oxford Paperbacks, 1972. Two collections of essays are K.B. Nowlan and T.D. Williams (ed.), *Ireland in the War Years and After*, Gill and Macmillan, 1969, and T. Moody and F.X. Martin, *The Course of Irish History*, Mercier, 1967. An 'official' history, published by the Stationery Office, is Hugh Shearman, *Northern Ireland*, HMSO, 1971. Two extremely good but very brief introductory pamphlets are Harold Jackson, *The Two Irelands*, Minority Rights Group's Report No.2, London 1971, and D.P. Barritt and A. Booth, *Orange and Green*, Northern Friends' Peace Board, Westmorland.
2. Beckett, *Making*, 222.
3. C.O. Byrne, *As I Roved out*, Irish Reprints, 1971.
4. A. Boyd, *Holy War in Belfast*, Anvil, 1969.
5. J.C. Beckett and R. Glasscock (eds.), *Belfast: Origins and growth of an Industrial City*, BBC, 1967, 47.
6. See Emrys Jones, *A Social Geography of Belfast*, Oxford University Press, 1960, 188.
7. J. Barrow, *Tour round Ireland*, John Murray, 1836, 36.
8. A fuller account of these riots is contained in A. Boyd's *Holy War*.
9. There was a surprising readiness on the part of politicians during the 1880s, especially those in the Conservative Party,

to admit that they regarded the Home Rule issue primarily as one from which political capital might be made. See, for example, Winston Churchill's biography of his father: Winston Churchill, *Lord Randolph Churchill*, Odhams, 1951, Chapter XIII.

10. J.C. Beckett *et al.*, *The Ulster Debate*, Institute for the Study of Conflict, 1972, 11.
11. Lyons, *Ireland*, 682.
12. Shearman, *Northern Ireland*, 16.
13. Beckett *et al.*, *The Ulster Debate*, 14.
14. Shearman, *Northern Ireland*, 174.
15. Terence O'Neill, *Ulster at the Crossroads*, Faber and Faber, 1969, 23.
16. Louis Boyle, *Statement on Resignation from the Unionist Party*, 1969.
17. More attention has recently been focused on the nature of the economic relationship between Britain and Northern Ireland, but very few publications have been devoted to the subject. A brief summary, however, appears in Martin Wallace, *Northern Ireland*, David and Charles, 1971, 121–57, and there is a discussion of public finance and services in R. Lawrence, *The Government of Northern Ireland*, London 1965.
18. M. Sheehy, *Divided we Stand*, Faber and Faber, 1955, 66.
19. Both these agreements were in respect to waterways which were situated between Northern Ireland and the Republic of Ireland.
20. Among the most interesting publications dealing with events following the Civil Rights campaign are Liam de Paor, *Divided Ulster*; Max Hastings, *Ulster 1969*, Gollancz, 1970; J.C. Beckett *et al.*, *The Ulster debate*; Paul Arthurs, *The People's Democracy*, Blackstaff, 1974. Essential reading is CMD 532, *Report on the Disturbances in Northern Ireland* (The Cameron Report), HMSO, 1959.
21. Paul Arthurs, *The People's Democracy*. This book is a useful account of the movement's development.

CHAPTER II: DEMOGRAPHIC BACKGROUND (pp. 25–47)
1. *Constitution of Londonderry.*
2. Alan Robinson, 'A Social Geography of Londonderry', unpublished thesis, Queen's University Belfast, 1967.
3. J. Barrow, *Tour round Ireland*, London 1836.
4. E. Jones, 'Belfast: a survey of the city', in *Belfast in its regional setting*, E. Jones (ed.), London, 1952. This book was

a pioneering description of the city's demographic growth, but should be read in conjunction with works of more recent commentators, especially J.C. Beckett and R. Glasscock, *Belfast*, BBC, London 1967.

5. *Report of Commission into Riots in Belfast*, 1857, 2.
6. John Darby and Geoffrey Morris, *Intimidation in Housing*, Northern Ireland Community Relations Commission Research paper, Belfast 1974, Appendix C.
7. Brendan Walsh, *Religion and Demographic Behaviour in Ireland*, Economic and Social Research Institute, Dublin 1970, 35.
8. Tom Hadden, 'Interlocking Ulstermen', *New Society*, 17 February 1972.
9. F.W. Boal and R. Buchanan, 'The 1969 Northern Ireland General Election', in *Irish Geography*, VI/1, 1969. Although other elections in Northern Ireland have not been analysed in a similar way, data on all previous election results are contained in Sidney Elliott, *Northern Ireland Parliamentary Election Results 1921–1972*, Political Reference Publications, Chichester 1973.
10. Rosemary Harris, *Prejudice and Tolerance in Ulster*, Manchester University Press, 1972. This book is a sociological study of a small village in South Ulster, and contains a number of interesting insights into relationships between the people who lived there.
11. HMSO, *Census of Population*, Preliminary report, Belfast 1971.
12. M.A. Poole and F.W. Boal, 'Religious Residential Segregation in Belfast in mid-1969: A Multi-level Analysis', in B.D. Clark and M.B. Gleave, *Social Patterns in cities*, London 1973, 14. This is the most up-to-date and detailed account of religious patterns in Belfast.
13. M.A. Poole and F.W. Boal, 'Residential Segregation'.
14. J.C. Beckett in J.C. Beckett and R. Glasscock (ed.), *Belfast*, 188.
15. The decline of Belfast's population is also marked over a longer period: in 1951 it was 443,671, in 1961, 415,856 and in 1971 it was 380,150.
16. Alan Robinson, *Social Geography*.
17. Alan Robinson, 'Londonderry, city of communities', *Community Forum*, 4/2, 1974. This article by a researcher who has been interested in the city for many years provides some understanding of the community spirit peculiar to Derry.

18. Tom Kirk, 'The Religious Distribution in Lurgan', unpublished thesis, Queen's University Belfast, 1967. Very few studies of small towns have been published but a number of relevant dissertations and theses are contained in the Geography department at Queen's University, which publishes annual lists of titles. See also J.H. Caldwell, 'Ballymena; an urban Ulster', *Fortnight*, 26 January 1972.
19. R. Ardrey, *The Territorial Imperative*, Collins, 1967.
20. Harold Jackson, *The Two Irelands*, Minority Rights Group Report No.2, London 1971, 10.
21. Independent Television Authority, *Religion in Britain and Northern Ireland*, London 1970, 13.
22. Boal's two surveys on territoriality in Belfast have been published separately, but he also wrote a comparison between the two surveyed areas. See F.W. Boal, 'Close together and far apart', *Community Forum*, 2/3, 1972.
23. F.W. Boal, 'Close together'.
24. Alan Robinson, 'Londonderry', *Community Forum*, 2/3, 1972.
25. F.W. Boal, 'Territoriality and Class: a Study of Two Residential Districts in Belfast', *Irish Geography*, 6/3, 1971.
26. Walsh, *Religion*, 33.
27. E. Jones, *A Social Geography of Belfast*, Oxford University Press, 1960, 155.
28. Brendan Walsh, *Some Irish Population Problems Reconsidered*, Economic and Social Research Institute, Dublin 1968, 7–16.
29. B. Kerr, 'Irish seasonal migration', *Irish Historical Studies*, III, 363–80.
30. Hadden, 'Interlocking Ulstermen'.
31. F.S.L. Lyons, *Ireland since the Famine*, Weidenfeld and Nicolson, 1971. 745.
32. Walsh, *Religion*, 17–18.
33. Walsh, *Religion*, 19–21.
34. Michael Poole, 'Residential Displacement in the Summer of 1969', *Fortnight*, August 1971.
35. Northern Ireland Community Relations Commission Research Unit, *Flight*, Belfast 1971.
36. Darby and Morris, *Intimidation*, Appendix C.
37. Darby and Morris, *Intimidation*, 66.
38. Darby and Morris, *Intimidation*, 72.
39. Both the examples mentioned actually occurred during

December 1972, the former in Derry and the latter in Belfast. Many more might be quoted.
40. Ardrey, *Territorial Imperative*, 244.
41. Darby and Morris, *Intimidation*, 73.

CHAPTER III: STATE INSTITUTIONS (pp. 48–79)

1. F.S.L. Lyons, *Ireland since the Famine*, Weidenfeld and Nicolson, 1971, 745.
2. A number of writers have produced data on local councils in Northern Ireland, demonstrating a pattern of bias by some councils, but some of these have given different figures for both the religious composition of local authority areas and the political affiliation of councillors. I have selected those collected by Derek Birrell (see D. Birrell, 'Religious Deprivation as a Factor in Conflict in Northern Ireland', in *The Sociological Review*, 20/3, August 1972) as the most reliable. His information was gathered from clerks of the various councils.
3. D. Barritt and C. Carter, *The Northern Ireland Problem*, Oxford Paperbacks, 1972, 42.
4. Terence O'Neill, *Ulster at the Crossroads*, Faber and Faber, 1969, 172.
5. See, for example, Brendan Dowling in *Fortnight*, 15 November 1974.
6. Surprisingly little has been written about the Mater hospital dispute, but a short summary is contained in Martin Wallace, *Northern Ireland*, David and Charles, 1971, 112–16.
7. The Special Powers act has been the subject of a number of publications. Among the most interesting of these are H. Calvert, *Constitutional Law in Northern Ireland*, Stevens and Son, 1968; Tom Hadden and Paddy Hillyard, *Justice in Northern Ireland*, Cobden Trust, London, 1973; and Don Carroll, 'The Search for Justice in Northern Ireland' in *New York Journal of International Law and Politics*, 1973. Hadden and Hillyard's publication also includes a useful survey of the administration of justice in Northern Ireland.
8. National Council for Civil Liberties, *Report of a Commission of Inquiry appointed to examine the purpose and effects of the Civil Authorities (Special Powers) acts*, NCCL, London 1936.
9. Government Information Service, *Press Release*, 22 November 1968.
10. Lyons, *Ireland*, 686.

11. James Callaghan, *A House Divided*, Collins, 1973, 55–6.
12. Calvert, *Constitutional Law*.
13. Nicolas Mansergh, *The Government of Northern Ireland*, Allen and Unwin, 1936.
14. Barry White, 'The State of the Police', in *Belfast Telegraph*, 21 September 1973.
15. HMSO *Report of the Advisory Committee on Police in Northern Ireland* (The Hunt Report), Cmnd 535, 1969, 29. The Hunt Report and the Cameron Report were the first two official inquiries which resulted from the Civil Rights Campaign. Both, and especially the Cameron Report, contain valuable background material on community tensions.
16. Central Citizens' Defence Committee, *The Black Paper–the Story of the Police*, CCDC, Belfast, 1973. The CCDC was a defence organisation based in the Falls Road district of Belfast which later concentrated on voluntary social provision for distressed families.
17. HMSO *Disturbances in Northern Ireland* (The Cameron Report), Cmnd 532, 1969.
18. G. Dobbie, 'Protectors and partisans, the police in Northern Ireland', Paper read at Lancaster conference on Northern Ireland, 1971.
19. HMSO *The Hunt Report*, 38. Chapters 8 and 9 of the Hunt Report and appendix V of the Cameron Report deal with the structure and functions of the Ulster Special Constabulary.
20. *Hunt Report*, 39.
21. H. Clarke, 'Why an Ulster Defence Regiment?' in *Solon*, 1/2, 1970.
22. Callaghan, *House Divided*, 90.
23. Callaghan, *House Divided*, 58.
24. *Andersonstown News*, 11 July 1973.
25. Aidan Corrigan, *Eyewitness in Northern Ireland*, Voice of Ulster Publications, 1969, 28.
26. Quoted in S. Riley 'Some Lawyers ask: Is the Law past Reproach?' *Sunday News*, Belfast, 8 May 1972.
27. Denis Faul, *Testimony to the Sub-committee on Europe of the House of Representatives of the United States of America*, Washington 1972, 196. The researches of Kevin Boyle, quoted in Hadden and Hillyard, *Justice*, point to a similar pattern.
28. E. Curran, 'Is Justice being done in Northern Ireland?' in *Belfast Telegraph*, 2 June 1972.

29. E. Curran in *Belfast Telegraph.*
30. Hadden and Hillyard, *Justice*, 62.
31. David Donnison, 'The Northern Ireland Civil Service', in *New Society*, 5 July 1973. Another article on the same subject is Michael McKeown, 'Civil Service Discrimination', in *Hibernia*, Dublin, 5 October 1973.
32. Barritt and Carter, *Northern Ireland Problem*, 96.
33. Northern Ireland Office, *Press Notice*, 6 July 1973.
34. Campaign for Social Justice in Northern Ireland, *Campaign Newsletter*, 1969.
35. Quoted in Martin Wallace, *Northern Ireland*, 117.
36. L. Symons and L. Hanna, *Northern Ireland: a Geographical Introduction*, University of London Press, 1967.
37. This map and table are reproduced from R. Cooper and T. O'Shea's 'Northern Ireland: A New Society survey of the social trends', in *New Society*, 7 June 1973, 555.
38. Brendan Walsh, *Religion and Demographic Behaviour in Ireland*, Economic and Social Research Institute, Dublin 1970, 33.
39. *Irish News*, 13 April 1948. Such statements are not uncommon. In 1963, for example, another Fermanagh Unionist, Alderman George Eliot said, 'We are not going to build houses in the South Ward, and cut a rod to beat ourselves later on. We are going to see that the right people are put into these houses and we are not making any apology for it', *Impartial Reporter*, Fermanagh, 14 November 1963.
40. *Cameron Report*, 56.
41. *Cameron Report*, 60.
42. Corrigan, *Eyewitness*, and Fermanagh Civil Rights Association, *Fermanagh Facts*.
43. Corrigan, *Eyewitness*.
44. Sunday Times Insight Team, *Ulster*, Penguin, 1972, 36.
45. *Irish News*, 11 March 1971.
46. This and the other quotations in this paragraph are taken from *The Cameron Report*, 55–67.
47. Derek Birrell *et al.*, *Housing in Northern Ireland*, Centre for Environmental Studies, London 1971, and J.G. Calvert, 'Housing Problems in Northern Ireland: A Critique', in *Community Forum*, 2/2, 1972, 18–20.
48. Richard Rose, *Governing without Consensus*, Faber, 1971, 294.
49. *House of Commons Debates*, (Northern Ireland), 61, c2372.
50. *Cameron Report*, 64.

51. Rose, *Governing without Consensus*, Chapter IX.
52. HMSO, *Third* and *Fourth Reports of the Northern Ireland Commissioner for Complaints*, 1970, 1971.

CHAPTER IV: POLITICAL PARTIES (pp. 80–112)
1. An account of Unionist politics during this period may be found in D. Savage, 'The Origins of the Ulster Unionist Party 1885–86', *Irish Historical Studies*, March 1961, XII, 47. The definitive description of the party's history, organisation and record is J. Harbinson, *The Ulster Unionist Party*, Blackstaff, 1973.
2. Defenders of the Orange Institution claim that its origins date back to 1688, thus attempting to establish a direct connection between Orangeism and the struggle for the Bill of Rights. This claim is significant in explaining the Institution's attitude to politics; although the Orange Order is nominally a religious organisation, Orangemen argue that the pursuit of religious liberty is also a political aim, just as it was in the 1680s. The claim for the Order's earlier origin is argued in M. Dewar, J. Brown and S. Long, *Orangeism*, Belfast, 1967, published by the Order. A more critical, and more anecdotal book is T. Gray, *The Orange Order*, The Bodley Head, 1972.
3. Richard Rose, *Governing without Consensus*, Faber, 1971, 257.
4. Harbinson, *Unionist Party*, 93. Harbinson's figure is based on an interview with Martin Smyth, Grand Master of the County Orange Lodge of Belfast.
5. Harbinson, *Unionist Party*, 90–91.
6. Quoted in M. Wallace, *Northern Ireland: 50 years of self-government*, David and Charles, 70.
7. L. Orr, 'The Orange Order', *Solon*, 1/2, January 1970.
8. *Fermanagh Times*, 13 July 1933.
9. D. Barritt and C. Carter, *The Northern Ireland Problem*, Oxford University Press, 1962.
10. T. O'Neill, *Autobiography*, Hart-Davis, 1972, 40.
11. *Belfast Newsletter*, 2 November 1959.
12. *Belfast Telegraph*, 10 November 1959.
13. *Belfast Newsletter*, 21 November 1959.
14. *Belfast Telegraph*, 14 November 1969.
15. O'Neill, *Autobiography*, 118.
16. *Belfast Telegraph*, 5 May 1969.
17. The essential source book for all election data on Northern Ireland from which most of the electoral information in this

chapter is taken is S. Elliott, *Northern Ireland Parliamentary Election Results, 1921–1972.* Political Reference publications, Chichester 1973. Also useful is J. Knight and N. Baxter-Moore, *The Northern Ireland Elections of the 1920s,* Electoral Reform Society, 1971.

18. See Patrick Marrinan, *Paisley, Man of Wrath,* Anvil, Tralee 1973.
19. Harbinson, *Unionist Party,* 224–25.
20. The paucity of information on the UVF is well illustrated by the only book published on the organisation, D. Boulton, *The UVF,* Gill and Macmillan, 1973.
21. *Belfast Newsletter,* 19 May 1966.
22. O. Dudley Edwards, *The Sins of our Fathers,* Gill and Macmillan, 1970, 119.
23. Institute for the Study of Conflict, 'Ulster, Politics and Terrorism', *Conflict Studies,* No. 36, June 1973.
24. The Sunday Times Insight Team, *Ulster,* Penguin Special, 1972. This book gives some account of the formation of the Provisional IRA.
25. IRA press statement announcing the end of their 1956 campaign, 1962.
26. The Ireland act, 1949.
27. There are two theses in the library of Queen's University Belfast which cover the history of the NILP from its foundation until 1969. They are J. Harbinson, *The History of the Northern Ireland Labour Party (1884–1949),* 1966; and J. Graham, *The Northern Ireland Labour Party (1949–c.1967),* 1973.
28. Quoted in N. Mansergh, *The Irish Question,* Unwin University Books, 1965, 242.
29. Graham, NILP, 45.
30. Little has been written about the Alliance party, but two useful newspaper articles are B. Bell, 'The Making of a Party', *Belfast Telegraph,* 26 April 1970, and M. Cummins, 'The Alliance Party', *The Irish Times,* 26 February 1972.
31. J. Macrae, *Polarisation in Northern Ireland,* Peace Research Centre, Lancaster, 1966.
32. A radical perspective of the Civil Rights campaign is given in E. McCann, *War in an Irish Town,* Penguin, 1974.
33. M. Hastings, *Ulster 1969,* Gollancz, 1970.
34. HMSO, *Disturbances in Northern Ireland* (The Cameron Report), Cmnd 532, 1969, 87.
35. P. Arthurs, *The People's Democracy,* Blackstaff, 1973.

36. M. Hastings, *Ulster 1969*, Gollancz, 1970.
37. One detailed description of the episode has been written; see B. Egan and V. McCormack, *Burntollet*, LRS Publishers, 1969.
38. For the events surrounding the UWC strike, see Ric Clark, 'Sixteen days in May', *Sunday News*, Belfast, 16 March, 23 March, 30 March and 6 April 1975.
39. F. Boal and R. Buchanan, 'The 1969 Northern Ireland election', *Irish Geography*, VI/1, 1969, 83.
40. B. White, 'John Hume', *Belfast Telegraph*, 14 September 1971.
41. Both books on the IRA which have been published deal with the period before the emergence of the Provisionals. They are, B. Bell, *The Secret Army*, Blond, 1970, and T.P. Coogan, *The IRA*, Pall Mall, 1970. A useful article on more recent events is S. Winchester, 'Along the Ulster Terror Trail', *The Guardian*, 23 June 1972.
42. S. Elliott, *Election Results*, 97.
43. S. Elliott, *Election Results*, 98.
44. J.L. McCracken in T. Moody and F. Martin (ed.), *The Course of Irish History*, Mercier, 1967.

CHAPTER V: CHURCHES AND SCHOOLS (pp. 113–39)
1. *Catholic Herald*, 1 June 1973.
2. *Irish News*, 2 June 1973. For a more detailed expression of this view see New Ulster Movement, *Tribalism or Christianity in Ireland*, NUM publication, 1973. Also a long debate in the correspondence columns of the *Irish Times*, November 1974–February 1975.
3. Richard Rose, *Governing without Consensus*, Faber, 1972, 427.
4. Independent Television Authority, *Religion in Britain and Northern Ireland*, Independent Television publications Ltd, 1970.
5. Northern Ireland General Register Office, *Census of Population*, 1961 and 1971.
6. Owen Dudley Edwards, *The Sins of our Fathers*, Gill and Macmillan, 1970, 193.
7. John Whyte, *Church and State in Modern Ireland 1923–1970*, Gill and Macmillan, 1971, 312. This book, although largely concerned with the Irish Republic, is essential reading for an understanding of the Catholic Church in Ireland.
8. E.B., 'The Church and Society', *This Week*, 3/33, 1972.

9. Quoted in Clifford Longley, 'Odd men out in all Christiandom', *The Times*, 21 February 1972, which is an erudite and thoughtful article on the political influence of the Churches in Ireland.

10. Quoted in Paul Blanshard, *The Irish and Catholic Power*, London, 1954, 232.

11. Emrys Jones, *A Social Geography of Belfast*, Oxford University Press, 1960, 172.

12. Tom Kirk, 'The Religious Distribution of Lurgan', unpublished M.A. thesis, Queen's University, Belfast, 1967, 150.

13. A. Mcgahey, 'The Irish Protestant Churches and Social and Political Issues 1870–1914', unpublished Ph.D. thesis, Queen's University Belfast, 1969.

14. Northern Ireland General Register Office, *Census*, 1971. In a feature article in the *Belfast Telegraph*, 4 March 1975, a spokesman for the Free Presbyterians estimated membership to be then in the region of 10,000.

15. *Church and Community: A Report to the General Assembly of the Presbyterian Church in Ireland*, Belfast, 1969.

16. Martin Wallace, *Northern Ireland*, David and Charles, 1971,

17. Anders Boserup, 'Revolution and counter-revolution in Northern Ireland', *Varldspolitikens Dagsfragor*, 1970, 1.

18. *Christian Advocate*, 20 August 1886.

19. Ian Paisley, 'Forum Debate', *Community Forum*, 1/1, 1971.

20. Louis Gardner, *The Resurgence of the Majority*, Vanguard Publications, 1970/71.

21. Patrick Marrinan, *Paisley, Man of Wrath*, Anvil, 1973.

22. *Report of the General Assembly of the Presbyterian Church in NI*, Belfast, 1950.

23. *Clergy Review*, February 1972.

24. *Belfast Telegraph*, 20 November 1971.

25. Act of Parliament 28, Henry VIII, c.15.

26. Quoted in Norman Atkinson, *Irish Education*, Figgis, Dublin 1969, 21.

27. Archbishop Boulter, *Proposal to Encourage Christian Schools*, British Museum MS. 21138, n.d.

28. Arthur Young, *Travels in Ireland*, London 1780.

29. John Magee; in *Aspects of Catholic education*, Irish News Ltd., 1971, 14.

30. *Report of the Commissioners of the Board of Education in Ireland*, Dublin 1812.

31. *Regulations of the Kildare Place Society*, Public Record Office, of Ireland, MS. 5626, 1871.

32. P. Cullen, 'Pastoral letter', *Freeman's Journal*, 10 November 1859.
33. Graham Balfour, *Educational Systems of GB and NI*, Oxford 1903.
34. *Nineteenth Century Review*, March 1924.
35. *Parliamentary Debates*, Northern Ireland, III, 114, 1921.
36. *Annual Register*, 1923.
37. *Interim Report of the Departmental Committee on the Educational services in Northern Ireland*, Belfast, n.d., 9.
38. M. Dewar, S. Long and J. Brown, *Orangeism: a New Historical Perspective*, Belfast 1967, 176.
39. *Belfast Newsletter*, 4 May 1929.
40. Quoted in Martin Wallace, *Northern Ireland*, 109.
41. Campaign for Social Justice in Northern Ireland, *Campaign Newsletter*, 13, 1971.
42. The material on educational divisions which follows in this chapter is discussed in greater detail in John Darby, 'Divisiveness in education: Northern Ireland', *Northern Teacher*, Belfast, Winter 1973.
43. D. Barritt and C. Carter, *The Northern Ireland Problem*, Oxford Paperbacks (reprint), 1972, 77.
44. HMSO, *Education in Northern Ireland*, 1972. Statistics are also provided in HMSO, *Educational Statistics*, which is published twice yearly.
45. In 1972 there were 5,628 students involved in teacher training in Northern Ireland. 3,876 of these (69%) were in the Colleges of Education.
46. Erskine Holmes, 'Public Opinion and Educational Reform in Ireland', unpublished M.A. thesis, Queen's University, Belfast 1968, 69.
47. Quoted in Martin Wallace, *Northern Ireland*, 111.
48. David Kennedy, in *Aspects of Catholic Education*, 44.
49. John Graham, *Divergent Thinking*, unpublished dissertation, Psychology Department, Queen's University, Belfast 1962.
50. Figures taken from the *Annual Reports* of the Catholic Chaplaincy, Queen's University, Belfast 1961–1971.
51. Alan Robinson, 'Education and Sectarian Conflict in Northern Ireland', *New Era*, January 1971.
52. John Magee, *The Teaching of Irish History in Irish Schools*, Irish National Teachers' Organisation, Belfast 1970. Republished by Northern Ireland Community Relations Commission, 1971, 5.
53. Lorna Hadkins, 'Textbooks', *Community Forum*, 1/1, 1971.

54. John Darby, 'History in the school', *Community Forum*, 4/2, 1974.
55. James Russell, *Some Aspects of the Civic Education of Secondary School boys in Northern Ireland*. NI Community Relations Commission Research Paper, 1972, 24.
56. John Greer, *A Questioning Generation*, Northern Ireland Committee for the Church of Ireland Board of Education, 1972.
57. *Practice '73*, Produced by the Education department, Queen's University Belfast 1973.
58. HMSO, *Education in Northern Ireland*, 1971.
59. John Boyd, *Visit to the School*.
60. John Salters, 'Attitudes towards Society in Protestant and Roman Catholic School children in Belfast', Unpublished thesis, Education department, Queen's University Belfast, 1970.
61. Vincent McCormack, 'Authoritarianism, Guilt and Political Attitudes in Two Groups of Different Denominations of Northern Ireland Schoolchildren', unpublished dissertation, Psychology department, Queen's University, Belfast.
62. One legislative attempt to resolve this dilemma was the announcement in 1974 by the Minister of Education in the Northern Ireland Executive, Basil McIvor, that he intended to introduce a third type of school—shared schools—which would be mixed-denominational. Shortly after the announcement in May, 1974, the Executive fell from office and McIvor's proposals into limbo.

CHAPTER VI: SOCIAL ORGANISATION (pp. 140–61)

1. Richard Rose, *Governing without Consensus*, Faber, 1971, 343.
2. Rose, *Governing without Consensus*, 344.
3. Simon Winchester, *In Holy Terror*, Faber and Faber, 1974, 35–6.
4. Research Services Limited, *Readership Survey of Northern Ireland*, RSL London 1970, Tables 1 and 2.
5. Gay Firth, 'Polar press', *Fortnight*, 14 May 1971, 10.
6. *Readership Survey*, Tables 3, 4 and 5.
7. Mary Davies, 'The Role of the Press in the Recent Northern Ireland Crisis', unpublished dissertation, London School of Economics, 1970. Another dissertation which supports Davies's general findings is A. Huczynski, 'A Content Analysis of English, Eire and Ulster Newspapers between August 11 and

August 16, 1969', London School of Economics, 1970.

8. Eamonn McCann, *The British Press in Northern Ireland,* Northern Ireland Socialist Research Centre, London 1971.
9. A useful series of articles on political newspapers and news sheets in Northern Ireland has been written by a librarian at Belfast's Linenhall Library. See Paula Howard, 'The Paper War', *Fortnight,* 11 January 1974, 25 January 1974 and 8 February 1974.
10. Rose, *Governing without Consensus,* 345.
11. Quoted in Rex Cathcart, 'BBC Northern Ireland: 50 years old', *The Listener,* 12 September 1974, 322.
12. Quoted in Cathcart, 'BBC Northern Ireland', 322.
13. Jay C. Blumer, 'Ulster on the Small Screen', *New Society,* 23 December 1971.
14. HMSO, *Second Report of the Northern Ireland Commissioner for Complaints,* H.C.2101, 1970.
15. *Fermanagh Times,* 13 July 1933.
16. *Belfast Telegraph,* 14 November 1959.
17. F.W. Boal, P. Doherty, and D.G. Pringle, *The Spatial Distribution of some Social Problems in the Belfast Urban Area,* Northern Ireland Community Relations Commission Research paper, Belfast 1974, 123–24.
18. Niall Duff, 'Community Self-Surveys', *Community Forum,* 3/1, 1973, 19.
19. Rosemary Harris, *Prejudice and Tolerance in Ulster,* Manchester University Press, 1972.
20. Tom Kirk, 'The Religious Distribution of Lurgan', unpublished thesis, Queen's University Belfast, 1967, 55.
21. Robert Taylor, 'Shopfloor Ulster', *New Society,* 25 May 1974, 434.
22. Kathleen Boehringer, 'Discrimination: Jobs', *Fortnight,* 14 May 1971, 5.
23. D. Barritt and A. Booth, *Orange and Green,* Northern Friends' Peace Board, Westmorland, 1972, 28.
24. Figures obtained from the *Annual Reports* of the Catholic chaplaincy, Queen's University Belfast, 1961–71.
25. Taylor, 'Shopfloor Ulster', 434.
26. Quoted in Andrew Boyd, *The Rise of the Irish Trade Unions,* Anvil Press, 1972, 96–97.
27. Taylor, 'Shopfloor Ulster', 434.
28. Rose, *Governing without Consensus,* 282.
29. So far, little has been written about this strike. The UWC published its *Ulster General Strike,* Belfast 1974; also see

Adam Roberts, 'Passive resistance in Ulster', *New Society*, 6 June 1974 and Ric Clark, 'Sixteen days in May', *Sunday News*, 16 March, 23 March, 30 March and 6 April 1975.
30. *Irish News*, 22 November 1972.
31. F.W. Boal, 'Territoriality on the Falls-Shankill divide', *Irish Geography*, VI/I, 1969, 43.
32. Harris, *Prejudice and Tolerance*, x.
33. Anders Boserup, 'Revolution and Counter-revolution in Northern Ireland', *Varldspolitikens Dagsfragor*, November 1970, 1.
34. Susan Starling, 'The Sociology of Voluntary Organisations in Belfast', unpublished dissertation, Geography department, Queen's University Belfast, 1970.
35. Kirk, *Lurgan*.
36. Northern Ireland Community Relations Commission, *Annual Report*, 1973.
37. See Sean Mackel, 'Cooperative and Industrial Self-help in Northern Ireland', *Community Forum*, 3/1, 1973.
38. The development of community groups in Northern Ireland is recorded in the two *Annual Reports* of the Community Relations Commission. See also, Community groups Conference, *Community Action: the way forward*, Derry 1974, and articles by Norman Goodchild, Raymond Johnston, Alan Robinson, Tom Lovett, Kathleen Kelly, Michael Morrissey and Jim Austin in *Community Forum*, 4/1, 1974.
39. The problem has captured the attention of many writers, poets and artists in Northern Ireland, and produced an artistic renaissance in the province, see 'The Northern Crisis', *Threshold* (Special issue), Belfast 1970; 'The Two Cultures', *Community Forum* (Special issue), 4/1, 1974, John Jordan, Northern Poets and Northern Politics', *Hibernia,* Dublin 1974.

CHAPTER VII: THEORIES (pp. 162–97)
1. G. de Beaumont, *L'Irlande sociale, politique et religieuse,* Paris, 1839, 1,198.
2. P. Sraffa (ed.), *The Works of David Ricardo,* IX, 1970, 145 and 153.
3. Quoted in Nicholas Mansergh, *The Irish Question*, Unwin University Books (revised edition 1965), 44.
4. Mansergh, *Irish Question*, 52. Professor Mansergh's book is a very useful description and discussion of a wide variety of nineteenth-century perceptions of the Irish problem.

5. Arthur Young, *Travels in Ireland*, London 1780.
6. Denis Barritt and Charles Carter, *The Northern Ireland Problem: a Study in Group Relations*, Oxford University Press, 1962.
7. C.D. Greaves, *The Irish Question*, Lawrence and Wishart, 1972, 116.
8. Anders Boserup, 'Revolution and Counter-Revolution in Northern Ireland', *Varldspolitikens Dagsfragor*. Anders Boserup was one of the first researchers to 're-discover' the Irish conflict, and his papers are among the most illuminating which have been written on it.
9. Robin Jenkins, *Conflict and Polarisation*, Peace Research Centre, London (mimeographed), 1968.
10. Anders Boserup, 'Power in a Post-Colonial Setting', *Peace Research Society Papers XIII*, The Copenhagen Conference, 1969.
11. Anders Boserup, 'Revolution and Counter-revolution', 1.
12. Peter Gibbon, 'Ulster: Religion and Class', *New Left Review*, No. 55, 1969, 28.
13. Anders Boserup, 'Power in a Post-Colonial Setting', 80.
14. W.G. Runciman, *Relative Deprivation and Social Justice*, Routledge and Kegan Paul, 1966, 11.
15. Derek Birrell, 'Relative Deprivation as a Factor of Conflict in Northern Ireland', *The Sociological Review*, August 1972, 338.
16. Derek Birrell, 'Relative deprivation', 339.
17. Liam de Paor, *Divided Ulster*, Penguin, 1970, 1.
18. Anthony Dickey discusses these first legislative attempts at tackling community problems in 'Anti-incitement Legislation in Britain and Northern Ireland', *New Community*, 1/2, 1972, 133–38.
19. J. Harrison, *The Scot in Ulster*, Blackwood, 1888, 100. Harrison also wrote: 'The difference is not accidental, not the divergence arising out of different surroundings, not even that springing from antagonistic religious training, but is the deeper stronger-marked cleavage of differing race. It is as distinct as between mastiff and staghound.'
20. *Punch*, 18 October 1862.
21. C. Wagley and M. Harris, *Minorities in the New World*, New York 1958.
22. John Rex, *Race Relations in Sociological Theory*, London 1970.
23. Robert Moore, 'Race relations in the Six Counties: Colonialism, industrialisation and stratification in Ireland', *Race*, 13, 1973.

258

24. F. Barth, *Ethnic Groups and Boundaries: the Social Organisation of Cultural Difference*, London 1969.
25. G. Simpson and J. Yinger, *Radical and Cultural Minorities*, Harper & Row, 1965, 20.
26. P. McNabb, 'A People under Pressure', unpublished paper read at Lancaster University, 1971.
27. William Lecky, *A History of Ireland in the Eighteenth Century*, Longmans, Green and Company, 1892, ii, 182.
28. L. Berkowitz, *Aggression: A Social Psychological Analysis*, McGraw-Hill, New York 1962.
29. Morris Fraser, *Children in Conflict*, Secker and Warburg, 1973, 113–14.
30. A development of this theory is discussed in C. McPhail, 'Civil Disorder Participation: a Critical Examination of Recent Research', *American Sociological Review*, 36, 1971, 1058–1073. McPhail postulates a deprivation-frustration-aggression theory, which is related to Northern Ireland in Derek Birrell, 'Relative Deprivation', 333.
31. R.S.P. Elliot and John Hickie, *Ulster: A Case Study in Conflict Theory*, Longman, 1971, 142.
32. J. Bayley, 'The Failure of Palliatives', *Community Forum*, 2/3, 1972.
33. G.B. Newe, 'Living together', *Community Forum*, 2, 3, 1972.
34. C. Lahinch, 'Rhodesia & the North—a parallel?' *This Week*, 15 June 1972, and E. Hughes, 'Has Swiss Experience Lessons for Ulster?', unpublished paper read at Lancaster University, 1971.
35. A. Greeley and P. Rossi, *The Education of Catholic Americans*, Aldine, Chicago 1966.
36. Northern Ireland Office, *Government of Northern Ireland*, Discussion Paper 3, HMSO, Belfast 1975.
37. North Eastern Boundary Bureau, *Handbook of the Ulster Question*, Stationery Office, Dublin 1923.
38. M. Tierney (ed.), *Daniel O'Connell: Centenary essays*, Dublin 1949. Another Southern Irish author who takes a similar view is M. Sheehy in *Divided we Stand*, Dublin 1955.
39. J. Magee, 'The Teaching of Irish History in Irish Schools', *The Northern Teacher*, 1970. Reprinted by the NI Community Relations Commission, 1971.
40. P. O Snodaigh, *Hidden Ulster*, The Gaelic League, Cavan, 1973. A strong attack on this booklet, supporting the Two Nations theory, was published in 1973 by the Workers' As-

sociation for a democratic settlement of the national conflict in Ireland. It is entitled *One Island Two Nations*.

41. New Ulster Movement, *Two Irelands or One?*, NUM, 1972, 5.
42. W. Carson, *Ulster and the Irish Republic*, Belfast 1957, 55.
43. Quoted in M. Heslinga, *The Irish Border as a Cultural Divide*, Van Gorcum, Assen, n.d.
44. L. Gardner, *The Resurgence of the Majority*, Vanguard publications, 1971. Two other articles which consider the Protestant position are Des Cranston, 'The Ulster Protestant Confused', *Cambridge Review*, 18 May 1973 and F. Wright, Protestant Ideology and Politics in Ulster', *European Journal of Sociology*, xiv, 1973, 213–80.
45. W.F. Moneypenny, *The Two Irish Nations*, London 1912, 17.
46. Nassau Senior, *Journals, Conversations and Essays Relating to Ireland*, I, London 1868, 22.
47. Quoted in Heslinga, *Irish Border*.
48. Estyn Evans, *Portrait of Northern Ireland*, Collins, 1951, 7.
49. J. White, 'Partition', *The Month*, XVII, 1957, 153.
50. Heslinga, *Irish Border*, 102.
51. The origin and growth of these problems have been analysed by the Commission's first director; see Hywel Griffiths, *Community Development in Northern Ireland: a case study in agency conflict*, Social Administration Department, New University of Ulster, Coleraine 1973.
52. A number of such voluntary organisations are described in David Bleakley, *Peace in Ulster*, Mowbray's, London 1972.

Index

263

Harland and Wolff shipyards, 129, 148, 149, 150, 166
Harris, Rosemary, on social relationships, 152–6; other references, 32, 45, 118, 140, 148
Hastings, Max, 61, 104, 105
Hedge schools, 124
Heenan, John Cardinal, Archbishop of Westminster, 121
Henderson, James, 81
Henry VIII, 123
Heslinga, M.W., 185–6
Higgins, John, 64
Hinduism, 134
Holmes, Erskine, 131
Home Rule, campaign to achieve, 7–8; other references, 60, 81, 82, 92, 98, 116, 127, 167, 175, 178, 183, 184
Hospitals Authority, 66
Hume, John, 104, 109, 133
Hunt Report, 23, 194; terms, 59–62

Incitement to hatred (Prevention of) act, 23, 170, 193, 195
Independent Television Authority, 115, 145
Independent Unionists, 89, 90
Independent Unionist Association, 90
Industrial development, postwar, 16–17, 67–8
Intimidation, 43–5
Ireland act (1949), 19
Irish Amateur Boxing Association, 154
Irish Congress of Trade Unions, 14, 150–1; Northern Committee, 150
Irish Free State, 12, 92; Civil war, 92; Relations with North and G.B., 17–19; 1937 constitution, 18
Irish League (Football), 153–4
Irish National Foresters, 156
Irish National Teachers' Organisation, 131
Irish News, 38, 96, 141–3
Irish Parliamentary party, 96
Irish Republican Army, in Northern Ireland, 92–5; 1956–62 offensive and effects, 13, 93–4, 97; influence of Civil Rights, 104; other references, 8, 9, 15, 44, 57, 60, 63, 91, 98, 164
Irish Republican Army (Officials), 94, 144, 168
Irish Republican Army (Provisionals),

144, 158, 191; formation, 22–4, 78, 94, 106; campaign, 107, 109–10
Irish Republican Brotherhood, 8
Irish Transport and General Workers' Union, 150
Irish Union Association, 96
Irish Volunteers, 5

Jackson, Harold, 25, 37
James I, 3, 170
Jenkins, Robin, 167, 168, 169
John XXIII, Pope, 121
Jones, Emrys, 40, 45, 118
Judiciary in Northern Ireland, 48–9, 63–5
Justice in Northern Ireland, 65

Keady, 32
Kennedy, David, 132
Kildare Place Society, 124
Kirk, Thomas, 37, 118, 152
Koestler, Arthur, 162

Labour party (G.B.), 9, 97
Lagan river, 45
Larkin, James, 175
Larne, 12
League of Nations, 187
Lee, G., and Taylor, R., 113
Leeds, 146
Legion of Mary, 155
Lemass, Sean, 14; meeting with Terence O'Neill, 20
Liberal party, (N.I.), 98–9, 102
Linfield F.C., 153
Lisbellaw, 87
Lisnaskea constituency, 53
Liverpool, 41, 170
Lloyd George, David, 41
Local government, 49, 50; franchise, 50–2; political composition, 52; bias and gerrymandering, 70–4; reorganisation, 190–1
Local Option candidates, 89
Lockwood Report, 35, 67
Logue, Michael Cardinal, Archbishop of Armagh, 117
London, 170
Londonderry, Viscount, 126–7, 130
Long, S.E., 127
Long Tower district of Derry, 38
Loyalists, 147, 151, 183–4
Loyalist Association of Workers, 107,

264